CANADIAN HOUSING POLICIES (1935-1980)

Albert Rose

University of Toronto

Butterworths

Toronto

© 1980 Butterworth and Company (Canada) Limited
         2265 Midland Avenue
         Scarborough, Ontario, Canada M1P 4S1
All Rights Reserved.
Printed and Bound in Canada.

The Butterworth Group of Companies:

Canada: Butterworth & Co. (Canada) Ltd., Toronto, Vancouver
United Kingdom: Butterworth & Co. (Publishers) Ltd., London,
                Borough Green
Australia: Butterworth Pty. Ltd., Sydney, Melbourne, Brisbane
New Zealand: Butterworths of New Zealand, Ltd., Wellington
South Africa: Butterworth & Co. (South Africa) Pty. Ltd., Durban
United States: Butterworth Inc., Boston
                Butterworth (Legal) Inc., Seattle

Canadian Cataloguing in Publication Data

Rose, Albert, 1917-
    Canadian housing policies (1935-1980)

Includes index.

ISBN 0-409-86315-7

1. Housing policy - Canada - History.
I. Title.

HD7305.A3R67   363.5′8′0971   C80-094402-X

Preface

In Canada housing has been a major economic and social policy concern for more than fifty years. During the 1930s, attention was directed to the miserable living conditions of those who suffered most from world wide depression and failure within Canadian resource/export industries. Canada's population at that time was about evenly divided between rural and urban areas and the full impact of the housing problem in an urban society had yet to materialize.

In the thirty-five years following the close of the Second World War the urbanization of our country has matched that of the United States, Great Britain, France and West Germany; by the end of this century Canadians will be almost totally identified in our statistical records as urban dwellers. The photographs of the 1930s, which have recently been appearing in new books for the edification of those who have known nothing but Western industrial affluence, now seem like interesting pictures drawn from the prints of the eighteenth and early nineteenth centuries. In short, although we have by no means grappled successfully with the problem of poor rural housing, our attention has turned since the beginning of the 1950s to the enormous problem of providing adequate housing for burgeoning urban populations; these have been swollen each year by most of the 150,000 to 250,000 newcomers from other nations, often far different in economic and cultural backgrounds.

It is not appropriate to continue the argument, so dear to politicians and social workers, that Canada is in the midst of a housing crisis. The truth is that throughout the twentieth century Canada has been in the midst of a continuous housing crisis. In his first book, Humphrey

Carver* analyzed the facts of Canada's housing production with respect to the best available data of the housing needs of Canadians from 1920 through 1945. It became perfectly clear that as a nation we had not, for a quarter of a century before the end of World War II, met the human and statistical criteria for decent and adequate housing accommodation.

Nevertheless, the major political parties in Canada, whether federal or provincial, did not see the matter of housing as an issue of significant concern for the vast majority of Canadian voters. In this judgment they were probably correct but by the close of the 1950s, following fifteen years of expansion in population (through a combination of one of the highest birth rates in the world and extensive immigration), this political judgment began to change. Canada had changed from a nation of tenants during the 1930s and early 1940s to one of homeowners by the late 1950s as a consequence of federal and provincial housing policies, legislation and initiatives.

By the end of the 1950s most major Canadian urban centres had exhausted their available raw land, not to speak of the supply of serviced land ready for construction of housing. It was foreseeable that a small group of relatively large producers of apartment dwellings would arise. Within the next decade (1959-1968) they accounted for as much as one-half to two thirds of the total new housing starts, with variations from region to region and from metropolis to metropolis.

Canadians reverted to a nation of tenants — this time in high-rise apartment buildings rather than in smaller structures — and the political climate changed as a direct result. There was tremendous concern among many groups about the very modest production of dwellings for low-income families during the years 1955-1964. These groups worked very hard to influence the Government of Canada and Central Mortgage and Housing Corporation to amend the National Housing Act towards the goal of substantially increasing the supply of housing for low-income individuals and families.

On the other hand, the provincial governments began to realize after 1964 how their political destinies were significantly tied to the quality of life in an urban environment. By 1967, John Robarts, the former premier of Ontario, cited as a strong argument for re-election his performance in the production of housing in general, and of public housing in particular, through the Ontario Housing Corporation. A year later, the new federal leader, Pierre Elliott Trudeau, had fulfilled one of his election promises by appointing Paul Hellyer, the man who placed second to him in the competition for leadership of the Liberal

---

*H. S. M. Carver, *Houses for Canadians* (Toronto: University of Toronto Press, 1948) p. 3-47.

Party, to direct the Task Force on Housing and Urban Development, whose work covered the period September 1968 to April 1969.

In 1970 the Government of Canada created a Ministry of State for Urban Affairs, with responsibility for the formulation of housing policy being implemented through the Central Mortgage and Housing Corporation in conjunction with the provincial government housing corporations and other agencies. In short, housing policy had arrived as a political weapon in the hands of members of the two senior levels of government. It was another five years before regional and municipal governments began to assume — after a diminution of responsibility for nearly twenty years — the kind of role in policy formulation and implementation originally assigned to them during the early postwar period.

My concern here not being mainly statistical, is with a description of the role of governments and the changing shifts and currents in policy which are a consequence of political, economic and social forces. Much of the material covering the years 1940-1968 (Chapter 3 and Appendix A) was originally drafted for the Canadian Conference on Housing held in Toronto during November 1968. A great deal has happened during the ensuing years with respect to government intervention in the housing market at all levels.

Housing policy has not merely arrived as a political phenomenon in terms of appeals to the electorate for favour or rejection, but is an important component of intergovernmental relationships, and a significant aspect of economic, social and political considerations at a time in Canadian history when the central issues are said to be those of inflation and unemployment. There are few segments of the Canadian economy in which price inflation has been greater and there has been no aspect of the inflationary process which has hurt or may hurt Canadians more significantly than its impact upon the production and distribution of housing accommodation for Canadians. There are few segments of the Canadian economy in which the burden of unemployment has been greater than in the construction industry, including the building of housing accommodation. There is a surplus of houses for sale in the early 1980s, yet many Canadian families are unable to afford accommodation.

From the outset, my objective has been to clarify the nature of Canadian housing policies, formulated by government and emerging from the struggle for hegemony between the various levels of government, primarily by tracing the history of legislation and its implementation. Members of the private residential housebuilding industry make decisions concerning their annual and five-year plans for land purchase and ultimate housebuilding activity; by doing so they may affect materially the supply and cost of housing. However, all their plans are very significantly influenced by the actions of government. That is not to deny that the lobbying or public information role of very large economic units in the housing industry may be considerable, or that their land acquisition policies have important economic and social consequences. It is rather to indicate the major emphasis of this work: government policies.

I cannot offer any simple or guaranteed solution to the dilemmas which face Canada, its provinces and municipalities, in the continuous efforts of providing adequate housing accommodation for various income groups in Canadian society. While I am all too conscious of our many deficiencies in this field, Canada also has much to be proud of in its record of accomplishment. The variety of regions and regional jurisdictions within the vast geographical area which is Canada and a whole gamut of international and national economic forces challenge our capacity to provide human and physical services for our people. To acknowledge that challenge is not to accept defeat.

In writing a book on a subject as complex as Canadian housing policies an author becomes obligated to a great many persons who offer advice, criticism and support. This book has been published with the help of a grant from the Social Science Federation of Canada, using funds provided by the Social Sciences and Humanities Research Council of Canada. Minor portions of chapter eight have been published elsewhere (Albert Rose, "The Impact of Recent Trends in Social Housing Policies," in *Urban Housing Markets: Recent Directions in Research and Policy*, edited by Bourne and Hitchcock and published by the University of Toronto Press, 1978). I would like to acknowledge the pioneering work of Peter Spurr (published by James Lorimer & Company), Michael Dennis and Susan Fish. I extend thanks to all Canadians who, by joining efforts with their fellow citizens, and by exerting pressure on their elected representatives as well as their appointed officials, have caused the development of better housing policies.

Albert Rose

Contents

I.   Housing Policies in their Political, Economic
and Social Contexts   1

II.   Essential Elements of a Canadian Housing Policy   15

III.   Housing Policy in Canada 1940-1968   27

IV.   National Housing Policies for Urban Canada:
The 1970s and Thereafter   43

V.   New Housing Policy Initiatives by Provincial and
Local Governments   69

VI.   Housing Policies in Ontario: A Case Study   101

VII.   Constraints Upon Policies and Programs   143

VIII.   Housing for Low-Income Families: The Importance
of Attitudes   163

X.   Canada's Housing Problem: Insoluble Crisis or
Intractable Dilemma?   181

Appendix A: Provincial Legislation in Housing and Urban
Renewal in the 1960s   201

Appendix B: Development of the National Housing Act   213

Index   215

CHAPTER 1

Housing Policies in Their Political, Economic and Social Contexts

Throughout the more than eleven decades of Canada's national existence, there have been few periods in which there were not expressions of concern about the housing and living conditions experienced by some Canadians. These concerns were expressed by elected representatives within local councils, by journalists, by church groups, by charitable organizations[1] and by individuals. In particular, the years prior to and after the First World War were marked by a great deal of interest in the orderly development of Canada's newly emerging cities and smaller urban centres.[2]

The untoward explosion which occurred in Halifax harbour in 1917 may mark the beginning of concerted public intervention and assumption of responsibility in the field of housing. This explosion destroyed a significant proportion of the housing stock adjacent to the harbour. As a consequence, a number of dwellings were built to be inhabited by families who had lost their homes; these houses remain inhabited today. Moreover, the problems consequent upon the disaster and the need for government intervention to assist disadvantaged families led directly to the creation of the first provincial housing authority, the Nova Scotia Housing Commission.

Nevertheless, with the exception of some housing which was built for veterans returning from the First World War under the terms of legislation passed by the Government of Canada, and 334 dwelling

1

units built by the Toronto Housing Company,[3] there was relatively little continuous governmental participation until the middle and late 1930s. During the 1920s, as Carver pointed out,[4] the Canadian economy was relatively buoyant and, in company with the United States, Canada enjoyed a period of unprecedented prosperity. Housing built during the 1920s was created by small builders (for purchase) within the private market. Insofar as Canadians thought very much about the housing conditions of those individuals and families in the lower half of the income scale, it was assumed that the "filtering-down" process worked satisfactorily. This assumption, long since discredited but widely held by more affluent members of the community to this day, involves the notion that when the well-to-do leave dwellings which they inhabit, presumably for more adequate housing, their previous dwellings are reduced in value and become available to those of lesser means. Those of moderate income who improve their accommodation by acquiring more space or elegance leave other houses which ultimately filter down to the very poor.

THE COMPLEXITIES OF HOUSING MARKET ANALYSIS

The field of housing is one of the most complicated aspects of modern industrial societies, if not the most complex. It may indeed be exceeded in scope and difficulty only by the field of health care. In western industrial societies, housing has become both a private activity in the market place and a public activity on behalf of those individuals and families who, due to insufficiency of resources, seem incapable of meeting their housing requirements. Such "resources" are usually considered to be financial, such as the proportion of income which can be devoted to housing without serious deterioration of the family's standard of living, but they may embrace such intangibles as motivation, the degree of sacrifice which an individual or family is prepared to make, and many other emotional aspects. (The nature of the house inhabited by a family, the neighbourhood in which it lives, and the amenities in that neighbourhood, are all components of the social class to which the family is considered to belong and some measure of the regard in which the family is held by its friends, relatives and neighbours.)

In a capitalistic market economy the housing industry, by definition, must produce for those who have the resources to take its products off the market, otherwise its entrepreneurs would be forced out of business. This has meant, and can only mean, that adequate housing is not provided automatically in western industrial societies for those persons with modest or inadequate resources. Under these circumstances governments have intervened and a variety of housing programs have been developed in Canada and in other countries to meet the needs of those who must be assisted by the resources of society as a whole.

The "government of housing", as Donnison has pointed out,[5] proceeds on a variety of levels of conceptualization. Many persons believe the provision of housing to be quite different, in philosophical terms, than the provision of food, clothing, household facilities, and other necessities of life. There is a moral problem faced by an important segment of the population which holds the view that there is something unethical in process when housing must be provided with state assistance unless there is some disadvantage within the individual and family which requires such assistance. In short, a disability must be recognized, examined and carefully evaluated before such assistance can be rendered and especially if it is to be provided for an extended period. This is simply one example of the attitudes many people maintain with respect to persons who are poor in industrial societies where poverty is no longer the norm.[6]

THE POLITICAL CONTEXT

No government is likely to take the requisite action to provide housing for those who require societal intervention unless there appears to be a political advantage or unless the pressure for action on the government in power is so strong that it can no longer be resisted. In Canada, the intervention of government in the 1930s was fundamentally a response to economic problems which spawned very significant political problems. The Conservative government, which appeared to be threatened with the loss of power as an election approached in 1935, passed a series of legislative measures described colloquially as "Canada's New Deal", presumably because they appeared to be emulation of American measures of 1933 and thereafter. The only piece of legislation which survived the test of constitutionality in 1935 was the Dominion Housing Act.[7] The fact that the legislation was passed is a reflection of political and economic circumstances; it cannot by any means be considered to be indicative of a conviction on the part of the then federal government that state intervention in the housing market was either normal or desirable.

The passage of the first National Housing Act in 1938 can be attributed to similar inducements as unemployment persisted under the new Liberal government and a further economic recession occurred in 1937-38.[8] The NHA was a political and economic act by a government hoping to stimulate employment by broadening the terms of the 1935 legislation. At no time prior to the Second World War did it appear to the majority of Canadians that governmental intervention in the field of housing was likely to persist and expand.[9] Viewpoints have since changed but it is still a moot point whether the majority of our citizens in the late 1970s view public activity in the field of housing as desirable, permanent and inevitable.

The first series of decisions must be taken at the local level, within municipal councils. Not only in federal nations like Canada or the United States but in a nation like the United Kingdom where there are no states or provinces, the fact remains that housing accommodation is provided, and very often financed in part, administered and managed, within the physical boundaries and the planning jurisdiction of a local government. By definition, the land upon which the housing rests is within a municipality or regional government; those individuals or families who require governmental assistance in meeting their housing requirements are residents and taxpayers of a locality or a regional governmental area. Local governments in most Canadian provinces have a good deal of "negative capacity" to forestall the creation of housing accommodation under governmental auspices if they are disinclined to favour such activities. These capacities rest in their powers to zone land, to regulate the pace and the specifics of urban development, and to develop standards of maintenance and occupancy within the existing housing stock.

In Canada, the provincial governments, as well, have substantial power to facilitate or to oppose inter-governmental activity within the field of housing. They have exercised these powers when they so chose and the fundamental political question remains the one enunciated previously: to what degree is there advantage to the government in power in engaging in this important economic and social activity around which so much controversy swells?

The great mistake which so many Canadians have made in considering the political context of housing policy consists in the naive view that once governments recognize a human need, they will move to take action as promptly as possible. The fact is that what is meant by "action" in the field of housing is a series of political and legislative decisions to devote a portion of scarce economic resources to this activity rather than to another. Sometimes this means diverting financial resources (to the housing activity) from the social services, from the health services, from the provision of educational facilities, and from basic municipal protective services; sometimes it means additional capital borrowing over and beyond the experience of previous years. It surely means the creation of administrative resources within government to handle the economic and technical questions which arise in the development of housing for persons and families of modest or low income.

THE ECONOMIC CONTEXT

The provision of housing accommodation is a matter of substantial economic significance in Canada. Between the early 1950s and the late 1970s the total annual investment in residential construction rose from about $2 billion to more than $11 billion.[10] Although the demand for new housing for purchase had not been strong in 1976 and throughout the first half of 1977, the number of housing starts in 1976 was at a record high (exceeding 273,000 units).[11] Unemployment in Canada exceeded 7 per cent of the labour force in the late 1970s; instability in the residential construction industry has greatly contributed to such unemployment.

Although most Canadians realize that provision of housing is an important economic activity within private industry as a whole, they are not fully aware of all the economic ramifications of the house-building industry and that all of the factors of production, land, labour and materials are involved in the provision of housing.

Moreover, those industries which produce the furnishings new home buyers often require (plumbing fixtures, appliances, furniture, carpets, bedding, linens and so on) will be affected by the degree to which the market for new housing is buoyant or otherwise. The policies of governments and the decisions of private entrepreneurs with respect to land use affect the supply of housing, the kind of housing produced and the level of housing costs at any one time. The degree to which residential housing is expanding has a profound effect upon employment in a number of related industries which supply building materials (lumber, cement, bricks, copper piping, oil burners, furnaces and the like). In short, the economic ramifications of the private and public provision of housing accommodation are widespread.

Under these circumstances I am always amazed at the naïveté displayed by many Canadians, including some politicians and social scientists, with respect to the economic position of housing in their analysis of housing programs and policies. Over the years I can recall the plaintive demands of citizens' groups, of social scientists, of elected and appointed officials and of voluntary organizations, that government not "use" housing as a stimulus or a deterrent to economic activity. Dennis and Fish have identified what they consider to be the first deliberate attempt by the Government of Canada in 1957 to use housing provision as an economic stimulant.[12]

The tragic aspect of this situation is the widely held belief that government can exercise its overall economic, monetary and social policies, without in any serious way affecting the provision of housing. It is not possible for the Government of Canada to exert its influence to vary interest rates or the money supply upward or downward without affecting mortgage rates, and these in turn have a profound effect on the capacity or willingness of Canadians to purchase new homes. In the latter part of 1976 and into 1977, the rediscount rate of the Bank of Canada was reduced on several occasions; soon thereafter rates on first mortgages from most lending institutions dropped by a similar percentage; in 1978 and 1979 the "bank rate" was increased ten times and, invariably, mortgage rates rose correspondingly.

Critics of government housing policies have customarily not been upset when rates were dropping but when it was apparently in the economic interest of the nation to raise interest rates (and thus mortgage rates) there were pleas by the aforementioned critics, to the federal government, to eliminate or ameliorate the influence of these changed economic policies in the field of housing. This cannot be done simply, although a number of assisted housing programs involving the subsidization of interest rates can be and have been undertaken to alleviate the impact of economic changes upon certain individuals or families within various housing markets.

There is a further dimension to the economics of housing which is more clearly understood than the interrelationships of monetary policy and housing activity, specifically the direct and indirect expenditures of government in housing provision. At the end of 1968 it was asserted in a formal report to the federal cabinet that

> a total of more than $12 billion in National Housing Act loans, grants and subsidies has been extended to provide Canadians with more and better housing in a suitable urban environment. It is by most standards an impressive record.[13]

More than $8 billion was committed in direct federal expenditures and CMHC loans between the end of 1968 to the end of 1978.

Canadians understand that loans are repaid and that direct expenditures are a relatively minor part of the total. Subsidies are more difficult to comprehend and have been a cause for concern by governments and resentment by the general public. Until 1973 the term "subsidy" generally referred to the difference between the rent-paying capacity of a tenant in public housing and the full economic cost of providing the accommodation, amortized over fifty years. Such subsidies were not substantial, in absolute current dollars, prior to the late 1960s. By the mid-1970s the annual dollar requirement in conventional assisted housing had approached $500 million, at least half of which was borne by the Government of Canada. At the same time, new programs had been developed requiring subsidies to home purchasers in the form of interest reduction loans and outright grants to purchasers to maintain monthly shelter payments at 30 per cent or less of gross family income.

There was in the late 1970s renewed concern about both per unit per month subsidy payments required by virtue of rapidly escalating housing costs, and total subsidy payments on an annual basis. I consider the subsidy question a serious policy constraint in Canadian housing for the next two decades at least.

THE SOCIAL CONTEXT

The determination of a national society, or a smaller community within it, to intervene in the housing market requires both implicit and explicit social commitments and underlying frameworks ranging from the philosophical to the quite specifically economic. Basically, the provision of affordable housing, adequate in quantity (space) and quality (physical and community amenities), for every individual and family, must be enunciated as a major social goal.

Canada, unlike a number of western countries, rather than formally presenting the fundamental goals of its housing policies, has instead relied on a statement of objectives associated with each new or altered housing program. This important omission has been clearly expressed by Wolman in his analysis of "housing as a social service".

> One of the less visible, but nonetheless important differences between British and American housing policy – and one which itself greatly helps to account for many of the other differences – is the view each country holds with respect to the appropriate responsibility of government in meeting the shelter needs of its citizens. The concept of housing as a social service appears frequently in discussions of British housing policy, while it is not a common frame of reference for debate on American housing policy.[15]

The word "Canadian" may be substituted for the word "American" in the quotation with entire justification. Nevertheless, the development of Canadian housing legislation by the federal and provincial governments, particularly since 1954, constitutes an undeniable social commitment.

Once this commitment is affirmed, the social questions assume the form of explicit socio-economic decisions. The major social question may be phrased as follows: "Who are to be the direct beneficiaries of publicly initiated housing policies and programs?" The obvious response must be: "Those persons and families in the greatest need of adequate housing." But how is need to be measured and priorities to be determined among those identified as "in need"? And how is such identification of those "in need" to be made in the first instance?

The first of the most logical techniques developed to answer these questions almost everywhere in the world consists of a careful observation and examination of the physical shelter and housing conditions of those who apply as tenants or purchasers of the new or rehabilitated housing to be provided. This assessment requires a staff of examiners or interviewers who must be trained to observe and rate the extent of physical deficiencies, to ask the proper questions of the residents and to seek relevant answers. This is particularly important when the impact of current living arrangements upon the physical and emotional health of family members is a part of the rating process in determining need.

The second technique in measurement of need and priorities among applicants (who, it is assumed, will generally exceed the number of available dwellings) is a determination of individual or family income or both. Information can be provided by the applicant or other members of the family, by the employer, if there is one, or by those agencies, usually governmental, which provide or supplement the basic income of the individual or family. The fundamental notion is, of course, that those in the poorest shelter and with the lowest income per household (sometimes considered per capita) should have the highest priority in the allocation of publicly provided housing. But to express this apparently fair and reasonable assumption without qualification is to gloss over a variety of social and administrative problems and issues.

What immediately comes to mind is the question of whether the alleged "need" should be expressed through a process of self-identification (application) or whether society should first identify those areas of clearly undesirable or "bad" housing in the community, develop a program to replace or rehabilitate such housing, if feasible, and allocate the new accommodation to the previous residents. The latter is the essence of the concepts of slum clearance and urban renewal. Those displaced by the clearance and rebuilding operations would naturally be the first to be rehoused. Such neat formulations soon run into the blocks which appear when criteria other than prior residence are taken into consideration. The most important of these is the income criterion. The assumption in Canada and the United States in the first postwar decade (1946-1955) that the residents of slum clearance or renewal areas would be "quite poor" was not borne out in practice. Some households were in poverty, some were not. Should all previous on-site residents have equal priority for rehousing?

The abovementioned experience raised sharply the whole question of the validity of the income criterion and also the question, "What is to be considered total family income for the purpose of determining eligibility and setting priorities for allocation of scarce accommodation?" Most governmental organizations determined eligibility by the total annual income for both individuals and families or by marginal tax (percentage of income for rent). During the 1950s, the Central Mortgage and Housing Corporation issued quarterly estimates of the total family income for various communities (said to be the upper limit of the lowest third of the family income distribution) beyond which applications for publicly assisted housing could not be accepted and current tenants would be encouraged to move out and seek accommodation in the private market.

Beyond these over-arching questions there are many problems implicit in the definition of family income. Most authorities in Canada and the United States developed systems of rental payment whereby rents were geared-to-income. Rents would increase as income increased (sometimes to a maximum proportion of 25-30 per cent of gross family income) and decrease as income decreased. Thus emerged the so-called "rental scale".

The first step in rent determination was thus income determination. The latter began usually with a recording of the total income of the head of the household, assumed to be the father of the family. But among low-income families, as the postwar decades passed, the principal income recipient was often the mother of the family – widowed, separated or deserted – and families headed by a woman became the norm among applicants for public housing. The question arose as to whether the principal source of income – a public social assistance payment – should be considered in toto for purposes of rent determination.

Among intact families headed by a male the question of secondary income recipients posed many difficulties. Should the part-time earnings of wives (mothers) be included in family income and if so, how much of their income? And what about the earnings of employed children, ranging all the way from the pin money of the child's newspaper delivery route to the full-time incomes of older teen-aged or young adult children who normally paid nominal amounts to parents for room and board? If these earnings were not included, in whole or in part, why not? It was not difficult to emphasize that one goal of publicly assisted housing programs was to enable families to re-organize or re-order their spending patterns, to save money if possible, and to leave public housing for the private rental or purchase market. Strict regulations governing income calculation might well inhibit attainment of these socio-economic goals.

As difficult as these administrative and social decisions were, they were overshadowed by the major questions of social objectives implicit in a large-scale public housing program. As the effort to increase the supply of publicly assisted housing units intensified throughout Canada during 1965-1974, the matter of the form and shape of physical structures on the one hand, and of the neighbourhood or community on the other, came to exercise paramount influence. The quickest way to acquire housing was to purchase buildings under construction by private entrepreneurs seeking liquidity in their investments. Moreover, rental units in high-rise multiple form offered hundreds of dwelling units rather than dozens usually available in low-rise, low or medium density developments.

Apartment buildings afforded housing described as bachelor accommodation and one- and two-bedroom apartments, for the most part. The housing authorities were committed to the prevention of overcrowding and thus could often not meet the needs of families with more than two to four children. In any case, there was the emerging question of the suitability of apartment dwellings for families with children. In the late 1960s there was an increasing volume of literature attributing disturbed family relationships and behavioural problems among children to high-rise apartment living.[16]

The question of "community" or "normalcy" within neighbourhoods dominated by public housing projects was equally important. Within some municipalities in Canada, school boards deplored the vastly increased number of children from low-income publicly-housed families, insisting that many children had fallen behind in the appropriate age-grade progression and related to this fact was the frequence of problem behaviour in classrooms.

This situation was merely one aspect of community. More important was the fact that public housing accommodation was increasingly populated by families dependent on one form or another of public assistance payments, general welfare assistance, family benefits or mothers' allowances, old age pensions and disability allowances. Moreover, the fact that applications from single parent families reached levels exceeding 50 per cent of all applications in many Ontario cities by the mid-1970s promised no return to "normal" communities composed of an appropriate mixture of self-supporting employed intact families, dependent intact families and self-supporting and dependent one-parent families. The notion of general normalcy in communities in which significant proportions of socially assisted housing units are located, cannot be stretched to encompass the notion of "villages of the poor".

A FUNCTIONAL APPROACH TO ANALYSIS

The complexities of housing policy analysis thus involve constitutional, political, economic, social and administrative considerations. In recent years a number of competent scholars and research organizations have attempted through analyses of the "housing problem" or the "housing crisis" (to cite the two most common phrases of concern in Canada) to devise housing policies they consider more appropriate in the light of changing circumstances.

At the beginning of the 1970s, as the federal government was contemplating the creation of a new ministry to be responsible for housing and urban affairs, the minister responsible for housing, Robert Andras, commissioned Harvey Lithwick, then Professor of Economics at Carleton University, to undertake a comprehensive examination of Canada's urban situation, including the organization and administration of its housing program. By 1972, under the direction of Dr. Lithwick, six research monographs had been published as well as a major review of the problems and prospects facing an urban Canada.[17] The second monograph in the research series was entitled "Housing in Canada".[18] There can be no question that under Dr. Lithwick's direction the empirical and theoretical framework essential to the development of a Ministry of State for Urban Affairs, which was ultimately created in 1971,[19] was well provided.

As these studies were in the process of publication and dissemination, a major research project was commissioned by Central Mortgage and Housing Corporation under the direction of Michael Dennis, then a member of the Faculty of Osgoode Hall Law School and Susan Fish, then Director of the Bureau of Municipal Research in Toronto. Dennis and Fish ultimately published their own report when the sponsoring organization either refused or was dilatory in its consideration of publication and dissemination. The approach in this major contribution to the analysis of housing policies in Canada is implicit within its title, *Programs in Search of a Policy: Low Income Housing in Canada*.[20] The major conclusions of the authors were that a great variety of housing programs had been initiated in Canada since the Second World War, that they had been ad hoc responses by the Government of Canada with or without the participation of the provincial governments, and that they failed to be based firmly on any clear policy direction by the federal government or the federal and provincial governments acting jointly.

In the view of one research organization, these major studies within the field of housing in Canada failed to recognize fully the basic characteristics of the housing sector. The most significant consideration is the fact that housing performs several significant functions.

> Housing performs at least four quite different functions in our society. It is a consumer good, providing shelter; it is an investment good, the only major investment of most families; it is an industrial sector, providing jobs and incomes for many; and it is a social good, which governments attempt to provide for all income classes.[21]

All of these several approaches to the analysis of Canadian housing were important contributions to the study of the subject. Nevertheless, the complex problems inherent within the provision of housing in Canada continue and while we are undoubtedly one of the best housed nations in the world, the questions raised by these analysts concerning the inadequacies of housing provision for a substantial proportion of our population remain unanswered. It is not suggested that I will provide the answer but in the analysis which follows, I shall trace the evolution of housing policies within Canada, not merely from the vantage point of the federal government but from the point of view of all three (or even four levels of government where regional governments exist) particularly since the end of the Second World War. I cannot accept the view that we have had housing programs to the exclusion of housing policies; I cannot accept the view that governments have failed the Canadian population seriously; I cannot accept the view that we cannot do better. Perhaps my examination of the history will provide some clues to the evolution of more adequate housing policies and programs designed to implement them.

NOTES

[1]D. C. Masters, *The Rise of Toronto, 1850-1890* (Toronto: University of Toronto Press, 1947) p. 127. An address by Miss Charity Cook, Tenth Canadian Conference of Charities and Correction, *Proceedings* (Toronto, October 1909) pp. 10-12. J. S. Woodsworth, *My Neighbor* (University of Toronto Press and Oxford University Press, 1911, reprinted 1972).

[2]Bureau of Municipal Research, Toronto: Bulletin 2, "Do You Care How the Other Fellow is Housed?", March 13, 1914; Bulletin 7, "Is the Solution of the Housing Problem a Civic Duty", April 1, 1914. D. W. Holdsworth, "House and Home in Vancouver: Images of West Coast Urbanism, 1886-1929", in G. Stelter and A. Artibise (Eds.) *The Canadian City: Essays in Urban History* (Toronto: McClelland & Stewart, 1977 – Carleton University Library).

[3]S. Spragge, "Early Housing Reform – A Confluence of Interests, 1900-1920", a paper delivered at the first Canadian Urban History Conference (University of Guelph, May 1977, mimeo) p. 12.

[4]H. S. M. Carver, *Houses for Canadians* (Toronto: University of Toronto Press, 1948) pp. 25-28.

[5]D. V. Donnison, *The Government of Housing* (London: Penguin Books Ltd., 1967) pp. 79-112.

[6]J. K. Galbraith, *The Affluent Society* (Boston: Houghton Mifflin Co., 1958) pp. 322-333.

[7]*Dominion Housing Act*, 1935, 25-26 George V, Chap. 58.

[8]*National Housing Act*, 1938, 2 George VI, Chap. 49.

[9]The Research Committee of the League for Social Reconstruction, *Social Planning for Canada* (Toronto: Thomas Nelson & Sons Ltd., 1935), pp. 3-39, 451-463.

[10]Central Mortgage and Housing Corporation, *Canadian Housing Statistics, 1978* (Ottawa: CMHC, March 1979) Table 24, p. 21.

[11]*Ibid.*, Table 1, p. 1. There were sharp reductions to 245,700 starts in 1977 and 227,600 in 1978.

[12]M. Dennis and S. Fish, *Programs in Search of a Policy: Low Income Housing in Canada* (Toronto: Hakkert, 1972), p. 130.

[13]Canada, *Report of the Task Force on Housing and Urban Development* (Ottawa: Queen's Printer, 1969) p. 6.

[14]Central Mortgage and Housing Corporation, *Canadian Housing Statistics, 1978* (Ottawa: CMHC, March 1979) Table 24, p. 21.

[15]H. L. Wolman, *Housing and Housing Policy in the U.S. and the U.K.* (Lexington, Toronto and London: Lexington Books, D. C. Heath and Company, 1975) p. 15.

[16]See M. Lipman, *Social Effects of the Housing Environment*, a background paper prepared for the Canadian Conference on Housing, October 1968, pp. 4-17; and H. N. Colburn, *Health and Housing*, similarly prepared, pp. 33-34. These papers were collected and published under the title, *The Right to Housing* (Montreal: Harvest House, 1969).

[17]Central Mortgage and Housing Corporation, *Urban Canada: Problems and Prospects*, a report prepared by N. H. Lithwick for the Minister Responsible for Housing, Government of Canada (Ottawa: CMHC, December 1970) pp. 236.

[18]L. B. Smith, "Housing in Canada," *Urban Canada: Problems and Prospects*, (Ottawa: CMHC, January 1971) research monograph 2, pp. 99.

[19]Dr. Lithwick became the first director of research for the new Ministry of State and remained in that position for nearly two years.

[20]M. Dennis and S. Fish, *op. cit.*

[21]R. Shaffner, "Housing Policy in Canada: Learning from Recent Problems" *HRI Observations* (Montreal: C. D. Howe Research Institute) No. 9, August 1975, p. 2.

CHAPTER 2

Essential Elements of a Canadian Housing Policy

INTRODUCTION

In recent Canadian history there has been much confusion about housing policy. The most serious and the most frequent charge to be levelled, particularly against the federal government, is that "there is no national housing policy." When the particular course of action adopted and pursued by one or more levels of government is unsuccessful in meeting the total problem under consideration, one suspects that the pronouncer of the dictum "there is no housing policy", is simply finding another way of saying that many individual, family, or group housing problems have not been solved satisfactorily either in quantitative or qualitative terms.

It is nevertheless true that it is very difficult for the student of housing affairs to decide when a particular government proposal, or apparent course of action, really represents housing policy or is merely a temporary palliative or pronouncement behind which stands no particular government support and conviction. During the past thirty years it has been alleged by many social scientists, politicians, and other students of the problem that the most prevalent governmental reaction to Canada's housing dilemmas may fairly be described as "housing by headline". This is meant to imply that during this period there have been far more pronouncements, newspaper articles, press releases, and other indications of concern and potential action than there have been specific governmental actions designed to meet our housing needs. In this welter of charge and countercharge, of proposal and counterproposal, of allegations of buck-passing from one level of government to another, the tremendous progress in Canada's housing situation since 1938-1939 tends to become lost, or at best dimmed, and the limits and scope of a housing policy become obscured.

The most important background fact in the Canadian housing experience is that Canada is a federal state. In 1867 the authors of our constitution determined that there would be a federal government with certain specific functions and a second tier of provincial governments with certain other specific functions. Unlike the situation in the United States, the residual powers were left with the federal governmen. In fact, the Government of Canada can legislate in any national emergency "for the peace, order, and good government" of all Canadians.[1] But, it must be emphasized that in a federal state the matter of housing policy is quite different from that in a unitary state like the United Kingdom. In Canada the first essential must be to determine where the constitutional responsibility lies, and once that legal interpretation is made clear and is accepted by the central government and the governments of the provinces, then, and only then, can the concept of policy begin to emerge. There can be no policy otherwise, unless what passes for policy is merely a course of action contemplated by one level of government in default of the rightful assumption of responsibility by another.

In this country the constitutional responsibility for the provision of housing to individuals and families has been assigned, by judicial interpretation, to the provinces under Section 92 of the British North America Act.[2] The assignment does not necessarily result in the acceptance of responsibility by these governments. Therefore, when some persons have insisted in recent years that Canadian housing policy has changed drastically by virtue of the assumption of responsibility by the governments of the provinces, such an assertion must be strongly challenged. Housing policy has not changed, if we can, indeed, admit that such policy existed. What has changed has been the adoption and pursuit of a course of action by a particular level of government (provincial) which, during the previous thirty years, had participated in this endeavour only to a very limited extent.

This kind of analysis emphasizes that there are essentials in the determination of a Canadian housing policy, and these essentials must be carefully examined and explained before we can proceed to understand the response to the national housing problem. The major essentials in Canadian housing policy are legislation, financial resources, responsibility for initiating action, and appropriate administration arrangements.

LEGISLATION

The determination of a particular course of action with respect to the alleviation of some aspect of the overall housing problem cannot take the form merely of a pronouncement by one or more levels of government that action will be taken. Nor is it sufficient to suggest that the government in question favours a particular approach or a particular view of the problem. Housing policy, as one definition suggests, requires a course of action adopted and pursued by a government, and the terms "adoption" and "pursuit" require, at the very least, the passage of legislation that enunciates specifically what the particular government is prepared to do about the problem. In this respect it might be argued that there has been a national housing policy in Canada since at least 1935, when the Dominion Housing Act was passed.[3] Since that time there have been three major National Housing Acts passed in 1938, 1944 and 1954; and in 1964 and 1973 a further series of major amendments which transformed the legislation[4]

The essence of federal legislation in housing is not very different from that of other federal legislation concerned with matters of national interest in some field of economic and social affairs. In a federal country, a major piece of legislation must afford an opportunity for the governments of the provinces, if they have the constitutional responsibility, to participate actively in the implementation of the particular course of action planned by the central government. These incentives may be as simple as the provision of financial resources, provided the governments of the provinces pass "enabling legislation" permitting them to sign agreements with the federal government on the matter in question. It is more usual, however, for the federal government to pass legislation which enunciates the essence of the central government's view of the problem and the nature of the potential solutions required to solve it. In addition, federal legislation customarily implies that certain standards of implementation and administration must be met if the provincial governments are to qualify for assistance – technical, administrative, accounting, financial – to be provided by the central government.

In a country like Canada, a major piece of federal legislation must provide the opportunity for every region to participate in the contemplated program. It should be possible for each region to develop, within appropriate limits, its own approach to the solution of the housing problem, an approach consistent with its history and traditions, its tastes and preferences, and its view of its own special needs.

It is conceivable that a course of action may be enunciated by government without the passage of specific legislation and that this declaration may be the expression of governmental policy. It is inconceivable, however, that policy can be implemented without the passage of legislation which makes it possible to pursue the prescribed action. Within the several National Housing Acts passed in Canada since 1938 it is possible to discern the philosophy underlying government housing policy. The legislation and the regulations written for such legislation really prescribe the beneficiaries for whom governmental action is intended and the conditions under which potential beneficiaries may, in fact, receive the support or assistance provided by the legislation. To this extent, legislation is not merely the legal execution of constitutional responsibility but can be conceived as both the social and economic dimensions of housing policy at the particular level of government responsible for its passage.

FINANCIAL RESOURCES

It is insufficient to pass laws without the provision of financial resources to implement the policies developed and proclaimed by the legislation. Moreover, the actual provision of government appropriations may be an indication of the intensity with which policy is meant to be implemented. Legislation is sometimes passed under pressure from citizens' groups, from business or trade associations, even from the elected representatives of other levels of government; but it may be the intention of the body which passes the legislation that it shall be merely a token acknowledgement of the need for governmental action.

In Canada, unlike the United States, the passage of legislation is usually accompanied by some specific indication of the amount of money intended to achieve the objectives of the legislation. For example, in both Part I (Housing for Home Owners) and Part II (Section 22 – later Part III, Section 23) of the National Housing Act of 1944, specific amounts of money, namely, $300,000,000 (1949) and $250,000,000 (1953), were specified as available for these particular portions. As time passed, these amounts were amended and when the National Housing Act of 1954 was passed, the amounts available were altered in response to changing legislation and increased demand. Therefore, there is no need in Canada for additional pressure to be brought, once the legislation is passed, to ensure that the appropriation is voted. Rather, the more serious concern is to ensure that the monies available and specified within the legislation are, in fact, spent. This assurance very often requires intense pressure upon one level of government to convince its officials and, indeed, to force them to develop programs for which the funds are apparently available through a higher level of government.

It would appear that the enunciation of a course of action by government has been accompanied by a specific appropriation of funds for the various programs possible within the new laws. This is not to suggest, however, that the amounts of money provided have been sufficient. In that aspect of Canadian federal housing legislation which is intended to encourage the assumption of home ownership through the provision of more generous mortgage terms than are available in the open market, governmental policy shifted during the post-war period from direct intervention (the provision of a portion of the mortgage loans themselves) to more indirect intervention (the guaranteed repayment of such loans if potential owners should default). As simple as this may seem, housing policy in Canada has been more evident in the field of mortgage financing of home ownership than in any other respect.

In the years following the passage of the National Housing Act of 1944 and throughout most of the ensuing decade, Part I of the Act provided that the Government of Canada would provide 25 per cent of the capital amount of an approved NHA mortgage loan at relatively low interest, namely, 3 per cent. The effect of this specific action has had so many important ramifications in our post-war housing experience that even today the full impact of the experience of the first post-war decade can scarcely be measured fully. Clearly, it was the policy of the central government to encourage the assumption of home ownership, in new construction only, through a programme which resulted in the lowest first-mortgage interest rates in our history. This was formed by not one but two forms of subsidy: direct lending of funds provided by the general taxpayer to several hundreds of thousands of privileged families, and the provision of such funds at an artificially reduced rate of interest.

Although it occupied only one short part of the federal legislation, a consequence of this set of policies was clearly the expansion of vast suburban areas adjacent to every medium-sized and large urban centre. The problems that have ensued, both for the governments and residents of suburban areas and the governments and residents of central cities which did not directly benefit from this encouragement to home ownership, are immeasurable. An adequate assessment of the pros and cons of this aspect of policy has not been published, and one must refrain from ascribing all forms of urban distress and all negative aspects of urban living to one specific set of policies. On the other hand, it is not sufficient for those who have defended such policies to argue that, in the long run, a vast growth of urban population resulted in an expansion of metropolitan economic development inconceivable in the years immediately after the end of World War Two. It can surely be argued that this is a case where housing policy in effect took over the responsibility of urban planning (in this case suburban planning) which has been the source of so much distress to social, economic and planning analysts.

At this point in the argument, the key aspect of the situation in the first postwar decade is that the financial resources were, indeed, made available. As total Canadian population expanded and urbanization progressed rapidly, it became apparent early in the 1950s that the policy of stimulating home ownership – in itself the advancement of a group of values which represented the collective judgment of elected and appointed officials – could no longer be supported with available governmental revenues. In re-writing the National Housing Act in 1953-1954, the government's decision to discontinue direct participation in mortgage lending at a subsidized rate of interest was no surprise to students of the subject at that time. The new legislation permitted the chartered banks to enter the mortgage field in so far as National Housing Act operations were concerned. In fact, the banks were formally advised that they must share in the provision of required financial resources. In order to enable a conservative banking system to participate in the pursuit of a course of action prescribed by government, a system of mortgage loan guarantees was instituted and, as is often the case, the ultimate consumer (in this case the home buyer) would provide the insurance premiums, in the form of a fee amounting to 2 per cent of the purchase price.

APPROPRIATE INITIATIVES IN THE FIELD OF HOUSING

The pursuit of a course of action (the implementation of policy) must begin somewhere. A statement of housing policy backed up by legislative and financial guarantees is by no means equivalent to the implementation of a policy unless someone, somewhere, takes the initiative. It has been stated many times that housing legislation in Canada is as good as that existing in any other western nation. There is no reason to challenge this contention because such an argument would be fruitless. The real test of housing policy is its translation into the provision of adequate physical and social space occupied by individuals or families who are in need of such accommodation. The failure of such housing policy, when and if it could be judged that a particular course of action had failed, is more properly attributed to lack of initiative than to lack of resources.

It was therefore fitting that in discussing the proposed 1949 amendments to the National Housing Act, which were to introduce Canada for the first time to the field of public housing for low-income families, the then minister of Resources and Development, Robert H. Winters, should stress that the new legislation could only be implemented by virtue of local initiatives. The federal minister made it perfectly clear that those forms of government which were allegedly closest to the tangible needs of people must take steps to meet those needs. The relationships emphasized by federal officials were, of course, federal-provincial relations.

Despite the triteness of the phrase, the municipalities are in fact the creatures of the provincial governments. Barring the extraordinary powers available during periods of war-time emergency, the federal government has no constitutional right to negotiate directly with local government. It was made clear, therefore, when Section 35 was before Parliament in November 1944,[5] that the federal-provincial agreements envisaged in this amendment to the Act depended upon local initiative. The amount of financial responsibility placed upon local governments was a matter for the provincial governments, after they chose to participate in the newly conceived federal-provincial partnership. Some provinces (Alberta, Quebec, and Prince Edward Island) did not choose to participate for nearly fifteen years.

Canada's housing history during the 1950s, as far as direct public intervention is concerned, can be described in terms of the existence or non-existence of local initiatives pressing for public participation in the available legislation and financial programs. Local initiative, subject to many and varied interpretations, is sometimes regarded as a purely voluntary effort on the part of private citizens and organizations directed towards influencing one or more levels of government to take appropriate action. This conception of local initiative is far too narrow. For example, in Halifax, where a substantial public housing program was mounted during the 1950s, the most important initiators were the mayor and the elected councillors of the city (these officials were advised by a competent city manager).

Perhaps this form of local government provides a structure in which the city manager, convinced of the need for urban renewal and an appropriate housing program, can draw more clearly to the attention of elected officials the needs of the community. Initiation in Toronto, however, has been less evident among elected and appointed officials but has, to a substantial degree, been the product of pressure mounted by voluntary community organizations such as: the Citizens Housing and Planning Association, from 1944 to 1949; the Metropolitan Toronto Branch of the Community Planning Association of Canada, from 1948 to the present; the Association of Women Electors; and other groups. In the late 1970s, with the creation of the City of Toronto Non-Profit Housing Corporation (City Home), this lack of "official" initiative was no longer a reality.

Each of these experiences (Halifax, Toronto, Vancouver,[6] et al) can be justifiably described as local initiatives. The legislative arrangements require that the local community has a clear recognition of need and a clear indication of the desire for the public assumption of responsibility to provide housing accommodation for low-income groups. This would seem to be an appropriate line of initiatives – a line running from the local manifestation of human need to those levels of government where the legislative and financial resources have been provided. The alternative approach, a line of action which would run from governmental bodies down towards the neighbourhood or the local community, is surely a paternalistic approach and moreover, one that could fail to recognize the differential quality of housing requirements from community to community and from region to region.

It must be recognized, of course, that what is called local initiative, whether citizen-based or council-based, can only flourish under certain favourable conditions. In a situation where a provincial government has decided, for whatever reason, that it does not consider housing to be of relatively high priority among all of its competing responsibilities, the atmosphere in which local initiative can develop is most restricted. In Nova Scotia, Ontario and British Columbia it was obvious that there was at least some recognition of the potentialities of the federal-provincial partnership. Although the line from local initiative to provincial acceptance of need, to the development of a federal-provincial agreement with respect to the construction of "housing projects for sale or for rent" in any Ontario community[7] was not smooth and uninterrupted, the general climate was favourable. In general it can be argued that this was also the case in Newfoundland, and to some extent in New Brunswick. In certain other provinces such as Alberta, Manitoba, and especially Quebec, the situation was quite different.

In certain provinces the required enabling legislation following the 1949 amendments, was not even enacted. In other provinces where enabling legislation was passed, unusually difficult financial requirements were prescribed, which effectively curtailed the nurturing of local initiatives in the development of housing programs. In those provinces where all or most of the 25 per cent provincial share of capital requirements and operating subsidies was passed on to the local municipality, such arrangements could hardly be regarded as "the pursuit of a course of action." A detailed assessment of the experience in the 1950s from province to province is not available, but it can be stated fairly that whatever progress occurred, in both physical and social terms, was very closely related to the climate in which voluntary and public initiatives at the local community level were fostered in some provinces or hampered to the point of discouragement in others.

EFFECTIVE ADMINISTRATIVE ARRANGEMENTS

Even where it can be assumed that all of the previously considered essentials of a national housing policy – legislation, financial resources, local initiative – were present and flowed smoothly towards the announced objectives, there was always the danger of long and frustrating delays and even the abandonment of specific programs because of the lack of administrative arrangements, both in the structural and personnel sense.

In the early years after World War Two, most provinces were ill-equipped to deal with the problems of urbanization which included housing, community planning, urban renewal, and the like. Most provinces did not have appropriate community planning legislation; most did not have appropriate legislation with respect to housing development; and, most did not have any clearly defined locus of responsibility within the provincial departmental structure where new programs could be lodged. In Ontario the entire field was the responsibility of two branches of the then Department of Planning and Development, first created in 1946. The Housing Branch was responsible for the administration of provincial legislation, such as the Housing Development Act of 1948,[8] and was soon assigned the role of provincial agent in the emerging federal-provincial partnership after 1949. The responsibilities of local government in the field of community planning were administered through the Community Planning Branch of the same department. Both of these branches were relatively new, modestly staffed and modestly financed; they were groping their way to an understanding and appreciation of the problems for which they were responsible, and were trying to devise administrative techniques for meeting them. Most other Canadian provinces were by no means as well equipped as Ontario to deal with the rapid expansion of urban areas after 1945.

The development of effective administrative arrangements cannot be conceived merely as a problem of governmental administration in the sense of allocation of responsibilities on organizational charts. There has been naive assumption on the part of the protagonists of public intervention, as well as by certain government officials, that the administration of housing programs is fairly straightforward. The fact is that in the first decade following the end of the Second World War there were very few people in Canada who had any experience in the administration of public housing programs; in the general field of housing itself such experience as existed was derived from the management of property administered by trust companies and a few owners of large multiple dwellings. After 1945 Central Mortgage and Housing Corporation was able to build up a substantial staff of well trained and experienced personnel; its main activities were, however, in the field of mortgage financing. Only gradually did the corporation acquire staff members who were interested in and knowledgeable about the disciplines of community planning, architecture, and social welfare.

Within the public services of the provinces there were few with experience relevant to the development of intergovernmental programs. Moreover, there were no substantial provincial housing organizations prior to the inauguration of the Ontario Housing Corporation in 1964.[9] Thus it was not possible to offer prospective public servants a clear and substantial career opportunity in the field of public housing. All across Canada in this field there were not more than two dozen full-time jobs, outside Central Mortgage and Housing Corporation, excluding clerical and maintenance staffs.

The administration of public housing requires far more than the knowledge and experience of a rent collector or a property manager. Those who are charged with the responsibility of administering dwellings provided for certain persons or families who qualify by virtue of low income, grossly inadequate current housing accommodation, some physical or emotional disability, large family size, or any combination of these several attributes, must be persons who have a clear understanding of both the objectives of the housing programs and of the culture of the families and individuals most likely to inhabit them.

There are basically two schools of thought underlying the case for public housing accommodation. One argues that the family requiring public housing is simply unable, for one reason or another, to earn the income necessary to acquire housing in the private market. These people are "a bit down on their luck", or the father lacks education or skill. For the second approach the argument is made that public housing should be viewed as assistance to the very poor such as: the elderly, families headed by a chronically ill or handicapped father, or families where there is no male head. Many persons believe that public housing should be restricted to those identified by this second approach. There is no reason why the two approaches cannot be blended – the distinction should be made between the independent and the dependent persons or families. Public housing accommodation should be available for income receivers who are self-supporting but whose incomes are simply insufficient to enable them to function in the private housing market as well as for very poor families. The critical factor is the blending of independent and dependent families within housing projects or neighbourhoods so that children may develop in an environment in which gross poverty is not the most distinctive characteristic.

It is true that lower class families are, generally speaking, different from families that are middle or upper class. Although not every individual or family is a part of the culture, there is a definite culture among lower-class families in Western urban industrial nations. Such individuals and families have a different set of values, a different set of relationships between members of the opposite sex, a different method of relating to and disciplining children, and a different attitude towards work and towards many other values commonly held by members of the middle class.[10] At the same time, many of the values and environmental circumstances which provide satisfactions and a basic cultural framework to the poor are found in slum, blighted, or urban renewal areas.[11] The removal of these families from such areas and their relocation in public housing projects does not necessarily solve many, or any, of their social and economic problems.

There is not yet any course at the university or technological college level in Canada designed to train housing administrators. When the largest federal-provincial housing authority in Canada (in terms of the number of dwelling units under administration), the Metropolitan Toronto Housing Authority, advertised for "housing administrators" in the spring of 1956 it received a great many more applications than the members of its board anticipated. For the most part, however, these applications came from persons already established in such fields as real estate, life insurance, property management within lending institutions, and from public servants who were not pleased with their progress in other fields of government activity. Only very few of the applicants appeared to have any understanding of what was involved in the administration of housing provided under governmental auspices. Some of these latter individuals had come to Canada following experience in local housing authorities in the United Kingdom, Hong Kong, and other parts of the British Commonwealth. There remains an urgent need for training programs to develop the large numbers of persons required in the field of housing administration.[12]

NOTES

[1]The British North America Act, 1867, (30 & 31 Victoria, c. 3). An Act for the Union of Canada, Nova Scotia, and New Brunswick, and the Government thereof: and for purposes connected thereunder. (March 29, 1867). Sec. 91.

[2]*Ibid.*, Sec. 92, 13.

[3]*Dominion Housing Act*, 1935, 25-26, George V, c. 58.

[4]*National Housing Act*, 8 George VI, 1944-45, c. 46, R.S.C. 1952, c. 188. An Act to Promote the Construction of new Houses, the Repair and Modernization of existing Houses, the Improvement of Housing and Living Conditions, and the Expansion of Employment in the Postwar Period.

[5]13 George VI, c. 30. An Act to Amend the National Housing Act 1944 (assented to 10th December, 1949) S. 35.

[6]The Vancouver Housing Association, founded before the Second World War, was perhaps the strongest and certainly the most durable citizens' housing organization in Canada.

[7]2-3 Elizabeth II, c. 23, *National Housing Act 1954*. An Act to Promote the Construction of new Houses, the Repair and Modernization of existing Houses, and the Improvement of Housing and Living Conditions, S. 36(1).

[8]*Housing Development Act*, Revised Statutes of Ontario, 1950, c. 174, Sec. 13(1) and 14.

[9]*The Ontario Housing Corporation Act 1964*, R.S.O., 1970, c. 317, S. 3(4).

[10]Oscar Lewis, *The Children of Sanchez* (New York: Random House, 1961) pp. xi-xxxi and 1-14.

[11]John R. Seeley, "The Slum: Its Nature, Use and Users," *Journal of the American Institute of Planners*, xxv, 1959.

[12]An Institute of Housing Management, with members drawn from both public and private housing management organizations, was created in Ontario in the mid-1970s and held its first annual meeting in November 1976.

CHAPTER 3

Housing Policy in Canada 1940-1968

A HISTORICAL PERSPECTIVE

Canadian public housing policies, in any coherent sense of the word, emerged as a consequence of the depressed economic activity of the late 1930s and the onset of the Second World War. (The official reaction to the disaster in Halifax harbour during World War One must be seen as a fortuitous incident.) There is, of course, some difference of opinion concerning the most appropriate date from which to build an analysis. The year 1929 is a favourite choice of many writers, for obvious reasons. In my view, however, the year 1941 is the date from which most of the mid-twentieth century programs of Canada and the United States can be appropriately measured. As the war effort accelerated Canada approached full employment. In the fall of 1941 prices of all goods and services, including rentals of housing accommodation, had advanced to the point where the federal government felt it necessary to impose controls under its war-time emergency legislation – controls over prices, wages, rents, and the allocation of materials.

By 1941 the federal government had also taken several significant steps which heralded the assumption of governmental responsibility in the housing field. Although the first National Housing Act had been passed in 1938, the opportunities for homebuilding were cut off by the onset of the Second World War. In 1941 a Crown corporation,

Wartime Housing Limited, was created by Order-in-Council to undertake the task of providing housing urgently required in many urban centres to accommodate workers attracted by governmental exhortation to work in wartime industries. Wartime Housing Limited can be seen now as a rudimentary federal housing agency, one of whose major tasks was direct negotiation with the elected and appointed officials of municipal governments. These negotiations produced a total of 45,930 dwelling units with an investment of $253,689,000 during the next nine years.[1] Nearly forty years later, most of the housing developed by this corporation remains in use in or adjacent to our cities.

Whatever its strengths and deficiencies, rent control as a facet of housing policy did represent an important federal intervention not previously experienced in the Canadian housing market. Its main significance was a recognition that the demand for scarce housing accommodation would continue to exceed the available supply during the war and probably thereafter. All the evidence in other countries pointed to the depressing effect that rent control would have upon the possible expansion of the supply of housing, but during the war the probability of any real expansion in the housing stock seemed quite remote. Rent control did continue into the post-war years and in some municipalities was retained, in whole or in part, until the late 1940s.

The Government of Canada passed the second National Housing Act in 1944, a much expanded and relatively comprehensive piece of legislation in contrast with the legislation of the immediate pre-war period. In retrospect, the Act appears like a declaration of faith in the nation's future in which housing policies would play a large role in post-war readjustment. In fact, the legislation did follow a major report of a special committee on post-war reconstruction known, after Professor Clifford Curtis of Queen's University, its chairman, as the Curtis Committee.[2] The Curtis Report, published in 1944, called for a recognition of the role of government, primarily that of the federal government, in the housing field, particularly with respect to the provision of housing for low-income families.

This report, which followed Canada's charter for post-war social security (the Marsh Report of 1943),[3] was a milestone in the enunciation of social responsibility by government. It must be reiterated that in the early months of 1944 the war was far from won, and it seems remarkable that the Parliament of Canada would enact legislation which, on the face of it, might appear premature. The very preamble of the National Housing Act of 1944, however, pinpoints the rationale for the legislation. The Act is described as "An Act to Promote the Construction of New Houses, the Repair and Modernization of Existing Houses, the Improvement of Housing and Living Conditions, and the Expansion of Employment in the Postwar Period". The emphasis on the expansion of employment in the post-war period makes it clear that the fundamental intention of the legislation was more economic – in terms of the avoidance of a post-war depression akin to that of 1919-21 – than a social concern with the well-being of all Canadians in terms of their housing requirements.

In the spring of 1945 the final link in this chain of future governmental organization for housing development was forged with the passage of the Central Mortgage and Housing Corporation Act.[4] This act created a federal housing agency in the form of a wholly-owned Crown corporation which was to administer the National Housing Act and thus the housing policy and program of the Government of Canada. The federal machinery for post-war housing expansion was complete.

Within the next five or six years Central Mortgage and Housing Corporation was to absorb or supersede all of the lesser agencies created during the wartime emergency, including Wartime Housing Limited.[5] The new agency, headed by a president and a vice-president and supported by a board of directors appointed by the Government of Canada, had all the attributes of a well-run business corporation and was designed to hide the potential iron fist of governmental intervention with a velvet glove of respectability or even financial profit. On this latter score the corporation has never disappointed the financial community.

INTERGOVERNMENTAL RELATIONS

Several important factors combined during the six years following the end of the war to make it possible for a strong federal role to emerge. The first of these was associated with the creation of a Crown corporation (CMHC) to administer the National Housing Act. Equally significant were the emergency powers granted to the Government of Canada in wartime and continued in substantial measure throughout the early post-war years. A shortage of consumer durable goods, building materials, steel, rubber, petroleum and other products vital to the growth of the national economy made it essential to continue certain wartime emergency powers and specific intergovernmental agencies.[6] In the early 1940s, Wartime Housing Limited negotiated directly with many municipalities and a pattern of relationships was established which continued, almost without question, during the early post-war years.

As the housing industry developed momentum by the second half of 1946, and the incomes and preferences of families began to reflect a higher level of expectations, Wartime Housing Limited was taken over by Central Mortgage and Housing Corporation and a new program was developed to take effect during the years 1947-1949. The intention of this new program, entitled Veterans' Rental Housing,[7] was to develop 10,000 dwelling units per annum of a more durable quality than that provided by Wartime Housing Limited (from an exterior point of view the main difference was the substitution of aluminum siding for frame construction, and full basements were deliberately provided). A serious attempt was made to provide permanent housing and once more, the federal government negotiated more or less directly with the municipalities concerned with little or no apparent objection from the respective provincial governments.

A third factor of considerable importance in the expansion of the federal role in the early post-war years was the obvious weakness of the provincial governments in these new fields of urban development. It has already been pointed out that the governments of the provinces were by no means prepared to assume their constitutional responsibilities in those areas of growth and development comprised by the term "urbanization". This must explain in part the lack of interference by provincial officials, elected and appointed, in the major federal-municipal housing programs of the 1940s. Moreover, these programs appeared to be the only way in which housing accommodation could be provided in Canada at that stage of political and economic development. Not only were the provincial governments unprepared, in the political and administrative sense, to play much of a role in housing policy, but their financial resources were quite inadequate to meet the new challenges they were forced to face within two or three years after the war.

Finally, the federal role was fostered by outright and fairly strong hostility to public housing programs, a hostility far more evident within the councils of local government and the legislatures of provincial governments than anywhere else in Canada. At the federal level, there was, by the late 1940s, at least a decade of major housing legislation, intervention in the housing market, direct negotiation with local governments for the construction of many thousands of dwellings, experience with certain social and community programs provided within Wartime Housing developments, and the operation of a substantial mortgage lending program supported out of tax revenues. The Marsh Report and the Curtis Report were further influences at the federal level that helped to weaken whatever antagonism existed towards public intervention in the nation's economy to achieve social goals through social service programs. There was never in Ottawa the strong anti-public housing lobbies which were evident in Washington from 1933 onwards.

In the Canadian cities and in the provincial legislatures, however, the situation was by no means so favourable. In many towns and cities there had been serious suffering by many thousands of families and individuals during the 1930s and not infrequent criticism of the manner in which financial assistance and work-relief programs had been handled. There was much dissatisfaction on the part of the unemployed and the needy as well as the staff members of the social and health services who had tried, under the most adverse circumstances, to help these people with the support of appropriate federal and provincial welfare legislation. At the same time, the four-fifths of the labour force who remained employed during those disastrous years found it difficult to accept the pleas of the disadvantaged. Rather, they were critical of what they considered to be wasteful measures of assistance to many persons whom they considered to be lazy and indolent.

Such attitudes towards the poor expressed themselves as opposition to the developing pressure for slum clearance and public housing programs during the last two years of the war and in the early post-war period. It was somewhat of a surprise to many people that the ratepayers of Toronto should endorse an estimated expenditure of nearly $6,000,000 on January 1st, 1947, for the Regent Park North low-income housing project.[8] Despite the favourable vote, there was fairly strong opposition to the assumption of responsibility by the City Council of Toronto in the absence of supporting provincial legislation and financial assistance. In other parts of Canada the situation was much the same. Although the opposition to public housing was never as vociferous, hard-hitting and vicious as it was in many urban areas in the United States, it nevertheless existed and discouraged local initiative, not only in the late 1940s but throughout the 1950s even after the passage of enabling federal legislation.[9]

In the two years following the war, then, intergovernmental relations in the field of housing were quite perfunctory. There was a clear, evident and strong federal role and assumption of responsibility enunciated in legislation and in administrative arrangements designed and enforced through Central Mortgage and Housing Corporation. There was a minor, weak, much less evident provincial role, even after the passage of Section 35 of the National Housing Act in November 1949, which depended on similar "enabling legislation" being passed in the provinces. Some provinces quickly took advantage of the new opportunities and developed appropriate machinery. Others did not and for some years operated under legislation and administrative arrangements which were at best makeshift or stunted in their growth and development.

At the local level there was confusion and consternation at the requirement that clear and definite local initiative must precede the utilization of the federal-provincial partnership within specific communities. The major cities and towns faced the same difficulties as the governments of the provinces, but, in addition, suffered from a series of disadvantages which they were less well prepared to overcome than their respective provincial hosts. At the local level there was opposition to public activity in the housing market, whether it be called slum clearance, urban redevelopment, public housing, or urban renewal. The residents of most neighbourhoods that were judged to be blighted or seriously deteriorating fought strongly against the expropriation and clearance of their homes, neighbourhood stores, and social and recreational facilities. They bitterly denounced official and press statements that they lived in a slum or a blighted area. At the same time, the residents of other neighbourhoods, both in the central city and the newly developing suburban areas, strongly opposed the location of public housing projects in their midst. They argued that they would be taxed not only in general but specifically for the welfare and educational requirements of downtown slum dwellers who had been foisted upon them for the general betterment of some other municipal organization.

In addition to this discontent and opposition from within, local governments faced very serious financial problems from the late 1940s through the late 1960s, and they continue to face significant financial dilemmas. Under the terms of the federal-provincial housing partnership, a municipality was required to bring "city services" (usually water and sewage facilities, street lighting and educational facilities) to the boundaries of a new public housing project and, in the case of schools, often within the large project site itself. These costs were burdensome enough to many municipalities but since in many provinces the local government was required to pay from 7½ per cent (Ontario) to, at most, 25 per cent of project costs (Alberta, Manitoba, and Nova Scotia) they were not the whole picture. During the 1950s, in return for these expenditures on capital and a similar share of operating deficits (rental subsidies) local governments might expect in lieu of taxes a payment which, they argued, was woefully short of meeting the real costs of local participation in an intergovernmental partnership.

Although it is true that despite these obstacles much progress was evident by the mid-1950s in Saint John's, Halifax, Toronto, Hamilton, Windsor and Vancouver – this list represents merely a handful of urban centres – in the great majority of municipalities little or no progress was evident before the mid-1960s.

In the light of the foregoing, it might be argued that it would be easy to identify a series of practical steps which could be described as "federal housing policies", "provincial housing policies", and "municipal housing policies". Unfortunately such an enterprise would be extremely difficult and unrewarding because none of the various governments in Canada ever really came forward with a clear statement of their goals and courses of action, or programs designed to attain given objectives over some period of years. There was no clear statement of what might be termed "federal housing policy", but a series of statements and pronouncements each year with respect to the overall housing situation and, in particular, with respect to the total number of dwelling units likely to be constructed, under construction, and completed during that year. Under the circumstances, the analyst can do no better than infer the most important elements of national housing policy from the enactment or amendment of legislation, and the encouragement or discouragement of various aspects of the total national housing program.

SIGNIFICANCE OF THE FEDERAL ROLE

Late in 1949, very soon after enactment of the federal-provincial partnership legislation, it became entirely clear that the federal government, through its agency, Central Mortgage and Housing Corporation, intended to play a strong and controlling role in the development of publicly-provided housing accommodation initiated anywhere in Canada, as seemed to befit its senior role in the provision of capital and operating subsidies. As the 1950s opened, a number of municipalities moved forward in their role as initiators of public housing programs. Evidence that the process of federal-provincial-municipal negotiation towards the creation of public housing would be a long and tedious affair, in which the dominant roles would be played by officials of the federal agency, began to accumulate. In an address to the Committee on Housing of the City of Kingston, Ontario, in 1954, I predicted that if the council of that city were to agree at that very moment to proceed with a request for the development of a substantial housing project intended to replace a deteriorated shack town which had recently become the responsibility of the city through annexation of part of an adjacent municipality, it would take five years before the assembled councillors would see a family occupy a dwelling unit. This prediction was borne out almost to the very letter, and is indicative of the length of time required to complete housing projects which accounts for much of the failure in Canadian public housing in the 1950s.

The federal role was based upon a clear and commendable objective of excellence for Canada's public housing program. By that time we had had the good fortune to observe nearly a half-century of British experience and more than a decade of American experience. Wherever a Canadian official might travel in these two countries, there were evident errors of omission and commission that it would be essential to avoid. A desire for excellence impelled the officials of Central Mortgage and Housing Corporation to develop a set of administrative procedures in which a local initiative might very soon bog down completely. It became an interesting exercise to list the number of steps and approvals through which a public housing project had to pass from the initial proposal at the local level to actual construction and occupation of the project by low-income families. The number of steps listed by the Metropolitan Toronto Housing Authority in 1961-1962, from local to provincial to federal to provincial to local approvals, back and forth a number of times, exceeded fifty. Under these conditions it was indeed remarkable that any public housing accommodation was built at all.

In retrospect, the main difficulty appears to have been the desire of highly trained and specialized officials of the federal agency to achieve excellence in the Canadian public housing program. This is by no means an undesirable objective, nor one to be discounted. The fact was, however, that excellence could only be obtained at the expense of quantity. Although this was not the only reason for Canada's modest quantitative attainment in public housing, it was an important consideration. The federal agency insisted on planning every step of the way, from the original municipal-provincial request to the ultimate appointment of a local housing authority to administer and manage the completed dwellings. The Architectural Division of Central Mortgage and Housing Corporation produced plans in the finest detail for such huge public housing projects in Canada as Lawrence Heights and Warden Woods in Toronto, Skeena Terrace and MacLean Park in Vancouver, Mulgrave Park in Halifax, and Jeanne Mance in Montreal. The results of the division's activity were noteworthy. Public housing projects were praised by architectural bodies, by visitors from other countries, and by local officials. Such praise and various architectural awards were won at the expense of a mass attack on the need for housing accommodation for the most disadvantaged individuals and families in Canadian urban centres.

Perhaps the techniques of the 1950s were fully justified on two counts: firstly, the absence of any appropriate provincial and local machinery to plan and design public housing programs or to implement such programs through the letting of contracts and the supervision of construction; and secondly, because the federal government was in fact paying the lion's share of the cost of such provision. It is clear that the first deficiency was in process of amelioration as the provinces attempted, in the late 1960s, to develop appropriate and adequate machinery through the device of the provincial housing corporation. At the same time, the federal government continued to put up a far greater percentage (90 per cent) of the required capital without any suggestion that it must seriously control the process of housing development because of this financial contribution.

In light of the substantial and powerful federal role in public housing, it might be thought that the Government of Canada was strongly in favour of a vast program of publicly provided housing for the lowest third of individuals and families in the national income distribution. As indicated previously, one can only infer the essentials of national housing policy, but it is safe to argue that the federal public housing policy was not consistent with the scope of the federal public housing role.

The best conclusion we can arrive at concerning national housing policy from 1945 through 1964 is that the Government of Canada was strongly in favour of the attainment of home ownership by every family. This goal was enunciated from time to time in Parliament and in the speeches of federal ministers, particularly those responsible for the operation of Central Mortgage and Housing Corporation. Moreover, the government and the officials of the corporation devoted much of their formal speechmaking and laudatory pronouncements to the encouragement of the house-building industry in its efforts to provide hundreds of thousands of homes for sale during the years 1946-1959. Every effort was made to provide adequate supplies of mortgage money, to manipulate the interest rate, and to set forth appropriate terms to encourage individual home ownership. Not only was mortgage money made available through the National Housing Act at rates lower than those prevailing in the money markets, but downpayments were successively reduced as loan amounts were increased. The period of amortization increased from fifteen years in 1946 to twenty, then twenty-five, and then to its present length of 35 years or more to enable lower-income families to acquire a home of their own. If anything, this was the heart of our housing policy during the past thirty years.

In the implementation of this course of action, Canada was transformed from a nation of tenants to a nation of homeowners, with the exception of Quebec. This was a fundamental revolution in our living patterns and a tremendous stimulus to the development of our national economy. Most of our population growth between 1951 and 1961 was located in old or new municipalities which developed on the fringes of existing towns and cities. During the decade in question population increased by 30.2 per cent, but in 17 metropolitan census areas it increased by more than 54 per cent. The population of the central city, as in the case of Toronto, declined, but the adjacent suburban areas increased prodigiously as houses became available.

The house-building industry came to represent a sizeable part of Canada's annual capital investment, absorbing 2 billion dollars per annum by 1965. Fluctuations in this industry affected, or were affected by, national economic and monetary policies. At least half-a-million jobs were directly involved with, and two or three times as many were dependent upon, the house-building industry, an industry devoted until the late 1950s to the production of one main product: the single family detached house on vacant land, the only type eligible for National Housing Act financing.

A national housing policy dedicated to a single objective neglected public intervention in rental accommodation for families in the lowest third of the income distribution. When a substantial degree of national resources and effort is devoted towards making every Canadian family a house owner, then there is a special kind of label, a special taint or blight to be placed upon those families who, despite all the favourable manipulations in the basic policy, cannot afford a house of their own. In such circumstances, the only possible conclusion to be drawn by many right-thinking men is that those who cannot benefit from these policies must be, in Galbraith's words, the victims of "case poverty".[10]

> Case poverty is commonly and properly related to some characteristics of the individuals so afflicted. Nearly everyone else has mastered his environment; this proves that it is not intractable. But some quality peculiar to the individual or family involved – mental deficiency, bad health, inability to adapt to the discipline of modern economic life, excessive procreation, alcohol, insufficient education, or perhaps a combination of several of these handicaps – have kept these individuals from participating in the general well-being.

These pervasive influences have taken a long time to overcome in the Canadian housing picture and it was only with the assumption of a stronger role by several provincial governments in the 1960s that the tide began to turn. Even so, progress can only be described as moderate in a nation in which, in the late 1960s, not more than 5 per cent of its annual housing starts of some 175,000 were devoted to public housing; and this proportion was attained only in 1967 after years of less adequate provision.

THE FIRST DECADE OF PUBLIC HOUSING: A SUMMING UP

Fifteen years of meetings and discussion, of speech-making and brief-writing, of presentations to provincial ministers, federal officials, local municipal councils, and groups of businessmen and service clubs, had resulted, by 1960, in the construction of not more than 10,000 to 12,000 public housing units, depending upon how the count was made. Some estimates of total public housing production included dwellings constructed for occupancy by elderly persons or so-called "limited-dividend" housing, other counts did not. It would be safe to insist that no matter how the estimate was derived, the total number of such dwelling units available for rent to low-income families did not exceed 15,000 in 1960.

Not only was there great discouragement at this meagre quantitative achievement of the years 1949-1959, but by this time Canada was in the midst of a severe economic recession which lasted well into 1963. Both the federal government and those provincial governments who had participated in the federal-provincial housing partnership during the 1950s discontinued their encouragement of additional programs and stood pat with those programs already under way and in the process of construction. The result was even greater discouragement for those voluntary associations and professionals who had hoped that a vast program of public housing activity would have been mounted by this time in many metropolitan areas. On the contrary, only thirty-eight dwelling units (the last to be completed in the Lawrence Heights project) were actually completed for occupancy by low-income families in the metropolitan area of Toronto during the years 1958-1963. Waiting lists grew only at a moderate rate because eligible families realized that it was futile to make application for accommodation that did not exist and for which there was no hope of attainment.

By 1961 it was clear to all interested parties that the federal-provincial partnership had collapsed. It was not only that its total accomplishment was grossly insufficient, but very little had been approved and no future programs were evident after the downturn in Canadian economic activity during the winter of 1957-1958. Under the circumstances, some persons concluded that the answer to the stalemate lay in an entirely different approach through an elevation of the role of the local housing authority. It was pointed out that such authorities in the United States had a great deal more power than similar bodies in Canada, that they raised their own funds at relatively low interest rates through the issuance of tax-exempt bonds, that they produced their own programs and plans for several years ahead (subject to the approval of federal and state authorities), that they acquired land, hired architects, developed plans, let contracts and, in general, acted as Central Mortgage and Housing Corporation was attempting to act on behalf of an entire nation.

In Metropolitan Toronto the drive towards a rejuvenated local housing authority was shaped by a number of lay and professional persons in the voluntary services and by elected and appointed officials at the political level. The chairman of the Metropolitan Toronto Council lent additional support to the creation of a new regional or metropolitan-wide Housing Authority which would absorb all existing authorities in the area: two organizations involved in public housing for families and two in the form of Limited-Dividend Housing Corporations devoted primarily to the production of housing for the elderly. In 1962 the view spread and gained credence that the federal government was prepared to amend the National Housing Act to encourage the growth and development of such comprehensive regional authorities[11] by permitting direct access to federal funds available under certain sections of the Act such as: Section 16 (Limited-Dividend), Section 23 (Urban Redevelopment), and Section 36 (Federal-Provincial Projects). Hopes were high at this time but they were dashed by a series of disasters, including the deaths of the federal minister responsible for housing affairs, the president of Central Mortgage and Housing Corporation, and the director of the Housing Branch of the Department of Economics and Development in Ontario.

In 1964 the Government of Ontario, aware that the National Housing Act would in fact soon be amended to encourage the assumption of significant responsibilities by local or provincial authorities, developed the concept of a provincial housing corporation and created this agency with the passage of the Ontario Housing Corporation Act in June 1964. In the same month, amendments to the National Housing Act revolutionized the approach to public participation in the provision of accommodation to low-income persons.[12]

THE 1964 AMENDMENTS: A TURNING POINT IN CANADIAN HOUSING POLICY

The 1964 amendments, which virtually re-wrote most of the social provisions of the National Housing Act, included the following significant changes.

1. A new Section 16A was added to authorize loans to non-profit corporations owned by a province, municipality or any agency thereof, or by a charitable corporation for the construction or purchase of a housing project or housing accommodation of the hostel or dormitory type for use as a low-rental housing project. This amendment may be considered to be a substantial expansion of the former Section 16, the so-called "limited dividend section", but of most significance is the implication that the governments of the provinces would enter into this specific activity.

2. Part III of the National Housing Act was re-titled "Urban Renewal" as distinct from its previous designation of "Urban Redevelopment". This part of the Act which had, from 1954, been comprised entirely of Section 23 was substantially re-written. This was the first time the phrase "urban renewal" was

written into the National Housing Act and Section 23 was broadened considerably to encompass a broad-gauge approach to the prevention and treatment of blighted and slum areas in urban municipalities.

Specifically, Section 23 was expanded by the addition of new Sections numbered 23A to 23F. These sub-sections were designed to cover, respectively, contributions for preparation of an urban-renewal scheme, contributions for implementing an urban-renewal scheme, loans for an urban-renewal scheme, insured loans for housing projects in urban-renewal areas, authorization for expenditures from the Consolidated Revenue Fund, and regulations. As far as the governments of the provinces were concerned, Sections 2A, B, and C were most important. Not only were the provinces clearly recognized as the authority which must approve local urban-renewal plans, but the federal government agreed to pay one-half of the costs of preparing and implementing such schemes. In addition, Central Mortgage and Housing Corporation recognized for the first time that implementation would require the employment of persons to assist in the re-location of individuals and families dispossessed of housing accommodation by urban-renewal programs.

3. Section 36 of the 1954 Act, which was the first portion of Part VI, entitled "Federal-Provincial Projects," was re-numbered as Section 35A and Part VI was re-titled "Public Housing". Although the federal-provincial partnership had been in force since the end of 1949, this was the first time that the phrase "public housing" had appeared in the National Housing Act.

   Section 35A was, in fact, a re-statement of the earlier federal-provincial partnership, with the addition of the possible inclusion of hostel or dormitory type housing accommodation in federal-provincial housing projects. The 75-25 division of financial responsibility in both capital costs and losses (subsidies) between the federal and provincial governments was continued unchanged.

4. The entire field of public housing operations was broadened substantially with the enactment of new portions of Section 35 numbered 35B to E. In Section 35B the term "public housing agency" was defined to include a corporation "wholly owned by the government of a province or any agency thereof", or "one or more municipalities in a province". This revised definition, along with the new financial provisions in Sections 35 C to E, brought the Canadian provinces directly into the field of public housing for the first time in our housing history.

   In Section 35C, Central Mortgage and Housing Corporation was permitted to make loans to assist a province, municipality or public-housing agency to acquire lands for public-housing projects. The maximum loan that might be made for this purpose was 90 per cent of the cost of acquiring and servicing the land. Since it was anticipated that a land-acquisition program would soon be followed by the construction of a public-housing project, loans under this section were expected to be for relatively short terms and in no case for more than 15 years.

This new Section was followed by another, Section 35D, which permitted the federal agency to make loans to provinces, municipalities and public housing agencies "to construct, acquire, and operate public housing projects". Loans made under this Section were to be subject to conditions similar to those applying to limited dividend housing companies and to non-profit corporations. In short, these loans could not exceed 90 per cent of the cost of the project as determined by the Corporation and would be for a term not exceeding fifty years from the date of completion or acquisition of the project. Finally, in the third new section, Section 35E, the federal Corporation was authorized to make contributions towards the operating losses of subsidized public-housing projects owned and operated by a provincial, municipal and public-housing agency for the benefit of persons of low income. The maximum federal contribution was set at 50 per cent for a period not in excess of fifty years.

In these new sections the National Housing Act was slanted in the direction of new forms of initiative by local or provincial governments. Clearly, the terms available in the completely revised Section 35 under the rubric "public housing" were far more favourable than the terms provided in the familiar federal-provincial partnership (although these provisions were retained as an alternative if desired by any provincial jurisdiction). The increase in the proportion of capital contributions was, of course, accompanied by a decrease in the proportion of subsidies which the federal government would pay; the amount of the subsidies however had rarely appeared to be a major consideration affecting the decisions on public housing of municipalities and provinces. The capital contribution, however, had been an important deterrent to local initiatives in most municipalities.

Although it may not have been apparent in June 1964, the amendments passed that month proved to be a turning point in Canadian housing history. From that time on the whole question of whether slum or blighted areas were to be cleared, the social questions accompanying the processes of re-housing and relocation, the whole question of whether low-income persons and families were to be offered decent and adequate housing at a price they could afford – these and numerous related social questions were put squarely in the laps of the provincial governments. Their response during the ensuing years has been a clear indication of their motivation, or lack of it, in the face of the most opportune circumstances ever put before the network of intergovernmental organizations in this country. The roles of these governments have become much clearer and, in the light of recent experience, it is now possible to speculate upon the respective roles of the three levels of government for the next decade or two.

NOTES

[1]O. J. Firestone, *Residential Real Estate in Canada* (Toronto: University of Toronto Press, 1951) Table 109, p. 488.

[2]Canada, Advisory Committee on Reconstruction, *Housing and Community Planning*, Sub-Committee Report, No. 4 (Ottawa: King's Printer, 1944).

[3]Canada, Advisory Committee on Reconstruction, *Report on Social Security for Canada*, prepared by L. C. Marsh, (Ottawa: King's Printer, 1943).

[4]Central Mortgage and Housing Corporation Act, 9-10 George VI, c. 15, 1945. The corporation began its operations on January 1, 1946.

[5]"Housing in Canada, 1946-1970," A supplement to the 25th annual Report of Central Mortgage and Housing Corporation (Ottawa: 1970) pp. 10-11.

[6]*Ibid.*, pp. 11-13.

[7]*Ibid.*, p. 12.

[8]Albert Rose, *Regent Park: A Study in Slum Clearance* (Toronto: University of Toronto Press, 1958) pp. 63-68.

[9]*Ibid.*, pp. 100-102.

[10]J. K. Galbraith, *The Affluent Society* (Boston: Houghton, Mifflin & Co., 1958) pp. 325-331.

[11]M. Dennis and S. Fish, *Programs in Search of a Policy: Low Income Housing in Canada* (Toronto: Hakkert, 1972) pp. 145-146.

[12]An Act to Amend the National Housing Act (1954). 13 Elizabeth II, c. 15, S. 8. June 1964.

CHAPTER 4

National Housing Policy for an Urban Canada: The 1970s and Thereafter

---

The development of housing policies for Canada, appropriate for the last three decades of the twentieth century, really began with the election of the first Trudeau government in 1968. Pierre Elliot Trudeau is an urbane man; he is also an urbanite, a native of the largest metropolitan area in Canada, whose thinking has been deeply influenced by the urbanization of this country since his birth in 1919. In the election campaign of 1968 the new leader of the Liberal Party promised very significant attention to the problems of Canadian cities. In August of that year, shortly after his election, Trudeau asked one of his best known cabinet ministers, Paul Hellyer, who had been given responsibility for housing, to lead a Task Force on Housing and Urban Development.

THE TASK FORCE ON HOUSING AND URBAN DEVELOPMENT 1968-1969

The chairman of the Task Force asserted that his approach would not be that of a Royal Commission which might take two or three years to investigate every facet of its terms of reference and produce a massive report. He emphasized speed and set as his goal the completion of a study within three to four months, and the production of a report within six months. The chairman was himself a housebuilder and land developer who had become independently wealthy: he had been first elected to the House of Commons at the age of twenty-five. He was known to be strong, energetic, impatient in some of his approaches; and many journalists suspected that his mind was already made up about solutions to Canada's housing problems. A seven-member task force was quickly assembled and set to work with a relatively small staff. In addition to Paul Hellyer, the members of the task force were Dr. Doris Boyle, Dr. Pierre Dansereau, W. Peter Carter, Robert Campeau, Dr. James Gillies, and C. E. Pratt.

Throughout the fall of 1968 it travelled from coast to coast and held hearings in a great many large and small urban centres as well as in certain rural areas. True to its chairman's word, the members of the task force swept into town like a whirlwind, occupied the local schoolhouse auditorium for several hours on one or more evenings, toured and visited housing projects, heard briefs which had been submitted in advance and the special arguments of voluntary organizations, and quickly swept out of town. In the course of its sessions the task force resorted to such unscientific strategies as asking for a show of hands to determine whether those in attendance wished to own their own homes rather than continue as tenants, roomers or boarders. In addition, the chairman commissioned certain studies from consulting firms who were provided with scarcely sufficient time to undertake acceptable research investigations. These methods were part of the reason for the debacle which ensued when the task force report was ultimately tabled in Parliament on January 22, 1969.[1]

The essential responsibility of the task force was to establish the requirements for and the limits of a federal role in the rapidly expanding urban society. It is entirely clear that both the prime minister and the chairman were convinced that the future of the Liberal Party lay in its response to the needs of an urban society. In 1961 the Census of Canada had reported that Canadians were 69.7 per cent urban dwellers; by 1971 this proportion had increased to 76.1 per cent.[2] Even without the benefit of the latter data, all parties in the House had the advantage of the projections of the Gordon Commission, which reported, in 1959-1960, that Canada would be almost entirely urbanized by 1990, if not some years before.[3]

In the 1960s the federal-provincial arrangements in the fields of housing and urban development had been oriented towards the provinces assumption of their constitutional roles. The federal government's responsibility was to provide financial resources within a series of programs which also required provincial and perhaps municipal contributions, to set standards that would create more or less similar patterns of inter-governmental relationships and of public housing throughout the nation, and to ensure that the requirements of the Naional Housing Act were met in both substance and spirit.

Within four years of the passage of the major 1964 Amendments to the Act, it was clear that these federal roles would consign the Government of Canada, and the party in power, to a minor position in a nation of thirty million or more urban dwellers. Urban development in Canada was bound to accelerate during the 1970s and 1980s if the nation's economic potential was realized, if the level of net immigration was maintained at some moderate level (say 150,000 to 170,000 per annum), and if Canada was to maintain its position as a nation with one of the highest living standards in the world, a major partner in the United Nations and NATO.

These were no longer the most significant agendas. The members of the task force received a substantial number of briefs from across the country, insisting that it was illogical and clearly irresponsible for the federal government to maintain Ministries of Agriculture, Fisheries, and Regional Economic Expansion without creating a ministry charged with the responsibility of providing adequate housing accommodation as well as the related urban infrastructure and services. I presented a brief to the task force on September 30, 1968 in which I argued the case for the creation of a federal Department of Housing.[4]

> It is incredible that in our Western industrial urban society housing and urban development continue to be one of the several (or part-time) responsibilities of a minister of the Crown . . . It must be admitted at once that the question of the locus of ministerial responsibility is by no means the major reason that Canada has failed to meet all the emerging requirements of housing and urban development during the past quarter-century. Nevertheless, the failure of the Government of Canada to create a department and to name a minister solely responsible for these developments seems indicative of an absence of urgency at the highest levels.

It was clear from the manner in which the task force questioned those who presented or responded to briefs that it was concerned with a number of quite specific concerns:

1. the failure of the Canadian housebuilding industry, Canadian financial institutions and the various levels of government to build adequate supplies of housing at prices that a substantial majority of families could afford to pay;
2. the failure of these institutions to meet the qualitative requirements of families; to build accommodation for very large families as well as for elderly couples; to build rental housing, particularly in apartment buildings, for families with more than two children;
3. the failure of intergovernmental programs to build more than a

token amount of housing leased on rent-geared-to-income scales for low-income families;

4. the failure of Central Mortgage and Housing Corporation to adapt quickly to changing requirements for housing accommodation and other aspects of urban development within a rapidly changing Canadian society; and,

5. the failure of the major urban planning organization within government, in conjunction with architects, private housing and development organizations, and those in the visual arts, to create more interesting, varied and pleasing designs for housing, new towns, and "satellite" communities.

The task force presented its report to Parliament right on schedule. Major recommendations covered financing, land costs and utilization, construction costs and techniques, social housing and special programs, urban development, administrative structure, and research, including the specific proposal that, "the federal government should establish a federal Department of Housing and Urban Affairs."[5]

The recommendations can be grouped under four main concerns: to facilitate and expand home ownership; to reduce the cost of housing; to de-emphasize the nature and role of public housing; to suggest the most appropriate forms of urban development during the last quarter of the twentieth century.

The recommendations designed to facilitate and expend home ownership included these proposals:

– that the maximum NHA mortgage be increased from $18,000 to $30,000;

– that the amortization period of an NHA loan be expanded from thirty-five to forty years;

– that a reduction in down payments lead eventually to the prospect of a nominal $100 down payment or no down payment;

– that the full benefits of NHA legislation with respect to mortgages on new homes be extended to the purchase of existing homes;

– that the insurance premium required on NHA mortgages, which amounted to 2 per cent of the purchase price, be reduced to 1 per cent; and,

– that private lending institutions be consulted once or twice a year by federal officials to insure that they made every effort to channel a sufficient proportion of their investment funds into residential housing.[6]

The task force proposed a series of measures which, over several years it argued, would cut the high cost of the main components of home ownership: land, building materials, fees, and the cost of mortgages. It proposed:

– that a capital gains tax be imposed on the speculative profits of

all land sales, including the possibility of a special tax where land transfers occurred without evidence of improvement;
- that the federal and provincial governments should remove all sales tax on building materials for residential construction, with the possibility that this change might begin with the introduction of rebates on materials used in "low-cost housing";
- that municipalities buy large quantities of land required for urban development within their boundaries and that the federal government make direct loans to them for this purpose;
- that an investigation be launched into restraint of prices in the building industry and unfair labour practices; and,
- that fees in real-estate transactions paid to brokers, salesmen and lawyers be reduced by some form of voluntary restraint.[7]

The report devoted ten of its eighty-five pages to a discussion of the inadequacies of some of the older and larger public housing projects in Canada and the social and economic evils that had developed among tenant families. It had been anticipated that, in the wake of the task force's visit to Toronto's Regent Park and Trefann Court, the report would blast large concentrations of publicly-housed families. Yet the recommendation that no more large projects be built had already been implemented by the Ontario Housing Corporation and was part of the philosophy of the other seven provincial housing corporations and two housing commissions in Canada.

In an analysis published within two weeks of the tabling of the report in Parliament, I argued that,

> The task force has clearly put forward a number of recommendations and proposals that can only be termed political. By any form of analysis they constitute an intrusion into the rights and responsibilities of provincial and local governments who, without doubt, are responsible for housing and physical planning within their geographical jurisdiction. The recommendation for forward purchase of land, the recommendation that local governments should be relieved by the provincial governments of at least 80 per cent of the cost of education, the recommendation that local governments (if they have not already done so) should adopt the National Building Code by 1970, the recommendation that regional governments should be set up throughout the nation and that these governments should assume the responsibility for purchasing and servicing land for urban development, the recommendation that municipalities should examine and alter their assessment procedures to ensure that speculation in land is no longer fostered by inadequate assessment procedures – all of these are the kind of proposals that Ottawa would choke upon if some provincial commission of inquiry were to recommend a closer examination and alteration of certain areas of federal jurisdiction to assist the meeting of a specific problem.
>
> It is my conclusion that one of the reasons for the formation of the task force was to take away from the new provincial housing corpora-

tions, particularly the successful Ontario Housing Corporation, some of the attention and kudos that have been gained through increasingly active provincial initiatives since 1965. . . . Ottawa has provided 90 per cent of the money but has had little of the credit. On the other hand, the complaints and criticisms about the chronic housing crisis throughout Canada have been focused on the federal government.[8]

Within a day or two of the tabling of the report there was major opposition to the recommendations from the general public, the provincial governments, the federal government and thus from within the Liberal Party of Canada. It was not immediately apparent that the Liberal caucus would take serious exception to the report, but within a week there was considerable division of opinion. Although the prime minister never stated publicly his opposition, it became obvious that he and his cabinet had rejected the recommendations of the task force. Within a few weeks Paul Hellyer resigned from the cabinet and within a year left the Liberal Party and crossed the floor of the House.

This outcome of the work of the task force is extremely curious, because the Hellyer Report laid the groundwork and developed the parameters of what became federal housing policy in the first half of the 1970s. Whatever the immediate political climate may have been following the presentation of the report, its salient recommendations have in fact been implemented. Moreover, they were implemented quickly, commencing with the creation of a Ministry of State for Urban Affairs in the 1970-1971 session of the twenty-eighth Parliament of Canada.

A MINISTRY OF STATE FOR URBAN AFFAIRS

A clear recommendation of the task force, that a federal Ministry of Housing and Urban Affairs be created, was implemented within eighteen months. Prime Minister Trudeau had initiated and authorized Ministries of State for a variety of purposes, including Science and Technology, Environment, and Urban Affairs, by a Proclamation of June 30, 1971. Robert K. Andras, was in fact, appointed early in 1970, but his first title was "Minister Responsible for Housing".

The minister's first major speech in the House delivered on April 21, 1970 set the tone for a variety of programs in the field of housing which, several years later, are still in the process of development. He proposed the following:[9]

1. A revised rent-to-income scale for public housing, including specific provisions that: (a) family size would be taken into account in arriving at rents through a reduction of $2 per month for each child after the second; (b) working wives would be

allowed to earn up to $900 per annum (up from the previous limit of $250) before such earnings would be considered income for the purpose of calculating rent; (c) incomes of one-parent families, for the purpose of calculating rents, would be reduced by up to $900 per annum to compensate for the fact that sole-supporting parents do not have the opportunities for additional earnings; and, (d) the maximum proportion of income required as rent in the higher income range would be reduced from 30 to 25 per cent.

2. Social and recreational facilities in both new and existing public housing projects would be eligible for federal assistance.
3. Duly constituted public housing tenant associations would be assisted with grants.
4. A model lease would be developed and incorporated within a revised manual of procedures for housing authorities.
5. Formal training programs in public housing management would be initiated in co-operation with the provinces.

The minister also placed a great deal of emphasis on housing design, location and density. On the question of tenant organization and involvement in the management of public housing, he stated,

> I am convinced that giving tenants some voice in the administration of their project is a matter of social justice and would help to encourage a new and healthier outlook all around and remove a major cause of many of the difficulties we have experienced to this time.[10]

It was established by Parliament that the new ministry, which was not a full-fledged department of the Government of Canada, would be responsible for housing policy. The Central Mortgage and Housing Corporation would be responsible for reporting through the new minister and he in turn would be responsible to Parliament. It was not considered sufficient, obviously, to establish a Ministry of Housing or even a Ministry of Housing and Urban Development; the designation "urban affairs" was surely a far broader-concept than any of the other titles suggested.[11] It is clear why the prime minister chose such wording, because no level of government was possessed of the constitutional responsibility in a field as conceptually vague and as boundless as "urban affairs"; though for forty years the major constitutional responsibility in the field of housing lay with the provincial governments. It is also clear that the term "urban development" was reprehensible. Perhaps the Liberal Party, conscious of the significance of rural affairs, was determined not to alienate its relatively modest support in rural areas and in the Western provinces by appearing to espouse urban development. Urban affairs surely encompassed more than simply development of our cities.

In its first decade the Ministry of State for Urban Affairs was in a process of evolution of role, responsibility and programs.[12] Although there had been no formal admission of conflict it was clear that the Central Mortgage and Housing Corporation came under strong attack by the new ministry. The corporation was placed on the defensive, and important staff positions were created by the minister and literally imposed upon the administrative structure of CMHC. The result was confusion, irritation, and conflict between the corporation and the ministry. In the minds of many parliamentarians and interested observers beyond the national capital, the creation of this ministry was an unproductive act.[13]

In his two years as minister, Robert Andras truly exercised supervision over a tooling-up process. The ministry was organized to assist him in policy formulation for the cabinet; a research division was created with sufficient funds to engage a substantial staff and a number of capable social scientists and urban affairs researchers; and, whether it wanted to be or not, the CMHC was reorganized. From the point of view of the critics of the corporation, it was dragged reluctantly into the second half of the twentieth century; to its devoted supporters, it was being emasculated by those forces within government which either opposed its role of the previous quarter-century or felt it should be replaced by some new structure developed within the ministry. There are many persons, within and without government, who sincerely deplore the allocation of socio-economic functions to Crown corporations as they are structures beyond the direct control of Parliament. From this point of view, the creation of a ministry that would exercise some control over the corporation, which had had a relatively free hand in policy formulation and implementation for a very long time, was a step in the right direction.

The first Minister of State for Urban Affairs implemented many of the proposals of the Task Force on Housing and Urban Development, but none was more important than the continued ban on urban renewal activities. In 1968 a substantial number of urban renewal schemes (probably more than thirty in all) were awaiting continued approval and funding in their respective municipalities. Mr. Hellyer, however, imposed a ban on further development of already approved projects pending completion of the study to be undertaken by his task force. It had been hoped that the new minister, following rejection of the Hellyer report, would restore the status quo in the urban renewal process or, at the very least, would enable those projects already underway to be completed. The government seemed to have accepted the view of the Hellyer task force that urban renewal was a damaging process, a process in which many low-income families were removed from traditional neighbourhoods, relocated elsewhere – sometimes in public housing but often in older, less desirable and sub-standard accommodation – and that better solutions needed to be found for the rehabilitation of the central core.[14] Be that as it may, the task force found no new evidence on the subject, nor did it present any solution to the problem of rebuilding the downtown areas of our major urban centres.

It was the ministry's view, apparently, that the positions adopted by the government during the period September 1968 to March 1969 should be continued pending further intensive studies of urbanization and housing policies. The principal study to emerge[15] was a serious condemnation of Canadian housing, planning and urban development policies over the previous three decades. Lithwick, in fact, rejected all the work of the previous quarter century – beginning with the amendments to the NHA setting up the federal-provincial partnership in November 1949 – as futile gestures which were at best anti-social. He had, of course, the advantage of hindsight, because as a relatively young academic (he had been an elementary school pupil in the post-war years) he could scarcely have appreciated the problems of passing new legislation and persuading the Canadian public in 1948-1949 that government should intervene in the housing market on behalf of low-income or disadvantaged families and individuals.

Lithwick's study was and remains the most comprehensive analysis of the process of urbanization ever undertaken in Canada. It was both highly conceptual and thoroughly empirical. The conceptual analysis was bolstered not only by the available data up to and including the censuses of 1961 and 1966 but also by detailed forecasts of such major components of urban development as housing demand and transportation requirements.

It is significant that the final section of this document, which became known as "The Lithwick Report", emphasized the notion of "policy" under the general rubric of "Urban Prospects and Policy". The section dealing with "housing in the urban future" forecast housing demand in eleven major metropolitan areas from Halifax to Vancouver to the year 2001. Total demand, moreover, was broken down between family and non-family.

The grim picture which emerged from the forecast visualized required additions to the housing stock for major metropolitan areas alone of more than 800,000 dwelling units in the 1970s, nearly 900,000 in the 1980s, more than 950,000 in the last decade of the century – a total of 2,651,000 between 1971 and 2001. This forecast, disregarding the requirements for the balance of the population residing outside the major metropolitan areas studied in 1970, meant a two-thirds addition to the total existent Canadian housing stock at that time.

Publication of the Lithwick Report and six significant research monographs created somewhat of a sensation in 1970-71 as Robert Andras began to interpret the federal role for urban affairs. Lithwick and some of his colleagues, as well as the minister, were in great demand to speak at universities, to participate in seminars, and to address annual meetings of major trade associations in the housing and building industry, until the awful truth emerged in late spring of 1971: neither Lithwick nor Andras had any real solution to the problems of urbanization and the enormous housing requirements of the last third of the twentieth century. In a seminar sponsored by the Centre for Urban and Community Studies at the University of Toronto, Professor Lithwick not only decried the value of most urban research in Canada (a good deal of which had been undertaken by members of his audience), but offered as a solution to the problem of urban growth federal restriction on immigration to Canada. His audience found this a very weak answer to the problem.[16]

Within a few months it seemed apparent that the impact of Lithwick's major analyses of urban prospects and policies had not been enthusiastically received by the cabinet (insofar as Robert Andras had presented the material to his senior colleagues). In a strongly worded statement issued to the press in early summer 1971, Professor Lithwick ceremoniously resigned from his post as Assistant Secretary (equivalent to senior Assistant Deputy Minister) in the Ministry of State for Urban Affairs. In his explanation he emphasized his frustration at the painfully slow evolution of federal housing policies and went so far as to indicate that he saw very little prospect of a strong federal initiative in controlling and directing the course of Canadian urban development during the balance of the century.

The second significant research venture by the Ministry was a contractual arrangement with Michael Dennis and Susan Fish. They embarked upon a major study of housing policies in Canada which apparently so disturbed the government in confidential draft form that the ministry was reluctant to publish it. A short time thereafter a full copy was leaked to one of the opposition parties in the House of Commons and a great many allegations based on it were made by the leaders of the two opposition parties. The government was firmly criticized for refusing to publish the document, and soon thereafter Dennis and Fish enlisted the services of a Toronto publishing house and issued their report.[17]

There is no question that the Dennis and Fish Report, as it became known, is the most comprehensive analysis of the housing problem in Canada since the publication of the Curtis Report in 1944.[18] The tone which permeates the entire report is one of frustration, anger and belligerence. The authors delve into several facets of the housing problem, including interest rates, the shortage of serviced land, and, inevitably, poverty and low-income among that substantial segment of Canadians whose housing accommodation is grossly inadequate.

Lithwick, as an economist, had berated not only politicians but his academic colleagues and predecessors for their gross neglect of the economics of urbanization. Dennis and Fish continued this onslaught on a wider front involving all social scientists and the entire society for its neglect of the requirements of low-income Canadians, presumably through an undying faith in the "filtering down" process whereby the better housing occupied by middle and upper-middle income groups eventually deteriorated and is made available to the lower-income groups. The authors were, however, fifteen years late in denying the validity of that ancient argument.

The greatest difficulty in accepting the analysis stemming from angry outbursts at the general stupidity and callousness of Canadians rests in the fact that with Dennis and Fish there is no middle ground. In their view, all Canadians have neglected the needs of the poor for decent and adequate housing accommodation; all politicians are primarily interested in rebuilding the core of our urban centres without regard for the impact on those residents who are most likely to be poor, elderly or members of families with many children; and all legislation has been grossly deficient because it is not intended to interfere with traditional housing market operations. In short, all politicians are hand-in-glove with all housebuilders, land developers and subcontractors, for the benefit of the few to the detriment of the needy. Perhaps the authors assumed that there was a significant need for a strong radical posture in describing, dissecting and re-assembling the components of our critical housing problem. They were not the first to make this assumption but in the late 1970s they retain the distinction of being the most strident of the critics. It is not difficult to understand that, if indeed he had initiated their study, Robert Andras was under no compulsion to engage in a masochistic exercise by distributing it widely under the government imprint.

In my view, Dennis and Fish ended up in exactly the same position as Lithwick in seeking new fundamental solutions to some of the most complicated problems in Canadian social and economic development. The concluding chapters of their report dealt with a so-called "comprehensive housing policy" and its administration. They insisted that there must first of all be a statement of national housing goals: providing equal access to decent housing for all Canadians, controlling housing price inflation, improving the environmental quality of all housing, conserving and upgrading the existing housing stock, maximizing the dignity and freedom of choice of the individual user of housing, and creating a decision-making process that is open to user input and whose centre of authority is as close to the user as possible.[19]

It is difficult for any student of the subject whose acquaintance predates 1968 to find anything new in these motherhood statements. Moreover, they imply on the one hand conditions which do not exist anywhere in the world (for example, "equal access to decent housing"), and a national economy which has full control of its development (for example, "controlling house price inflation").

There is no doubt that Dennis and Fish had an important impact upon new federal housing legislation passed in 1973 and upon the general posture of federal spokesmen in housing and urban affairs. Their report drew sharp attention to the socio-economic inequities in the provision of housing in Canada. It emphasized and documented the gross disadvantages of Canadian individuals and families in the lower half of the income scale. It pointed to conflicts between national policy statements on the one hand and national housing programs on the other; and between several departments of the Government of Canada whose policies affect housing and urban affairs, and Central Mortgage and Housing Corporation. In short, *Programs in Search of a Policy* provided a sufficiently long and difficult agenda for the new Ministry of State for Urban Affairs that the latter could well have occupied itself in a decade of policy responses; but time and events do not stand still and new situations in the housing market were soon to push the report into the background.

THE 1973 AMENDMENTS TO THE NATIONAL HOUSING ACT

The sequence of dramatic events since the election of the first Trudeau government in 1968 – the appointment of the Task Force on Housing and Urban Development and rejection of its report; the appointment of Professor Lithwick, the publication of several major research monographs and rejection of Lithwick's recommendations; the appointment of Michael Dennis, publication of the Dennis and Fish monograph and rejection of its policy recommendations – led to a clear expectation of major changes in federal legislation. In 1972 the second Minister of State for Urban Affairs, Ron Basford, introduced into the House a draft bill containing a series of important new initiatives, all of which died on the order paper when the prime minister called an election for early fall. The fact that the Trudeau government was returned with only a two-seat advantage over the Conservative Party and was forced to rely on the New Democratic Party to maintain its position as the Government of Canada had two important consequences for prospective housing legislation. On the one hand, widespread political confusion made it inevitable that amendments to the NHA would not be among the highest priority legislation; on the other hand, the enormous interest of the NDP (which held the balance of power) in all forms of social legislation ensured that new housing legislation could not be long delayed.

Early in 1973 Parliament passed a substantial series of amendments to the NHA (which continues to be cited as the *National Housing Act, 1953-54*, c. 23, S. 1). A detailed examination of the 1973 consolidation reveals 36 amendments.[20] Many of the changes are in the nature of legislative housekeeping and require no further explanation. Let us turn to the minister's exposition of what he termed "New National Housing Act Programs".[21] In a strong effort to make the most of the 1973 amendments, ten new programs were identified. These will be described in the order in which they appeared in the minister's publicity kit distributed widely throughout the country.

(1) Assisted Home Ownership (new Sections 34.15 and 34.16)

These sections were introduced into the Act under Part IV.2 as "Loans to Facilitate Home-Ownership". In a real sense, such changes derived from Central Mortgage and Housing Corporation's traditional responsibilities in the field of direct lending whereby loans could be made to individuals living in geographical areas where conventional mortgages were not available. The major change, however, is simply that the AHOP was directed towards lower-income families with one or more dependent children. The minister's explanation of objectives and methods was as follows.

> Assistance is provided in accordance with a graduated scale of adjusted family incomes. As family income decreases in the income scale, assistance increases progressively. Following interest rate adjustments down to CMHC's lowest rate, a maximum grant of $300 per annum is available to make further reductions in monthly charges.

> The objective is to enable families to own a house without spending more than 25 per cent of their gross income in meeting the monthly costs of mortgage loan repayments and municipal taxes. Regular home-owner housing, housing built on leased land or condominium forms of housing all qualify under the program.[22]

AHOP was considered by both federal and provincial officials to have been a substantial success and a significant legislative innovation. There are, in fact, two parts to the "assistance" available under the scheme: firstly, an interest reduction loan (literally a second mortgage) designed to reduce the effective rate of interest from current levels to 8 per cent. The intent was to reduce the amount of total family income required to meet debt service charges within a 25-30 per cent ratio of shelter costs to gross income,[23] depending upon the specified maximum sale prices in difficult localities. The loan is repayable after six years. The second form of assistance to the purchaser was a direct grant (originally $300 per annum) to a maximum $750 per annum to further reduce the burden of shelter costs on moderate-income families. This grant could bring families with incomes of $800-$900 per month into the market. Success of these concepts is attested to by the action of the governments of Nova Scotia (1974-1975) and Ontario (1976-1977) to add an additional grant to the subsidy. In Ontario's case a further $750 per annum was possible in the first year, one implication being the potential entry into home ownership of families with $7,000 – $8,500 per annum.

CMHC attributed an important part of the successful 1976 home-building program to AHOP in its assessment of that year's activity:

> Housing starts in 1976 totalled 273,203 units, up from 231,456 in 1975 and above the previous record of 268,529 in 1973 . . . Private institutional lending for new residential construction increased from $4.7 billion in 1975 to $6.5 billion in 1976, or by 38 per cent. This increase was almost entirely attributable to increased NHA activity, and particularly to the AHOP and ARP (Assisted Rental) Programs . . . The demand for mortgage funds for new residential construction was strong throughout 1976 . . . The strength in the second half of the year was due in large part to the AHOP and ARP Programs.[24]

The danger in AHOP rests in its fundamental reliance on continued price inflation in the Canadian economy. For the low or moderate-income purchaser of an AHOP-financed home there are two important requirements which come into sharp focus six years after purchase. First of all, repayment of the interest reduction loan must commence in the seventh year, and at the rate of interest then prevailing. This rate could be 3 to 5 percentage points higher than the 8 per cent rate for the first five years. Clearly, the purchaser needs a substantially higher income than the one prevailing at the time home ownership commenced. Inflation will likely be a prerequisite to the attainment of such income. The second requirement is a sufficient rise in all prices and thus allowable or attainable incomes, to permit the purchaser to maintain a reasonable debt service ratio.

The future did not bode well for AHOP participants. If the prospects for new growth and development and thus the prospects for expanded employment were encouraging, the assumptions governing the program might be reasonable. All the forecasts of the late 1970s, however, appear to indicate that economic growth for the early to mid-1980s will be relatively modest and that unemployment will remain at a level of 8 per cent. Taking this into consideration, it is doubtful that appropriate housing policies can be devised to meet the needs of all income groups given statistical projections of an additional 150,000 families and/or 220,000 households being formed per annum.[25]

(2) Non-Profit Housing Assistance (new Section 15.1)

The purpose of this amendment is "to make it easier for non-profit housing organizations to develop housing projects." Loans may be made to non-profit corporations of three types: those constituted exclusively for charitable purposes, co-operative associations whose members will make up the majority of those who will occupy the housing, and housing co-operatives owned entirely by a municipality or an agency of a municipality. In all cases the loan may be in an amount equal to the total lending value of the project.[26] Moreover, CMHC is enabled to make an additional contribution not exceeding 10 per cent of the capital cost of projects developed by any of these three types of non-profit co-operatives.

(3) Co-operative Housing Assistance

The act was amended in several sections to extend the provisions for co-operative housing and various forms of assistance were added to make it easier for low-income families and persons to obtain housing through co-operative associations. In the past only recognized formal co-operative associations were enabled to secure loans. The 1973 amendments encouraged groups of individuals to organize themselves in co-operatives not only to build new housing but to purchase existing housing and to rehabilitate it.

(4) Neighbourhood Improvement Program (new Part III.1, S. 27)

In the 1973 act NIP follows immediately upon part III, "Urban Renewal". This new program is thus a broadened and more deliberate extension of the traditional concepts of clearance and renewal. The new section begins,

> For the purpose of improving the amenities of neighbourhoods and the housing and living conditions of the residents of such neighbourhoods, the corporation may make contributions and loans pursuant to this Part to or for the benefit of municipalities in a province.

In the first instance, however, CMHC is required to enter into an agreement with a province for the purposes just described. This requirement has become known loosely as "the master agreement" which, the legislation states, sets out the criteria governing the selection of neighbourhoods and, in general, prescribes the procedures under which applications are made.

Under the heading "Neighbourhood Eligibility", the 1973 kit states:

> The criteria whereby municipalities and neighbourhoods may participate in this program are set out in agreements between the federal government and each of the provincial governments.
> In general, however, it is expected that participating neighbourhoods will have the following characteristics:
> 1. They will be predominantly residential although they may contain local stores, schools, banks, churches, small businesses and perhaps some non-conforming uses of land;
> 2. A significant proportion of the existing housing stock is in need of improvement and repair in order for it to comply with minimum standards of health and safety;
> 3. Most of the housing in the neighbourhood is occupied by people of low to moderate income;
> 4. The available social and recreational amenities are considered to be inadequate.

In the minister's presentation to Parliament and in a variety of speeches and background papers released by the ministry, NIP is fundamentally the logical expansion of legislation which dates from 1944 in the Canadian housing annals. Some of the very language of Section 12 of the National Housing Act, 1944 and Section 23 of the National Housing Act, 1954, appears almost intact in the 1973 Amendments which offered two apparently new programs described as a "neighbourhood improvement programme" and a "residential rehabilitation programme".[27]

The federal contribution through CMHC is identical with the 50 per cent available thirty years ago for "acquisition and clearance of sub-standard neighbourhoods". The major difference is that NIP does not contemplate clearance (except as indicated below) but obviously, from its very title, is intended to emphasize "improvement". The federal contribution is made with respect to the costs of selecting appropriate neighbourhoods, acquiring parcels of land for low-income family dwellings of low density, the acquisition and clearance of land for social or recreational facilities, the construction of such facilities, and so on. The contribution is also intended to assist in the relocation of persons whose accommodation is lost through neighbourhood improvement and, finally, the municipal staffing of the entire process. These forms of encouragement and financial assistance encompassed within NIP had been available for some time.

Since 1964 the federal government had also contributed to the costs of improved municipal and public utility services in designated urban renewal neighbourhoods. This contribution is continued at the rate of 25 per cent but was expanded to include the acquisition and clearance of land "where the existing housing is not consistent with the planned general character of the neighbourhood". Central Mortgage and Housing Corporation may make further loans of up to 75 per cent of the costs incurred by municipalities which participate in a Neighbourhood Improvement Program.[28]

(5) Residential Rehabilitation Assistance Program (Part IV.1)

Rehabilitation as a concept has been a part of the National Housing Act since 1944 and has been one of the least successful aspects of federal housing legislation. The intent in 1972-1973 was to provide a fillip to this aspect of traditional legislation by encouraging the maintenance and improvement of existing housing stock. It has always been recognized that the vast majority of housing accommodation in Canada has been in the form of existing housing, much of which is forty to fifty years old or even older.[29]

In 1973 RRAP was described as a new program. It is difficult to comprehend the newness of the program because it did little more than specify more clearly the nature of eligibility for federal assistance and a new approach in the form of "forgivable loans". In the previous three decades the major problem with the rehabilitation section of the Act was that those persons who most required financial assistance for repair and improvement of owner-occupied accommodation were the least likely to borrow money, even under relatively generous terms, because they tended to be in families of low income or elderly persons or both. Moreover, those dwellings owned by absentee landlords were not likely to be repaired, since the cost of improvements would mean that rents would need to be raised; in most cases, the landlord could not see this prospect in the neighbourhoods in which he owned such accommodation.

The minister's program of 1973 specified that eligible homeowners could not earn more than $11,000 per year. Up to $5,000 per dwelling unit could be borrowed at a less than the normal rate of interest (this represented an increase in the maximum lending value of $1,000 per dwelling unit, whereas for nearly two decades $10,000 per dwelling unit had been available under the United States legislation).[30] If the Canadian homeowner earned less than $6,000 per annum, a portion of the loan did not have to be repaid provided that the owner continued to occupy and maintain the accommodation. In the range $6,000 to $11,000 per annum the forgiveness portion was progressively reduced as income increased.[31]

Landlords who agreed to accept rent controls were also eligible for assistance under RRAP, together with non-profit corporations and co-operatives. There was, however, a very important restriction: the dwellings to be rehabilitated, whether owner-occupied or owned by absentee landlords, had to be located in Neighbourhood Improvement Program Areas; if they were in other areas they could be included only by special agreement with the province concerned. Non-profit corporations and co-operatives, however, could purchase older accommodation, renovate it, and make it available regardless of its location.[32] A good deal of the additional funds allocated in recent years are, in fact, accounted for by the activity of non-profit housing corporations.

In 1973 the NHA was amended by the addition of the important Section 34.1(3), which stated that no loan would be made under RRAP unless the province of the municipality "has adopted occupancy and building maintenance standards satisfactory to the Corporation".

(6) Land Assembly Assistance

The minister announced as his "sixth programme", assistance available under Sections 40 and 42 of the NHA to provinces and municipalities wishing to assemble and develop land for residential and associated purposes, or "to establish land banks for future development of a predominantly residential nature". The language of Section 40(1) is almost word for word the language incorporated in Section 35 of the NHA in the significant amendments of November 1949. What, then, is new about land assembly when in the Metropolitan Toronto area, for example, such vast land acquisitions as Malvern, Bathurst-Lawrence, Keele and Steeles (now accommodating both York University and a major public housing development known as Edgeley Village) were undertaken between 1950 and 1952?

Since 1964 there has been a great deal more emphasis on the concept of "land banking", which appeared so beneficial in its potential that it could scarcely be opposed by politicians, public servants, and members of voluntary organizations. The objectives of land assembly assistance included an improvement in the supply of land, a reduction in the rate of interest with respect to the cost of serviced land, and a program which would be scaled and timed "to assist the implementation of municipal, regional and provincial growth policies". What is involved in attaining these objectives is simply the forward purchase of land, since the price of land in a rapidly urbanizing society is bound to increase. The costs to government in the acquisition and clearance, and the ultimate subsidies required to provide housing accommodation to needy families, will also increase considerably. The great difficulty was that by 1973 relatively little land was available for land banking. Spurr has demonstrated that all the major housing development organizations operating in the Montreal, Toronto and Vancouver metropolitan areas either owned or had under option vast acreages of undeveloped or serviced land.[33] Despite the assistance of the land assembly provisions of Section 42, land banking opportunities were severely limited.

(7) New Communities Program (Part VI.1)

This relatively new legislation expanded the concept of federal-provincial agreements which had been originally introduced in November 1949 for the purpose of providing housing for rental to low-income families. The scope of federal-provincial agreements had been broadly expanded in 1954 and again in 1964, but in 1973 the legislation included for the first time the acquisition of land "for a new community, including land to be used for transportation corridors, linking the community to other communities, or for public open space in or around a new community or separating it from any other community." Such agreements could include assistance in undertaking the planning of a new community and the design and installation of utilities, and other services required for its development.

It must be clear that a "New Communities Program" is an obvious and significant federal thrust in the emerging picture of Canada as an urbanized nation. The Task Force on Housing and Urban Development was quite aware of British and American experiments in the development of new communities, and Paul Hellyer in particular made a number of public addresses on this subject. Long before the report of the task force was tabled, its chairman was on record as an advocate of "satellite communities" and his report of January 1969 included recommendations on the subject. In that sense the inclusion of a New Communities Program in the 1973 amendments is a further example of the government's implementation of the recommendations of the task force, despite the formal rejection and ignominy suffered by its chairman.[34]

(8) Developmental Program

In Part V of the act, "Housing Research and Community Planning", an amendment to Section 37 was introduced to enable the federal government to play a more significant role in the development of new and innovative solutions to Canadian housing problems. This read,

The corporation may undertake or cause to be undertaken projects of an experimental or developmental nature that may assist the corporation in the formulation and implementation of a housing policy designed to meet the needs of the various communities in Canada.

The ministerial statement defined the developmental project as one in which new forms of housing, new community designs, new methods of providing services, and new social relationships "are put into practice, so that their efforts can be seen and tested." The fact is that financial assistance for research in these areas has been available since the introduction of Part V in the act. The particular specification of the notion of a developmental program was not included but there is certainly a good deal of evidence that many innovations in community planning have been delineated in social research funded by CMHC.[35]

(9) Housing for Indians on Reserves

The Government of Canada has a specific responsibility for Canadian status Indians who live on reserves, and this responsibility has included the provision of new housing within the programs of both the Department of Northern Development & Indian Affairs and the Central Mortgage and Housing Corporation. Section 59 of the NHA was amended in 1973 to authorize the corporation to "make loans to Indians, as defined in the Indian Act, for the purpose of assisting in the purchase, improvement, or construction of housing projects on Indian reserves." The objective of this change was to extend to Indians access to housing by the provision of a mini-program of residential rehabilitation on the reserves.

(10) Purchaser Protection

Finally, the minister indicated that it was the policy of his government "that home buyers should benefit from the same kind of protection available to purchasers of other goods in today's economy." In short, the government was examining the possibility of developing a national warranty system and to this end amended Section 8.1 of the NHA.

Section 8 had previously made it possible for the corporation to make a contribution to a purchaser from the Mortgage Insurance Fund when the builder had failed to complete the construction of a house which was insured through the provisions of the National Housing Act. The purpose of the contribution had been restricted to enable the purchaser to complete construction of the house. In 1973 the legislation was amended to include bankruptcy of the builder prior to completion of a unit. Central Mortgage and Housing Corporation could make available to the prospective purchaser sufficient funds to discharge any liability which he had incurred with respect to liens or "privileged claims affecting the house." This change was a major step in the direction of a home warranty system but the minister expected that further efforts would be required, and he indicated that the government intended to proceed with a "home protection development plan".

In 1976 the Government of Ontario passed legislation to enable the Housing and Urban Development Association of Canada (HUDAC) to establish a warranty program.[36] Builders were required to join the scheme and to pay a fee for participation, or forfeit certain opportunities within the building programs of the Ministry of Housing and the Ontario Housing Corporation. The legislation protects the purchaser of homes built by members of the plan by guaranteeing that certain deficiencies attributable to the work of the construction company will be rectified. There is no similar legislation in other Canadian provinces but there are warranty plans and programs in which HUDAC and other organizations play important roles and assume significant responsibilities.

A BRIEF ASSESSMENT

In 1973, there was clearly an intention on the part of the ministry and its senior agency, CMHC, to pursue certain traditional initiatives with more vigour and flexibility. For the most part, the programs themselves are more flexible interpretations of legislation dating back to the National Housing Act of 1944. For example, the Neighbourhood Improvement Program is a modern version of slum clearance and urban renewal and the Residential Rehabilitation Assistance Program is the modern version of the home improvement loan program which first became available with the inclusion of Part IV, Home Improvement and Home Extension loans, in the 1944 act.[37]

The recent additions to the program raise a further caveat which may be more significant than an assessment that could be interpreted by federal officials as mere quibbling over words. The fact is that all these programs are administered by the Central Mortgage and Housing Corporation. It is never clear to either the casual or the professional observer of such federal-provincial programs whether federal officials, for whatever reason, are fully or only partially in support of programs introduced by the ministries concerned. It was not at all clear that the Ministry of State for Urban Affairs and the CMHC were at one which each other as policy agency and implementation agency respectively.

Nor was it clear that the regulations in such fields as neighbourhood improvement and residential rehabilitation would be interpreted any more flexibly than legislation that had been on the books for at least a quarter of a century.[38]

Such municipalities as Vancouver, Edmonton, Winnipeg, Windsor, Toronto, Ottawa, Montreal, Saint John, Halifax, and St. John's have all been deeply involved in the processes described first as "Slum Clearance" (Section 12 of the NHA 1944), then as "Urban Redevelopment" (Section 23, NHA 1954), and later as "Urban Renewal" (Section 23, NHA 1954, as amended 1964). They did not approach NIP in the mid-1970s with the great enthusiasm of an explorer coming across a new diamond field or a new gold mine. Many forms of encouragement and financial assistance encompassed within NIP had been available for some time. Many approaches had been made during the past twenty years by municipalities through their respective provincial governments to the federal government through its agency, CMHC.

Some approaches had been fruitful, some had been abortive or frustrated, and some had been facilitated and proved to be disastrous programs. The general impression of provincial and local governmental reception of Ron Basford's announcements in 1972-1973 was that they were not greeted with enthusiasm or open arms by elected and appointed provincial and municipal officials. Nevertheless, NIP is here and apparently has a thrust that is different; in particular, it is more concerned with social consequences than with the urban renewal schemes developed in accordance with the stipulations of Part II of the NHA 1954, as amended.

Despite the early skepticism with which the 1973 amendments were greeted, there has been, as the statistical data attest, a substantial upsurge in municipal and provincial activity within the two major programs customarily referred to as NIP and RRAP.[39] It is not a question of further legislative changes.[40] Rather, it is clear that modifications of the regulations and a "selling job" by the minister and his associates stimulated increasing interest, particularly within local governments in every province and on the part of citizen-initiated housing co-operatives.

NOTES

[1]Canada, Report of the Task Force on Housing and Urban Development (Ottawa: Queen's Printer, 1969) pp. 85.

[2]Science Council of Canada, *Perceptions 1: Study on Population and Technology* (Ottawa: Information Canada, 1975) Table 1, p. 13; Table 3, p. 15.

[3]Canada, *Report of the Royal Commission on Canada's Economic Prospects* (Ottawa: Queen's Printer, November 1957) pp. 97-122.

[4]Albert Rose, *A Brief to the Task Force on Housing and Urban Development* (Toronto: mimeo., September 30, 1968) p. 1-2.

[5]Canada, *Report of the Task Force on Housing and Urban Development*, p. 72.

[6]*Ibid.*, pp. 26-37.

[7]*Idem.*, pp. 37-45.

[8]Albert Rose, "Paul Hellyer on Housing: Fact or Fiction?" (*The Globe and Mail*, February 5, 1969) p. 7.

[9]Robert K. Andras, "Statement on Public Housing Program", House of Commons, April 21, 1970, pp. 10.

[10]*Ibid.*, p. 9. The matter of grants and the matter of a voice in the management of public housing were closely related. Tenant associations required funds to develop programs of interest to tenant families and to convince provincial housing corporations or local housing authorities of their representativesness and their capacity to share in a variety of managerial tasks.

[11]The report of the Hellyer task force recommended a "Department of Housing and Urban Affairs". The prime minister and the cabinet rejected both the notion of such a department and inclusion of "Housing" in the title of the new ministry.

[12]Late in 1978 Prime Minister Trudeau announced its abolition, presumably in deference to the wishes of the provinces and re-named the corporation, Canada Mortgage and Housing Corporation.

[13]In 1976, for the first time one person, William Teron, was appointed to the senior position in both the Ministry (as secretary, equivalent to deputy minister) and the Central Mortgage and Housing Corporation (as president). The latter post Mr. Teron had already held for some three years. This dual appointment was clearly intended "to heal wounds" and to tie the corporation more closely to government policy in urban affairs.

[14]M. Lipman, "Relocation and Family Life" (Toronto: University of Toronto, unpublished doctoral dissertation, 1968). In a study of the Alexandra Park Urban Redevelopment Project in west-central Toronto, Lipman found that displaced home-owners were forced to add substantially higher amounts to their mortgage debt after expropriation and purchase of another house in a different neighbourhood.

[15]N. H. Lithwick, *Urban Canada: Problems and Prospects* (Ottawa: Central Mortgage and Housing Corporation, December 1970).

[16]Lithwick spoke at the University of Toronto on February 10, 1971.

[17]Michael Dennis and Susan Fish, *Programs in Search of a Policy: Low Income Housing in Canada* (Toronto: Hakkert, 1972).

[18]Canada, *Report of the Advisory Committee on Reconstruction* (Ottawa: 1944), Vol. IV.

[19]Dennis and Fish, *op. cit.*, p. 349.

[20]R.S. c. N-10, 2. 2-59; 1973. c. 18, S. 1-21.

[21]Government of Canada, Central Mortgage and Housing Corporation, *New National Housing Act Programs*, 1973, not paged.

[22]First program description, August 1973.

[23]To about $11,000-$12,000, per annum.

[24]Central Mortgage and Housing Corporation, *Canadian Housing Statistics, 1976* (Ottawa: CMHC, 1977) pp. viii-x.

[25]Central Mortgage and Housing Corporation, *Canadian Housing Statistics, 1975* (Ottawa: CMHC, 1976) Table 110, p. 88.

[26]"Total lending value" is a concept utilized by mortgage appraisors to indicate the maximum amount upon which a loan may be based. It is usually less than market values.

[27]Albert Rose, "Relevance of NIP to Inner-City Areas", *Presentation to the Centre for Urban and Community Studies*, (Toronto: University of Toronto, mimeo., September 1973) pp. 27.

[28]Nevertheless, between 1973 and 1976 grants under NIP (NHA, Sec. 27.2) exceeded $143 million and loans to the provinces under Sec. 27.5 approached $32 million. See *Canadian Housing Statistics*, 1976, Table 70, p. 62.

[29]Albert Rose and Donald F. Bellamy, *Rehabilitation of Housing in Central Toronto*. A report submitted to the City of Toronto Planning Board, September 1966, pp. 1-10.

[30]The maximum amount which could be borrowed under RRAP was increased to $10,000 in October 1976. The rate of interest was 8 per cent.

[31]In 1973 one-half of the maximum loan, that is, $2,500 was forgivable. When the loan maximum was increased to $10,000, the forgivable portion was increased to $3,750. The borrower literally earns a forgivable portion at the rate of $750 per annum and thus reaches the maximum in five years.

[32]Home improvement activity increased greatly in dollar volume under RRAP between 1973 and 1978; $319 million were committed in loans by the latter year. See *Canadian Housing Statistics, 1978*, Table 72, p. 64.

[33]Peter Spurr, *Land and Urban Development* (Toronto: James Lorimer and Co., 1976) pp. 111-113; table A-7, p. 411; and table A-8, p. 412. Spurr's report, described as "a preliminary study", was commissioned by CMHC in part during 1972-73. The author offered the completed study to the corporation in August 1974 and was hired to develop it for publication. In 1976 CMHC decided not to publish it and James Lorimer and Co. made it available to the public.

[34]Report of the Task Force on Housing and Urban Development, *op. cit.* p. 75. In effect, the amount committed between 1973 and 1978 for the program now described as Community Resources Organization (Sec. 36G) was less than 1.9 million. See *Canadian Housing Statistics, 1978*, Table 72, p. 64.

[35]A particularly significant example would be the study by A. J. Diamond, "Density, Distribution and Costs" (University of Toronto Centre for Urban and Community Studies, April 1970, mimeographed) pp. 289.

[36]*Ontario New Homes Warranties Plan Act*, 1976, proclaimed by Order-in-Council 3365-76, in effect from December 31, 1976.

[37]Although there has been much greater dollar activity under RRAP since the 1973 amendments, the restriction that borrowers must be residents of NIP areas was a serious deterrent. In 1976 fewer than forty individual homes in the City of Toronto were improved with RRAP assistance. (Interview with Director of Community Development, City of Toronto, May 27, 1977).

[38]Canadian Council on Social Development, *Housing Rehabilitation.* Proceedings of a conference held November 1973 (Ottawa: CCSD, December 1974) pp. 27-29, 106-108.

[39]Between 1973 and 1978, NIP Grants (Section 72.2) amounted to nearly $202 million and loans (Section 27.5) to more than $64 million. *Canadian Housing Statistics, 1978*, Table 72, p. 64.

[40]"There were no legislative changes to the National Housing Act during 1976." *Canadian Housing Statistics, 1976*, Housing Legislation and Policy, p. xiv.

CHAPTER 5

New Housing Policy Initiatives by Provincial and Local Governments

The report of the federal Task Force on Housing and Urban Development and the implementation of some of its important recommendations cast a serious chill over the development of provincial housing policies at the close of the 1960s. There had been feverish activity within a number of provinces, particularly in Ontario during the years 1967-69. I felt that the report of the task force was, in substantial measure, aimed at the Ontario Housing Corporation and its rapidly increasing program of governmental housing activity within Canada's largest province.[1] This allegation was not denied by Paul Hellyer or by officials of CMHC. Rather, the Government of Canada proceeded to initiate a new Ministry of State for Urban Affairs while continuing the freeze (originated by Mr. Hellyer) on more than thirty urban renewal projects across Canada, most of them located within Ontario.

During the years 1970-72, provincial housing programs were thus virtually at a standstill as provincial officials attempted to ascertain and measure the significance of new federal initiatives. On the one hand, Robert Andras (the first minister) began to release modest funds to complete work already underway in urban renewal projects; on the other hand, in the conventional public housing field, the OHC alone was absorbing nearly 98 per cent of all available federal funds by 1969-70. It was certain that the new provincial housing corporations elsewhere in Canada would have a claim on these funds and, unless the total allocation by the federal government was increased (through CMHC), the Ontario program would be bound to suffer. At approximately this time the first initiatives from the Quebec Housing Corporation were ready and the President of CMHC announced that $150 million would be made available per annum to the QHC without the necessity of formal approval of each specific program.

This agreement seriously upset the relationships that had been established between the Ontario Minister of Economics and Development (Stanley Randall), the president of CMHC (Herbert Hignett), and the Minister of State for Urban Affairs (Robert Andras). Ontario felt that, at the very least, it had undertaken its responsibilities since 1964 in strict accordance with federal housing legislation. It had accepted the necessity to seek approval by the CMHC for every housing project in the province in which work was undertaken or was to be undertaken. Within Metro Toronto this involved dozens of approvals following a multitude of inspections: first, of proposals, plans and prices; second, of construction; and finally, of the condition of the particular building or grouping of houses prior to formal take-over by the OHC. These intergovernmental arrangements were well understood in Ontario, since they had been initiated in part during the days of the federal-provincial program at the beginning of the 1950's.

At the very most, what Ontario wanted was the same treatment as that accorded to Quebec through its agency, the Quebec Housing Corporation. This meant that the Government of Ontario would seek a commitment by the CMHC for a block of funds for public housing purposes (whether for rental by families or senior citizens, or for land assembly and servicing of land); and block funding not for only one fiscal year but for three to five years in advance, as was the hope of the new Minister of Economics and Development, Allan Grossman, who had been designated by the Premier of Ontario as Minister responsible for Housing.

This was the climate early in the 1970s as the new amendments to the NHA began to take shape and as the full impact of major federal initiatives in housing policy formulation began to be felt. Although there was considerable irritation, tension and a serious retardation in the rate of progress towards meeting the needs of low-income families and elderly persons throughout the country, the major positive effect was the examination and re-examination of provincial housing policies.

Table I
Statutes for Housing and Planning

FEDERAL

National Housing Act, R.S.C. 1970, c. N-10
  as amended by 1973-74, c. 18, 1974-75-76, cc. 38, 82.

ALBERTA

The Alberta Housing Act, R.S.A. 1970, c. 175
  amended 1971, c. 46; 1972, c. 51; 1973, c. 54; 1974, c. 34; 1975, Bill 13.

The Municipal Government Act, R.S.A. 1970, c. 246
  amended 1971, c. 74.

The Planning Act, R.S.A. 1970, c. 276
  amended 1971, c. 84.

BRITISH COLUMBIA

The Housing Act, R.S.B.C. 1960, c. 183.

Department of Housing Act, 1973, c. 110.

The Municipal Act, R.S.B.C. 1960, c. 255
  amended 1961, cc. 43, 59; 1962, cc. 36, 41; 1963, c. 42; 1964, c. 33;
  1965, c. 28; 1966, c. 31; 1967, c. 28; 1968, c. 33; 1969, c. 21; 1970,
  c. 29; 1971, c. 38; 1972, c. 36.

MANITOBA

The Housing and Renewal Corporation Act, R.S.M. 1970, c. H160
  amended 1970, c. 86; 1971, c. 14.

The Municipal Act, 1970 (Man.), c. 100
  amended 1971, cc. 27, 81, 82; 1972, cc. 22, 41, 42.

The Municipal Board Act, R.S.M. 1970, c. M240
  amended 1970, c. 92; 1972, c. 81.

The Planning Act, R.S.M. 1970, c. P80.

The Real Property Act, R.S.M. 1970, c. R30
  amended 1970, c. 90; 1971, c. 82; 1972, cc. 37, 82.

NEW BRUNSWICK

The New Brunswick Housing Act, 1967.

The Community Planning Act, 1960-61 (N.B.), c. 6
  amended 1963 (2nd Sess.), c. 13; 1964, c. 18; 1965, c. 12; 1966, c. 152;
  1968, c. 21; superseded by 1972, c. 7.

The Municipalities Act, 1966 (N.B.), c. 20
  amended 1967, c. 56; 1968, c. 41; 1969, c. 58; 1970, c. 37; 1971, c. 50;
  1972, c. 49.

Table I (continued)

NEWFOUNDLAND

The Housing Act, 1966, S.N., c. 87. An Act to incorporate the Newfoundland and Labrador Housing Corporation, April 25, 1967, cited as the Newfoundland and Labrador Housing Corporation Act, R.S.N., 1970, c. 249.

The Local Government Act 1966 (Nfld.), c. 31
amended 1966-67, c. 15; 1968, c. 19; 1969, c. 37; 1970, c. 33; 1971, c. 56.

The Urban and Rural Planning Act, 1965 (Nfld.), c. 28
amended 1969, c. 55.

NOVA SCOTIA

The Housing Development Act, R.S.N.S. 1967, c. 129
amended 1969, c. 52; 1970-71, c. 45.

The Home Owner's Incentive Act, R.S.N.S. 1970-71, c. 1.

The Municipal Act, R.S.N.S. 1967, c. 192
amended 1968, c. 41; 1969, cc. 60, 61; 1970, c. 54; 1970-71, c. 52; 1972, c. 46.

The Planning Act, 1969 (N.S.), c. 16
amended 1970, c. 87; 1970-71, c. 71.

The Towns Act, R.S.N.S. 1967, c. 309
amended 1968, c. 58; 1969, cc. 77, 78; 1970, c. 72; 1970-71, c. 59; 1972 c. 55.

ONTARIO

The Housing Development Act, R.S.O. 1970, c. 213;
as amended by 1972, c. 129; 1974, c. 31; 1976, Bill 64.

The Ontario Housing Corporation Act 1964, c. 76;
R.S.O., c. 317.

The Ministry of Housing Act, 1973, c. 100;
as amended by 1974, c. 14.

The Municipal Act, R.S.O. 1970, c. 284
amended 1971, c. 81 and c. 98, s. 4 Sched. para. 23; 1972, cc. 121, 124, 169.

The Planning Act, R.S.O. 1970, c. 349
amended 1971, c. 2; 1972, c. 118.

Table I (continued)

PRINCE EDWARD ISLAND

The Prince Edward Island Housing Authority Act, 1966;
R.S.P.E. 1974, c. 33; repealed by the Housing Corporation Act, 24 Eliz.
II, 1975, c. 14.

The Planning Act, 1968 (P.E.I.), c. 40
amended 1969, c. 35; 1970, c. 38; 1971, c. 30.

The Town Act, R.S.P.E.I. 1951, c. 162
amended 1952, c. 45; 1953, c. 46; 1959, c. 26; 1960, c. 42; 1961, c. 39;
1963, c. 31; 1964, c. 32; 1966, c. 41; 1968, c. 55; 1970, c. 51; 1971, c. 56.

The Village Service Act, 1954 (P.E.I.), c. 39
amended 1956, c. 45; 1957, c. 37; 1959, c. 31; 1960, c. 46; 1961, c. 43;
1962, c. 39; 1963, c. 35; 1964, c. 36; 1965, c. 28; 1966, c. 45; 1968,
c. 60; 1969, c. 51; 1971, c. 56.

QUEBEC

The Quebec Housing Corporation Act, (Loi de la Société d'habitation du
Québec) 1966-1967, c. 55;
as amended by 1971, c. 56; 1971, c. 57; 1974, c. 49.

The Cities and Towns Act, R.S.Q. 1964, c. 193
amended 1966-67, c. 54; 1968, cc. 17, 53, 54, 55; 1969, cc. 55, 56; 1970,
cc. 46, 47; 1971, c. 55.

The Municipal Code
amended 1963, c. 65, s. 5.

SASKATCHEWAN

The Housing and Urban Renewal Act, 1966,
repealed by the Saskatchewan Housing Corporation Act, 1973, R.S.S.
c. 93.

The Senior Citizens' Home Repair Assistance Act, 1973, R.S.S., c. 103.

The House Building Assistance Act, 1974, c. 45
repealing the Acts of 1970 and 1972.

The Community Planning Act, R.S.S. 1965, c. 172
amended 1967, c. 92; 1968, c. 12, 1970, c. 9.

The Housing and Urban Renewal Act, 1966 (Sask.), c. 53
amended 1967, c. 30; 1968, c. 31.

The Urban Municipalities Act, 1970 (Sask.), c. 78
amended 1971, c. 63.

Source: I. M. Rogers, *Canadian Law of Planning and Zoning* (Toronto: Carswell
1973). Amended by the author to include certain additional Housing
Statutes and updated to 1975-76.

A PERIOD OF PROVINCIAL RE-EXAMINATION:
LEGISLATION AND SOUL-SEARCHING

The provinces were forced to examine the adequacy of their legislation as quickly as possible after 1970 and, if necessary, to amend it to meet the new conditions occasioned by the policies which Paul Hellyer had initiated and which the first Minister of State for Urban Affairs had begun to translate into federal and federal-provincial programs. A tabulation of governing legislation is presented in Table I to indicate, first of all, the activity which transpired to bring order out of near chaos.

A quick glance at this compilation of legislative enactments will indicate that there were a great many amendments to existing legislation throughout the country in 1971 and 1972. In the western provinces – with the exception of Saskatchewan which passed legislation in 1973 – the basic legislation received important changes in those years. In three of the Maritime Provinces there was an entirely new Community Planning Act, and in Nova Scotia all the basic legislation governing housing development was amended between 1970 and 1972. This was also the case in Ontario, and in Quebec with the exception of its basic municipal code. It is clear that the provinces were attempting to fit their legislative structure within the new formulations put forward by a federal government which proposed to play a substantial role in the future urbanization of a very wealthy, very diverse and thinly populated nation.

The second major element in this picture of housing policy formulation which took the form of a process of soul-searching, is perhaps best illustrated by the detailed exposition that follows on the course of events in Ontario. In defence of this approach it is argued that Ontario is virtually a major state within the Canadian nation. So much attention has been paid to the cultural differences and aspirations of the people of Quebec that the concept of two nations – Canada on the one hand and Quebec on the other – has restricted the thinking of most people. Ontario's place in the nation has tended to be based more on the fact that most of its population is English-speaking rather than a recognition of its own special significance.

Ontario had a population of more than eight million persons in the late 1970s, approximately equal to that of Sweden and close to the total combined populations of Norway and Denmark. This province is by far the wealthiest in the country in terms of total physical product and the gross provincial product measured in dollars. Per capita income is above that of any other province;[2] the rate of unemployment until recent years has been below that in any other province; and, while the labour force has expanded substantially as a result of natural growth and immigration, total employment has expanded more or less in the same proportion. In short, Ontario is a nation-state with vast resources and with far less dependence on one type of resource than any other province in Canada. The reference to the Scandinavian countries was deliberate to indicate that the standard of living in Ontario is of the same order as that of major Scandinavian countries purporting to maintain the highest living standards in the world and which have developed tremendously imaginative and effective housing policies.

The situation that developed in Ontario from 1971 through 1974 constitutes one model of progression towards the evolution of appropriate housing policies. It is not so clear that the same route was followed formally in any other province, but it would appear from legislative changes and from the statistical data available that, at least in certain formal and informal ways, the same set of procedures was followed in what I have called the process of "soul-searching". In Ontario this process occurred in the following apparent sequential progression.

1. In November 1972 the Premier of Ontario, William Davis, appointed an Advisory Task Force on Housing Policy chaired by Professor Eli Comay, Faculty of Environmental Studies at York University (formerly the Commissioner of Planning for the Municipality of Metropolitan Toronto). The task force submitted its report and several supporting monographs, as well as a variety of commissioned studies, on July 27, 1973.

2. The Government of Ontario created a Ministry of Housing through the passage of the *Ministry of Housing Act* on October 25, 1973. Premier Davis appointed Robert Welch, formerly the Policy Minister for Social Development, as the first Minister of Housing in Ontario.

3. The Ministry of Housing issued *Housing Ontario '74* described as "an initial statement of policies, programs, and partnerships."

The report of the Advisory Task Force on Housing Policy proposed not only the creation of a Ministry of Housing but, further, that the Government of Ontario should de-centralize the administration and management of housing programs whenever a municipality felt capable of undertaking these responsibilities. The major documentation required to demonstrate such capacity was the development of a local, municipal, or regional housing policy.[3] Early in 1974 the City of Toronto issued a study entitled, *Living Room*,[4] which purported to be the city's statement of housing policies and capabilities to undertake its responsibilities, not only in the management but in the development of a housing program. The Ministry of Housing apparently recognized the city's capability; in late spring, 1974 the City of Toronto created its first Department of Housing and appointed a Commissioner of Housing with the same status as that of other major departmental heads.

In May 1974 the Municipality of Metropolitan Toronto issued an *Interim Metro Housing Policy* in draft form and described it in two parts as a housing policy suitable for the entire metropolitan area of Toronto with its two-and-a-half million inhabitants. The potential conflict in housing policies between the constituent municipalities in the lower tier of the two-tier regional government and the upper tier, as represented by the Metropolitan Council in Toronto, had not yet been resolved in the late 1970s.

An examination of the major documents produced in Ontario during the years 1973-1977 constitutes one appropriate way of presenting the evolution of provincial and local housing policies.[5] The wealth of documentation is not available for any other province, yet the manner in which the progression has occurred is likely to be repeated in many other jurisdictions in our country.

PROVINCIAL INITIATIVES OUTSIDE ONTARIO

Since 1968, when the Canadian Conference on Housing included representatives from eight housing corporations, the two provinces which were lacking such administrative devices have developed new or stronger administrative organizations. The Saskatchewan Housing Corporation was created in March 1973 and the British Columbia Housing Management Commission in December 1967; but the latter was relatively inactive until amendments were made to the *British Columbia Housing Act 1960*. These amendments took effect in June 1970 and made it possible to undertake a variety of new programs in the mid-1970s.

All ten provinces are now identical, at least in terms of the apparent superstructure governing the development of housing policies and the implementation of housing programs within the respective provinces. This is not surprising in view of the fact that all must perforce operate within the umbrella of the National Housing Act and must seek the substantial financial resources available through the federal legislation, particularly since the amendments of 1973 and 1975.

Nevertheless, the essential data released by the CMHC indicate that there has been a substantial reduction in the activity of most provincial governments as far as housing for low-income groups is concerned. Table II indicates first of all that 1970 was the banner year for financial assistance to low-income groups from the federal agency through the provincial organizations during the decade 1965-1974. This tabulation, drawn from data in *Canadian Housing Statistics*, previously entitled, "Aids to Low Income Groups", was retitled in the 1976 edition. The

Table II
Housing Assistance Programmes[6] (by type of dwelling) 1969-78 Canada

Period	Single-Detached Dwellings	Multiple-Dwelling Structures	Total
1969	1,348	27,450	28,798
1970	1,803	52,533	54,336
1971	5,354	41,212	46,566
1972	5,701	29,819	35,520
1973	5,366	24,484	29,850
1974	9,008	25,004	34,012
1975	17,643	61,857	79,500
1976	22,192	68,428	90,620
1977	17,414	85,899	103,313
1978	9,048	38,728	47,776

substantial increase in the figures commencing 1975 is due to the inclusion of activity under Section 6 of the NHA whereby approved lenders may make insured loans. This recent substantial statistical change is primarily a reflection of increased activity in condominium apartment structures. In my opinion, inclusion of the data for Section 6 seriously weakens the phrase "housing assistance programs".

Similarly, the data for Table III are not entirely comparable because of the aforementioned inclusion of Section 6 data in 1974 and thereafter. It would appear that there was a substantial recovery in every province and for the nation as a whole after 1973. Most of the new dwelling units, however, were not for rent to low-income groups in traditional public housing programs; rather they were for sale to families in the lower half of the middle income group ("families of modest or moderate income"). It is important not to be deceived by statistical tables which indicate a three-fold increase in the number of dwelling units produced in Canada under "Housing Assistance Programs".

This table indicates that the major reason for the downturn in the production of public housing for low-income groups prior to 1974 lay in the trend away from multiple dwellings, particularly in the provinces of Quebec and Ontario. There had been an important increase in the production of single detached homes, but a fourfold increase from 1969 to 1973 did not compensate for a more than 60 per cent drop-off in multiple dwellings from 1970 through 1973. For Canada as a whole, housing for low-income groups dropped by about 50 per cent during these four years. This is significant evidence of the critical problems which faced those individuals and families who fell in the lowest third of the income distribution.

Table III

CMHC aids to Low-Income Groups[7] (number of dwelling units by provinces and types of dwellings)

Province	1971 Single-Detached Dwellings	1971 Multiple-Dwelling Structures	1971 Total	1972 Single-Detached Dwellings	1972 Multiple-Dwelling Structures	1972 Total	1973 Single-Detached Dwellings	1973 Multiple-Dwelling Structures	1973 Total
Nfld.	142	345	487	109	106	215	199	450	649
P.E.I.	91	52	143	158	118	276	96	49	145
N.S.	1,083	1,761	2,844	761	1,753	2,514	610	1,266	1,876
N.B.	396	509	905	273	710	983	188	273	461
Que.	1,694	14,110	15,804	1,927	5,602	7,529	2,802	2,049	4,851
Ont.	60	15,208	15,268	169	12,187	12,356	366	11,105	11,471
Man.	380	4,252	4,632	398	2,451	2,849	344	876	1,220
Sask.	1,116	343	1,459	1,550	753	2,303	1,068	499	1,567
Alta.	420	2,663	3,083	441	1,952	2,393	358	1,671	2,029
B.C.	102	2,567	2,669	225	2,414	2,639	551	2,896	3,447
CANADA*	5,524	41,846	47,370	6,102	28,102	34,204	6,638	21,293	27,931

*Includes Yukon and Northwest Territories.

Source: CMHC, *Canadian Housing Statistics, 1973* (Ottawa, March 1974) Table 51, p. 44.

Table III (continued)

Province	1974			1975			1976		
	Single-Detached Dwellings	Multiple-Dwelling Structures	Total	Single-Detached Dwellings	Multiple-Dwelling Structures	Total	Single-Detached Dwellings	Multiple-Dwelling Structures	Total
Nfld.	921	831	1,752	480	1,333	1,813	764	1,536	2,300
P.E.I.	166	232	398	283	109	392	223	11	234
N.S.	1,307	988	2,295	1,616	1,941	3,557	1,131	954	2,085
N.B.	608	1,226	1,834	1,020	1,494	2,514	1,520	849	2,369
Que.	5,378	4,321	9,699	9,132	15,346	24,478	10,924	14,782	25,706
Ont.	2,744	11,366	14,110	1,374	24,513	25,887	1,841	27,542	29,383
Man.	747	1,229	1,976	651	4,807	5,458	534	3,756	4,290
Sask.	1,271	1,230	2,501	1,453	2,256	3,709	1,687	4,199	5,886
Alta.	369	1,579	1,948	204	3,026	3,230	169	3,874	4,043
B.C.	1,618	4,896	6,514	1,371	6,606	7,977	3,239	9,255	12,494
CANADA*	15,180	28,015	43,195	17,933	61,623	79,556	22,304	67,009	89,313

*Includes Yukon and Northwest Territories.

Source: CMHC, *Canadian Housing Statistics, 1978* (Ottawa, March 1977) Table 52, p. 46.

Table III (continued)

Province	1977			1978		
	Single-Detached Dwellings	Multiple-Dwelling Structures	Total	Single-Detached Dwellings	Multiple-Dwelling Structures	Total
Nfld.	678	1,185	1,863	447	456	903
P.E.I.	171	192	363	119	301	420
N.S.	1,127	3,322	4,449	786	1,048	1,834
N.B.	874	633	1,507	683	564	1,247
Que.	5,976	16,366	22,342	2,678	7,142	9,820
Ont.	1,724	35,289	37,013	1,445	21,099	22,544
Man.	546	5,711	6,257	424	3,046	3,470
Sask.	2,467	3,531	5,998	1,224	1,635	2,859
Alta.	545	9,225	9,770	219	2,696	3,188
B.C.	3,254	11,693	14,947	1,481	1,741	3,222
CANADA*	17,636	87,420	105,056	9,621	40,117	49,738

*Includes Yukon and Northwest Territories.

Source: CMHC, *Canadian Housing Statistics, 1978* (Ottawa: March 1979) Table 57, p. 51.

Table III presents a more detailed breakdown revealing that between 1972 and 1973 total dwelling units declined in all provinces except Newfoundland and British Columbia. It may be concluded that the new corporation in British Columbia and the allocation of substantial resources by a new government elected in 1972 made the difference. In most provinces the decline was substantial. In Quebec it was more than one-third; in Ontario it was approximately 7 to 8 per cent.

In almost every respect the years 1971-73 revealed a substantial decline by comparison with 1969 and 1970. The reasons for this downturn at a time when total housing production throughout Canada rose dramatically were provided earlier. The confusion after 1969 – the creation of the Ministry of State for Urban Affairs and the indecision of the successive ministers and their senior officials after 1970-71, the use of housing as a factor in curtailing the progress of inflation in the years 1969-71 – combined to worsen drastically the housing situation of low-income groups in our country.

The data for the years 1974-77 indicate a substantial increase in governmental activity. The title of the relevant Table was changed, however, from "CMHC Aids to Low-Income Groups" to "NHA Activity for New and Existing Housing". These statistical manipulations seem to be based upon the notion that the federal government desired full statistical recognition for all its interventions in the housing market. If this is an accurate presumption it must have been embarrassing to discover that the number of units assisted dropped from more than 105,000 in 1977 to less than 50,000 in 1978 (a decline of 52.6 per cent). These facts presaged a crisis which deepened in 1979 and has become intolerable in the early 1980s.

A reading of the annual reports and other material published by the various provinces in recent years does, nevertheless, support the view that they were concerned with the plight of low-income families and individuals, and particularly with the needs of older people. The following description of activity within the several provinces is presented in geographical order by province, from west to east.

British Columbia

Governmental housing activity in British Columbia took a form unique among the provinces. Although a B.C. Housing Management Commission had been created at the end of 1967, its only responsibility was to operate and administer existing federal-provincial public housing projects. The two local housing authorities, the Vancouver Housing Authority and the Prince Rupert Housing Authority, were disbanded. The government of Premier W. A. C. Bennett was cautious in its expansion of the public housing stock and clearly was opposed to the concepts underlying public intervention in the housing market. With the election of a new government in 1972, a number of significant changes occurred.

A Department of Housing (rather than a ministry) was created on November 15th, 1973. On January 10th, 1974 the Department acquired a private housing construction company, known as Dunhill Development Corporation Limited, "to expedite matters."[8] Dunhill was described as "a British Columbia company with an excellent reputation in the building development and construction field."[9] The B.C. Housing Management Commission was reconstituted with "a fresh mandate".

> Thus, for the first time in the history of British Columbia, the provincial government assumed a meaningful responsibility for the provision of adequate and reasonably-priced housing for residents of the province.[10]

The Housing Management Commission planned an entirely new approach to its responsibilities in January 1975. It dispatched a letter to all public housing tenants, indicating that a new rent-to-income scale had been created for the purpose of changing the image of public housing. On January 13th, 1975 it introduced a rent supplement program which, it stated, had among its basic objectives the integration of persons and families in different income ranges, "normalization" of public housing programs in the community, housing alternatives for low-income groups and, hopefully, public acceptance of governmental activity. In the late months of 1974 there was considerable correspondence on this subject between the "Minister of Housing" in Victoria and the Minister of State for Urban Affairs in Ottawa. On August 9th of that year, Lorne Nicolson declared in a letter to Barnett Danson,

> The program is designed to cover a much broader social mix, permitting projects to become better integrated (without stigma) into the surrounding community. It will replace the existing public housing rent scale in British Columbia and will also be applicable by agreement with CMHC to co-operative and non-profit housing developments.[11]

Senior citizen housing had not previously been covered in British Coumbia by a rent-geared-to-income scale so the rents of single elderly persons were to be reduced and the rents for elderly couples were to be increased, although a number of allowable income exemptions were reported.

The federal minister responded with approval and indicated that provincial governments may deviate from the "federal rent-to-income scale" so that local conditions and needs can be better met. He stipulated, however, that the federal share of subsidies shall be based on the lesser amount resulting from the application of the "federal and provincial rental scales".[12] Mr. Danson wrote again on June 30th, 1975 to indicate that agreement had been reached between the Government of Canada and the Government of British Columbia concerning the social and income mix for public housing in the province. His statement is an important affirmation of policy which presumably applied to all provinces.

> Within a Section 43 NHA project, 95 per cent of the units would be reserved for low income families as defined in the National Housing Act (50 per cent of those in greatest need from the lower third of incomes within a market area and 35 per cent of those in greatest need from an income range above the lowest third to a level where 25 per cent of the income equates with current market rents for new comparable accommodation).
>
> An allocation of 5 per cent may be made to families of higher income, at market rents.[13]

The first annual report of the Department of Housing and the 1974 Dunhill Corporation annual report were equally optimistic. The department stated that "by the end of 1974 the provincial housing ministry, with all its housing and mortgage programs, was involved in financing over two-thirds of the housing starts in British Columbia, in one way or another."[14] Dunhill reported that by the end of 1974 the total number of dwelling units completed, in progress or planned was 2,984.

A residential land lease program was promised under a new Leasehold and Conversion Mortgage Loan Act. British Columbia was involved in a reduced interest rate program (which preceded the federal AHOP Program) whereby interest could be reduced to as little as 5 per cent by way of a so-called free loan.[15] During its first year of operation the Department of Housing was involved in 258 projects of varying types and sizes.[16] The public housing rental stock showed a substantial increase with about 1,400 new units for a total of 6,200 under management in mid-1975. The expectation was a stock of 10,000 units by mid-1976.

With the defeat of Premier David Barrett and the New Democratic Party late in 1975, a good deal of the apparent staff enthusiasm disappeared. A major study of housing problems in the province prepared by Karl Jaffary for the previous government was shelved.[17] The senior staff person of the B.C. Housing Management Commission was dismissed. Responsibility was assigned to the new Minister of Housing and Municipal Affairs. Reports for 1976 from the Department and from Dunhill were not available late in 1977. Thus it can be conjectured that British Columbia, like other provinces had dampened its enthusiasm for direct public housing activity and turned its attention to new programs designed to facilitate home ownership for moderate income families. This conjecture is strengthened by the data presented earlier in Table III.

Alberta

Amendments to the Alberta Housing Act at the beginning of the 1970s affirmed continuation of the Alberta Housing and Urban Renewal Corporation as a corporation with the name, Alberta Housing Corporation. In the 1973 annual report of the AHC three aspects of the overall situation were emphasized. Alberta was the first province to sign an agreement with the federal government for implementation of the Neighbourhood Improvement Program. Housing for senior citizens received emphasis with almost 1,000 self-contained units approved for construction in 1973. The corporation was also responsible for elderly persons' housing in "lodges", which have characteristics of both homes for the aged and nursing homes. In the year-end review 392 beds were approved. Finally, the report emphasized that 340 public housing units (family housing) were already under construction or planned for 1974.[18]

An examination of housing programs in Alberta reveals the full galaxy of such programs available through federal-provincial cooperation, with two unique additions to such a list. The customary array was described as: Public Housing, Federal NIP, Staff Housing Program, Rural and Native Housing Program, Land Assembly and Development, Direct Lending Program, Senior Citizens Housing, Federal Assisted Home-Ownership Program, and Métis Housing Program. Housing for certain staff members of government who must live in remote areas and a Self-Help Métis Housing Program appear to be unique, although it is not clear whether the latter falls within the Rural and Native Housing Program (National Housing Act, Section 40.1).

The results of this apparent activity were described in a review entitled, a "Fifteen Month Review and Financial Statement" which covered the period January 1974 to March 31, 1975. By the time this report was made public early in 1976 the Alberta Housing Corporation had been reorganized, following a study by management consultants, whereby AHC was decentralized into separate north and south regions, each headed by a vice-president. The chief operating officer of the corporation is termed the President, responsible to the Minister of Municipal Affairs who is Chairman of the Board of Directors of the corporation.

In the fifteen month period, 1,078 self-contained units and 856 beds in lodge accommodation were approved under the Senior Citizens Housing Program. An additional 209 public housing units were approved and assistance was granted for 146 homes for Métis. Under the Direct Lending Program 2,470 loans were approved for the construction of 2,646 dwelling units. Within the Corporation's Land Assembly and Development Program, eighteen land banks and/or land development projects had been devised to assist municipalities. Moreover, the new NIP Program was underway in six cities and three districts.[19]

It is interesting to note that within this province, subsidiaries are divided on the following basis: federal 50 per cent, provincial 40 per cent and municipal 10 per cent. In Ontario the division is on a 50 – 42½ – 7½ basis.

Saskatchewan

Administration and control of all property acquired under the Housing and Urban Renewal Act, 1966, were transferred to the new Saskatchewan Housing Corporation in 1973. In its first annual report covering the period March 16 to December 31, 1973, the SHC carefully separated its powers to assist low-income families and individuals from its powers to help social assistance recipients.[20]

During its initial year the corporation placed priority upon public rental housing for low-income families and senior citizens, "with particular emphasis on the housing needs of the latter".[21] Construction of an additional 1,100 public housing units was approved during 1973. The total stock under administration at December 31, 1973 was 2,048 units composed of 1,457 for families and 591 for senior citizens. The report stated that five new programs had been developed in that first year: Senior Citizens Housing Repair Assistance Program, Residential Rehabilitation Program, Direct Lending Program, Non-Profit Program, and Subsidy and Self-Help Program.

A year later the corporation reported that its internal administration had become departmentalized as follows: Loans and Grants, Finance and Administration, Municipal Programs, and Research and Information. The first annual agreement under NIP had been signed and participation of twelve municipalities had been approved.[22] A great increase in public housing and housing activity generally, was claimed. In 1974 construction began on 519 units, with 570 dwellings actually completed. The total inventory in public housing was 2,578 dwelling units at December 31, 1974.[23]

In Saskatchewan both capital funding and subsidies were distributed on the following basis: federal 75 per cent, provincial 20 per cent and municipal 5 per cent. This distribution implies that the corporation was utilizing Section 40.2 of the National Housing Act rather than Section 43 which was normally favoured by the provincial corporations.

It is evident that in the mid-1970s the SHC emphasized promotion of the federal AHOP Program. In a special publication describing the program in June 1975, it emphasized that the province had agreed to offer subsidies over the then CMHC maximum of $600 per purchaser. The SHC noted that it would increase these subsidies by up to $628 per year, thus reducing the annual income requirement to $6,787 if families were willing to pay up to 27 per cent of gross income for a home, the price of which did not exceed $31,000 in Regina ($30,000 in Saskatoon).

Manitoba

In February 1976 the Manitoba Housing and Renewal Corporation issued its eighth annual report since its incorporation in 1967.[24] It emphasized that new programs introduced in 1974 included NIP and the Rural and Native Housing Program. In addition, assistance was made available to first-time home buyers in the form of both grant and mortgage subsidies.[25]

Six main avenues of operation were recorded by the MHRC: Land Assembly, Rental Programs, Purchase Programs, Renewal Programs, Research, and New Towns. By the end of 1975 the corporation had land banked 4,717 acres including 3,554 in the Winnipeg area.[26] Under the Elderly and Infirm Persons Housing Act, capital grants had made low rents possible; the current inventory at December 31, 1975 was 2,666 dwelling units. It is noteworthy that, in its annual report, the corporation admitted that it had entered rent supplement programs in both Winnipeg and northern Manitoba because of waiting lists of one to two years' duration for public housing accommodation.

The Manitoba corporation appeared from its reports to be active in all facets of its "main avenues of operation." It had purchased housing in the Rural and Native Housing Program; it had assisted Continuing Housing Co-operatives on leased land; it had been involved in AHOP since January 1974; and, with the first NIP agreement signed in 1974 it was involved in that program as well as RRAP.[27]

The statistical results of this substantial activity are impressive. At the close of 1975 the number of dwelling units committed were: in Family Public Housing, 4,945, including 2,037 in Winnipeg; in Elderly Persons Public Housing, 5,687, including 3,857 in Winnipeg; in Rural and Native Housing, 922; and, in Elderly and Infirm Persons Housing 2,666, including 1,578 in Winnipeg. Manitoba's record in a variety of housing assistance programs, with particular emphasis upon public housing, is all the more impressive when its population of just over 1 million persons is considered.[28] Moreover, the province initiated two unique experimental structures designed to accommodate handicapped persons. The public housing project named Ten Ten Sinclair in Winnipeg is designed to accommodate people confined to wheelchairs. It was opened in October 1975 and contained 75 one-bedroom suites. The Manitoba Housing-Kiwanis Centre of the Deaf is a six-storey, 200 unit building opened in January 1976.

Prior to 1969, funding of public housing for both capital and subsidies was on the basis of the following distribution: federal 75 per cent, provincial 12½ per cent, and municipal 12½ per cent. This was changed in that year to 90 per cent federally funded and 10 per cent provincially funded (NHA, S. 43), with the municipalities making no contribution to either capital or operating costs. There were, however, ninety local housing authorities with municipal representation at the close of 1975.

Quebec

The Quebec Housing Corporation Act 1967/67 was amended in both 1971 and 1974. An annual report covering the years 1972-73 was issued by the QHC in April 1974. Although Quebec was by that time involved in many facets of governmental intervention in the housing market, the statistical results were not impressive.

In the previously presented tables[29] of NHA activity for new and existing housing, it was clear that the number of units listed under the heading "Aids to Low-Income Groups" declined significantly in the province from 15,804 in 1971 to 6,888 in 1973 before a statistical recovery occurred in the ensuing years by virtue of the inclusion of the activity under the NHA, Section 6.

In a more detailed breakdown of housing assistance programs under the National Housing Act covering the entire post-war period, 1946-1976, the most salient data revealed that Quebec was second to Ontario in every aspect of social housing activity. As the second most populous province this should perhaps have been the case but in terms of activity per thousand of population, Quebec did not keep pace. Table IV presents some of the significant statistics.

The Quebec government was clearly not pleased with this record and commissioned a Task Force which submitted a report in January 1976.[30] *Report on Housing in Quebec* consisted of an analysis of the

Table IV

Housing Assistance Programs Under the National Housing Act, Canada Quebec and Ontario (1946-1976)

Total Housing Activity*	*Quebec*	*Ontario*
New Housing		
Number of Loans	40,417	32,661
Number of Units	119,483	179,157
Hostel Beds	32,366	35,231
Existing Housing		
Number of Loans	2,154	3,646
Number of Units	4,912	11,287
Hostel Beds	2,833	2,815
Entrepreneurial Activity Under Section 15 ***(Limited Dividend)***		
New Housing		
Number of Loans	239	371
Number of Units	27,941	40,754
Hostel Beds	47	527
Existing Housing		
Number of Loans	163	3
Number of Units	1,747	165
Hostel Beds	18	–
Loans and Contributions to Non-Profit Corporations ***and Continuing Co-operatives***		
Loans for New Housing		
Number of Loans	247	144
Number of Units	6,692	7,875
Hostel Beds	16,268	5,538
Loans for Existing Housing		
Number of Loans	37	466
Number of Units	380	1,768
Hostel Beds	2,438	1,530
Federal-Provincial Rental Housing Projects ***Under Section 40 (75% to 25% Basis)***		
New Housing		
Number of Projects	1	82
Number of Units	796	6,599
Existing Housing		
Number of Projects	–	2
Number of Units	–	436

Table IV (continued)

Loans for Public Housing Projects Under Section 43

(90% to 10% Basis)	Quebec	Ontario
New Housing		
Number of Loans	397	1,077
Number of Units	23,852	77,906
Hostel Beds	174	732
Existing Housing		
Number of Loans	12	54
Number of Units	380	5,215
Hostel Beds	–	–

Loans by CMHC Under Assisted Home Ownership and Rental Programs, NHA, 1973-1976

	Quebec	Ontario
Assisted Home Ownership Program (AHOP)		
Number of Loans	434	85
Number of Units	434	85
Assisted Rental Program		
Number of Loans	1	1
Number of Units	8	17

*Includes activities under the following Sections of the National Housing Act: Loans to Entrepreneurs and Non-Profit Corporations (Sections 15 and 15.1), Public Housing (Section 43), Student Housing (Section 47), Assisted Home-Ownership Programmes (Sections 34.15, 58 and 59), Co-operative Housing (Section 34.18), Federal-Provincial Rental and Sales Housing Projects (Section 40), and Loans by Approved Lenders (Section 6). All sub-sections in Table IV are included within the grand total of housing activity.

Source: CMHC, Canadian Housing Statistics 1976, Tables 53-58, pp. 47-51.

housing situation in general and offered a proposal to the government for a general housing policy. It proposed that 300,000 homes be constructed in five years, that an additional 360,000 homes be restored and repaired within ten years and that 30,000 acres of land "be made suitable" (serviced) within five years.[31]

The report concluded that the market mechanisms as well as the existing governmental programs function well in the case of single-family dwellings (presumably for sale), but the operation had suffered from a shortage of tenement homes at low prices (rentals) throughout the entire province. The Task Force attributed this shortage to several factors: increase of needs, deterioration of existing housing and the slowing down of construction. It emphasized that the gap is widening between the ability to pay for a reasonable standard of living and the rising cost of new houses. Construction costs increased 100 per cent between 1972 and 1975 while the rate of interest rose from 9 to 12 per cent.

The task force stated that in 1975-76 the Government of Quebec was spending about $32 million for programs of the Quebec Housing Corporation and $28 million for industrial development, water and sewerage. It affirmed that a realistic budget would include, approximately, $42 million for new programs and $38 million for renovation (rehabilitation).[32]

New Brunswick

The New Brunswick Housing Corporation issued an annual report in mid-1975 covering the fiscal year 1974. By March 31, 1975, 2,920 dwelling units were under administration and 532 were at varying stages of construction in 35 municipalities. It should be noted that the population of the province was 675,000 in that year. The development program of the corporation was concentrated on the housing needs of the elderly and emphasized the completion and occupation of the first senior citizens' developments in Bathurst and Fredericton and the first senior citizens' hostel project. Within the previous two years the corporation had designated 356 senior citizen units for low-income residents who required supplementation by virtue of their inability to obtain "decent housing in the private sector."[33]

Particular emphasis was placed upon the renovation of older projects. In this connection, New Brunswick had embarked upon a unique activity in which social assistance recipients participated in a work activity program to upgrade public properties. While interesting, this development has roots within the original poor law philosophy which has dominated social development in the Atlantic provinces since the 18th century. The report made clear the linkage between the needs of persons in poverty for a variety of social services and their requirements for decent housing.

> While social development has been traditionally relegated to a subordinate role, the Corporation recognizes a need for an expanding social delivery service and negotiations are continuing with other governmental and private service agencies.[34]

In none of the recent annual reports of other provincial corporations is the linkage between social services and housing accommodation so clearly delineated. In most provinces the housing authorities are careful to separate these two fundamental requirements.

In New Brunswick the corporation's development division described a "very active land banking program" as a major function. It emphasized that public housing units fell in the fiscal year 1974 to 176 starts compared to 387 in the fiscal year 1973 "due to tendered construction costs of public housing units extending to inaccessible levels" (*sic*)[35] On March 31, 1975, the New Brunswick Housing Corporation was administrating 2,108 completed and occupied units (1,235 for families and 873 for senior citizens), together with 127 rental supplement units (81 for families and 46 for senior citizens), plus the original federal-provincial family units in St. John and Moncton, numbering 685 – a total of 2,920. At that time, only ten additional family units were under construction, whereas 212 senior citizen units and 310 rent supplement units for senior citizens were under construction.[36] As in several other provinces, the emphasis has shifted from accommodation for families to housing for senior citizens.

The province issued a mimeographed, undated document (probably in 1975) entitled, *Housing Programs in New Brunswick*. This document was designed to distinguish newly emerging provincial programs, including assistance to individuals for home improvements and mortgage assistance for new construction, from new federal-provincial programs, including AHOP, the Rural and Native Housing Program, and the Co-operative Housing Program. In the AHOP Program New Brunswick was prepared to supplement the federal grant by $300 per annum and in certain special cases, by as much as $500. Seventy units of new construction were planned for 1975. Under the Rural and Native Housing Program the province had approved 400 grants in 1975, either for rehabilitation or for new construction. Co-operative housing activity was underway in four cities with 400 dwellings planned in 1975.

Nova Scotia

The Nova Scotia Housing Commission in the annual report for the 1973 fiscal year emphasized that it had introduced an interim form of Assisted Home Ownership under the NHA amendments of 1972 and 1973. The province was prepared to add a provincial grant to the federal assistance to reduce the required family income to as little as $5,000 per annum.[37]

Construction had been started during the period under review on an additional 533 dwellings for senior citizens in 25 communities. By contrast, a mere 158 houses for families were commenced in six communities. At the end of fiscal 1973 the local housing authorities in the province had approximately 3,800 dwelling units under management.[38] The commission revealed that it would embark upon a survey of the external conditions of all residential buildings in communities with a population of 2,000 persons or more.[39]

A year later the annual report for fiscal 1974 highlighted five major events. It reported a new enabling agreement had been reached with CMHC to enable co-operative housing companies to operate with increasing mortgage amounts and subsidies. At the same time the province signed its first agreement under the Neighbourhood Improvement Program.[40] By the end of the fiscal year the cities of Halifax, Dartmouth and Sydney had renewal programs for implementation under NIP.[41]

In the public housing field 572 starts were recorded for senior citizens' housing in 21 communities, nine of which were embarking upon their first such construction, but the Low Rental Family Housing Program was in serious difficulties.

> The government moratorium on this program continued in effect with the result that only 216 starts were made during the year on projects approved prior to the imposition of the moratorium.[42]

The government's decision to suspend the development of public rental housing for families was based upon substantial increases in the cost of construction. The provincial government felt that the subsidies consequent upon such costs over the fifty-year mortgage term would be significant. At the same time, the demand for such housing continued to increase because of rising costs in the private housing market.[43]

The commission had signed a new agreement with the federal government under the AHOP Program. At that time the federal subsidy was $300 per annum (later increased to $600 and in 1976 to $750 per annum). Thus, the provincial subsidy was then set at an additional $300 per annum. Higher maximum mortgage limits were set for co-operative builders and 795 units of co-operative housing were approved in fiscal 1974.

Nova Scotia continued to place emphasis upon its Land Development Program. In the year under review, 553 lots were released with an additional 179 anticipated later in 1975. The commission reported considerable land assembly activity.[44]

Prince Edward Island

Canada's smallest province (1976 population: 120,000) reported enthusiastically that fiscal 1973 had been a year of housing activity with starts at a record pace. The Prince Edward Island Housing

Authority emphasized substantial activity for senior citizens' housing, home improvement, social housing and home ownership – yet it cautioned that the year under review was one in which the cost of building or repairing homes increased dramatically. Moreover, it was a year in which the amount of inexpensive serviced land grew even more scarce.[45]

The province's own Home Ownership Assistance Program had a direct input into 40 per cent of the housing starts during fiscal 1973.[46] During the year the new federal AHOP Program was accepted and applicants were directed to available federal assistance wherever appropriate. The Authority reported that in fiscal 1974 it expected to sign agreements respecting NIP and RRAP.

P.E.I. maintained a Home Improvement Assistance Program which was associated closely with a social rehabilitation housing program undertaken in co-operation with the Department of Social Services of the province. This unique program made available up to $4,000 assistance per dwelling for the rehabilitation of residences belonging to welfare recipients.[47]

The annual report of the P.E.I. Authority is far more detailed than those of most other provinces and clearly reflects the pride of a small province in its extensive involvement in federal-provincial housing programs. The roster of program areas included eight distinct sections reflecting a considerable effort on the part of a small population with few resources but with significant housing problems.[48]

At the close of fiscal 1973 Prince Edward Island had completed 409 senior citizens' units in 26 locations. The annual report stated that "the 409 units gave P.E.I. 32.3 senior citizens' dwelling units per thousand persons 65 years of age or over. This figure compares favourably with the 1971 Canadian average of 13.7."[49]

In the field of public family housing the figures are not nearly so impressive. Rent-to-income housing operated by voluntary local housing authorities was originally created under the NHA, Section 40, on the basis (for both capital and subsidies) of the following distribution: federal 75 per cent, provincial 12½ per cent, and municipal 12½ per cent. For fiscal 1973 the province took over the municipal share. Nevertheless, just 16 family dwellings were completed that year and at March 31, 1974 only 90 family housing units were under administration in the entire province. In mid-1975 a mimeographed report was issued by the re-named Prince Edward Island Housing Corporation.[50] The annual report of the authority for fiscal 1974 was issued about the same time.

The new document of mid-1975 was a comprehensive review of all programs within the province under four major headings: Home Ownership and Home Construction, describing the Co-Operative

Housing Program, the Social Housing Program, and the Rural Poor and Native Housing Program.[51] The second major heading entitled, Home Rehabilitation, described the social rehabilitation program and rural home rehabilitation program. The third category was rental accommodation, including senior citizens' housing, homes for special care and family or public housing. Finally, the document contained a description of municipal and land programs, including the Neighbourhood Improvement Program and a land assembly and development program.

The difficulty with the provision of rental housing for families was further re-inforced when it became clear that no new dwellings were constructed in fiscal 1974. The report stated,

> As with all our deep subsidy programs, the Housing Authority is giving careful consideration to the financial costs of the Family Housing Program. Rapidly rising construction and maintenance costs, together with other demands being placed on provincial funds, make a re-assessment of the program a necessity. In many cases, home ownership programs such as AHOP and Co-operatives, may provide a more effective and acceptable housing alternative to low-income families.[52]

Newfoundland

The Newfoundland and Labrador Housing Corporation carries out its responsibilities for the operation and management of subsidized rental housing through the St. John's Housing Authority, Corner Brook Housing Corporation and three direct management offices. The corporation designs and builds the housing with loans through the appropriate Sections of the National Housing Act, but operating losses are shared equally with the federal government; there is no municipal contribution.

In documents issued in the early-1970s, the corporation listed nine separate programs, the first of which is the aforementioned Subsidized Rental Housing. In addition, a program, entitled, "Housing for Needy Individuals", is under direct management in cooperation with the provincial Department of Social Services. This latter program is akin to others in the Atlantic provinces but is not found in the programs operated from British Columbia to Ontario.

A program, entitled, "Rental Housing – General" is akin to the staff housing program in the province of Alberta. In Newfoundland, the corporation builds or acquires housing for rental to support industrial development and to house government employees, particularly members of essential professions such as doctors, dentists and welfare officers.[53]

Land banking and land assembly are emphasized by the corporation which, with the assistance of the relevant Sections of the NHA, will make loans to municipalities for land development, repayable over three to five years. The corporation is also involved in the development of so-called industrial parks, using both provincial funding and assistance from the federal Department of Regional Economic Expansion.

Newfoundland entered into its first agreement under the federal AHOP program for fiscal 1974 and agreed to make available a grant of $300 per annum for appropriate applicants in addition to a similar amount of federal assistance at that time. Financially, the corporation is engaged in mortgage lending in smaller communities and rural areas not well-served by conventional lenders. This latter program began in 1971 with direct provincial funding at $6 million and reached $15 million within two years. In 1974 a cost-shared program was initiated with 882 loans amounting to $13.4 million. The federal and provincial contributions were 75 per cent and 25 per cent, respectively.

In mid-1975 the government announced that Newfoundland had recorded, in 1974, its highest ever number of housing starts (4,911), "in a year when starts in Canada were substantially down."[54]

ANALYTICAL SUMMARY

This detailed review of housing policies and programs throughout the Canadian provinces (not excluding Ontario which is the subject of the following chapter) reveals a number of significant shifts in the first half of the 1970s, disclosing trends which continued into the latter half of the decade and extend into the 1980s. There can be little doubt from the multitude of new legislation enacted and amendments to previous legislation, that every province, in its own way and on the basis of its special political and social philosophy, attempted seriously to deal with the housing requirements of its people.

The legislative changes were required in large part because of amendments to the National Housing Act enacted in 1972 and 1973. Programs such as NIP, RRAP and AHOP offered much more flexibility to the provinces than in the past and much greater opportunity to demonstrate physical and statistical results in terms of projects undertaken, dwellings renovated and new and existing dwellings purchased by moderate-income families. The most important factor influencing provincial governmental housing policies in the 1970s was the essential requirement to take advantage of federal programs, even though they represented a political and social shift away from the emphases which were implicit in the legislative amendments of 1964.

It would be quite incorrect, however, to imply that federal legislation forced any provincial government to disavow its political philosophy in the interest of receiving federal financial assistance. It seems to be quite clear that the basic philosophy underlying the new federal programs instituted in the first half of the 1970s was almost entirely consistent with the principles underlying provincial approaches to the solution of housing problems.

The traditional approach to the provision of housing accommodation for low-income families, which was the basis of the 1949 NHA amendments, strengthened by the new National Housing Act 1954, and its major review in 1964, had fallen from favour by the early 1970s. In part, this was because the original federal-provincial partnership, legislated in November 1949, had failed to produce the mass of housing accommodation required to meet the needs of low-income families.

The Ontario Housing Corporation demonstrated conclusively after 1965 that the new funding arrangements in Section 43 of the NHA could produce vast quantities of rental housing, but most of the other provinces were either unsuccessful in their attempt to duplicate the response of the OHC or their housing corporations were wary of some of the social and economic pitfalls which the OHC encountered. Above all else, by the late 1960s and the early 1970s the experience in Ontario revealed extremely difficult problems of housing management when large numbers of families eligible for public rental housing were accommodated in relatively large projects. There can be little question that most provincial corporations moved slowly and deliberately in the late 1960s observing on the one hand, the enormous increase in the public housing stock in Ontario, and on the other, the need to create a substantial bureaucracy to develop, construct, operate and manage a vast stock of publicly-owned dwellings for rental.

By the mid-1970s it was evident that a very important shift had occurred involving selectivity by the provincial housing corporations, including OHC. Public housing for families was out of favour not merely because of the problems involved in its construction and administration but because two new, important groups of persons with housing needs had come to the fore: senior citizens and sole-support mothers with dependent children. The preceding review of provincial housing activity from British Columbia to Newfoundland showed clearly that recent annual reports placed emphasis upon the needs of senior citizens and the development of new programs to meet these needs. Every province stated that in one way or another it had a program entitled, "Senior Citizens Housing", although titles varied across the nation. The numerical results recorded in successive annual reports revealed that housing for the elderly was expanding both in number of dwelling units and in number of municipalities involved, but also that family housing had virtually ceased.

This phenomenon was not the apparent heartless policy shift that it seemed to be, particularly to organizations of public housing tenants. What had happened was a major socio-economic and philosophical shift, away from rental housing and in the direction of home ownership. The initiation of AHOP in 1973 proved to be far more significant than its proponents anticipated. There can be little doubt that thousands of moderate-income Canadian families were enabled by this program (based upon a federal-provincial agreement renewed from time to time by each province) to assume the responsibilities of home ownership.

The statistical results are impressive but the ultimate economic and social consequences are potentially dangerous. The emphasis placed by both the federal and provincial governments upon this program was made clear when AHOP was amended in 1975/76 as a part of a program put forward by the Government of Canada "designed to produce one million new housing units over the next four years."[55] The minister stated that AHOP would be made available to any Canadian household of two or more people wanting to buy moderately-priced housing and to keep their monthly payments equal to those of an 8 per cent mortgage. This provision removed the requirement that the purchasers be a couple with one or more children. At that time the conventional mortgage lending rate was 12 to 12½ per cent.

At the same time the special grants designed to keep monthly payments under 25 per cent of gross income were increased from $600 to $750 per annum. In addition, as before, the reduction in effective market interest rate took the form of a loan which was interest-free for the first five years and repayable with interest after a year of grace, that is, commencing with the seventh year. In the view of many observers, this program is a time bomb because it depends, for its fulfillment, upon the continuance of rising incomes and thus assurance that purchasers will be able to repay in due course. No one had yet suggested what might happen if they could not pay.[56]

The provincial housing corporations in the 1970s were particularly interested in land banking and land assembly for a variety of purposes within their jurisdictions. It is particularly interesting to note that almost every province quoted its acquisitions of land in its publications of the mid-1970s at the very time when Ontario, with very substantial land acquisitions, was determined to carefully and deliberately get out of the land banking business in favour of its municipalities.

Finally, it became a fact in the decade 1965-1974 that every province made a real effort to accept responsibility and to undertake programs to meet some of the housing requirements of its citizens. This was quite untrue prior to 1964. In the ensuing decade a great deal was attempted, sometimes with success and sometimes with little results. Both the electors and their elected representatives seemed dedicated to do something about this most complex of all Canadian socio-economic problems. Nevertheless, with the onset of the 1980s, they still appear to be seeking the least painful solutions when there are really none without significant expenditure of time, effort and money.

NOTES

[1]cf. *supra.*, chapter IV., p. 64.

[2]Statistics Canada, *Income Distributions by Size in Canada 1977* (Ottawa: August 1979) Table 2, pp. 40-41. Preliminary data for 1978 continue to reveal a slight lead over Alberta in average but not median incomes.

[3]Grants are available from the Ministry of Housing to assist in the development of a municipal housing policy statement. The ministry will also provide assistance in obtaining housing data and has established study guidelines. Only upon approval of a housing policy statement may a municipality proceed with municipal land development under the Housing Development Act. Cf. "Housing Programs in Ontario", *Housing Ontario*, Vol. 20, No. 1, January/February 1976, p. 6.

[4]*Living Room: The City of Toronto's Housing Policy* (Toronto: Housing Work Group) December 1973.

[5]Vid. *infra*, chapter VI.

[6]Central Mortgage and Housing Corporation, *Canadian Housing Statistics 1978* (Ottawa, March 1979) Table 55, p. 49. Includes activities under the following Sections of the National Housing Act: Loans to Entrepreneurs and Non-Profit Corporations (Section 15 and 15.1), Public Housing (Section 43), Student Housing (Section 47), Assisted Home Ownership Programmes (Sections 34.15, 58 and 59), Co-operative Housing (Section 34.18), Federal-Provincial Rental and Sales Housing Projects (Section 40), Assisted Rental Programme and Graduated Payment Mortgage (Section 58), and Loans by Approved Lenders (Section 6).

[7]Includes activities under the following Sections of the National Housing Act: Loans to Entrepreneurs and Non-Profit Corporations (Section 15 and 15.1), Public Housing (Section 43), Student Housing (Section 47), Assisted Home-Ownership Programmes (Sections 34.15, 58 and 59), Co-operative Housing (Section 34.18), and Federal Provincial Rental and Sales Housing Projects (Section 40). CMHC, *Canadian Housing Statistics, 1973*, (Ottawa: March 1974), Table 51, p. 44.

[8]British Columbia, Department of Housing, *First Annual Report* (Victoria, January 1, 1975) p. 9.

[9]*Ibid.*, p. 9.

[10]*Idem.*

[11]Letter from Lorne Nicolson, Minister of Housing to Barnett Danson, Minister of State for Urban Affairs, August 9th, 1974.

[12]Letters from Barnett Danson, Minister of State for Urban Affairs to Lorne Nicolson, Minister of Housing in British Columbia, October 1, and October 3, 1974.

[13]Letter from Barnett Danson to Lorne Nicolson, June 30th, 1975.

[14]British Columbia, Department of Housing, *op. cit.*, p. 6.

[15]*Ibid.*, p. 12.

[16]*Ibid.*, p. 15.

[17]British Columbia, *Housing and Rent Control in British Columbia*. A report prepared by the Interdepartmental Study Team on Housing and Rents. (Vancouver: October 1975) pp. 450.

[18]Alberta Housing Corporation, *Annual Report 1973* (Edmonton: 1974) pp. 3-4.

[19]Alberta Housing Corporation, *15-Month Review and Financial Statement,* January 1, 1974 – March 31, 1975 (Edmonton: 1976) p. 5.

[20]Saskatchewan Housing Corporation, *Annual Report 1973* (Regina: 1974) p. 3. Cf. Saskatchewan Housing Corporation Act 1973, S. 13(i), (iv).

[21]*Ibid.*, p. 5.

[22]Saskatchewan Housing Corporation, *Annual Report 1974* (Regina: 1975) p. 6.

[23]*Ibid.*, p. 9. The figures for total inventory do not accurately reflect the change since the end of 1973.

[24]Manitoba Housing and Renewal Corporation, *Annual Report 1974/75* (Winnipeg: 1976).

[25]*Ibid.*, p. 4.

[26]*Ibid.*, pp. 5-6.

[27]*Ibid.*, pp. 8-9.

[28]CMHC, *Canadian Housing Statistics, 1976* (Ottawa: March 1977) Table 119, p. 94. The estimated population for 1976 was 1,028,000.

[29]Tables II and III.

[30]*Habiter au Québec*, January 1976, (mimeographed, auspices and publisher not given, January 1976) p. 15.

[31]*Ibid.*, p. 3-6.

[32]*Ibid.*, p. 9.

[33]New Brunswick Housing Corporation, *Annual Report 1974/75* (Fredericton: 1975) p. 4.

[34]*Ibid.*, p. 2-4.

[35]*Ibid.*, p. 6.

³⁶*Ibid.*, p. 9.

³⁷Nova Scotia Housing Commission, *Annual Report* (for the fiscal year ending March 31, 1974) (Halifax: 1974) p. 5.

³⁸*Ibid.*, p. 11.

³⁹*Ibid.*, p. 15.

⁴⁰Nova Scotia Housing Commission, *Annual Report* (for the fiscal year ending March 31, 1975) (Halifax: 1975) p. 5.

⁴¹*Ibid.*, p. 13.

⁴²*Ibid.*, p. 9.

⁴³The Nova Scotia Housing Commission, *Annual Report* (for the fiscal year ending March 31, 1974) p. 9.

⁴⁴The Nova Scotia Housing Commission, *Annual Report* (for the fiscal year ending March 31, 1975) p. 11.

⁴⁵Prince Edward Island Housing Authority, *Annual Report* (for the fiscal year ending March 31, 1974) p. 13. Housing starts for the province were 1,240.

⁴⁶*Idem.*

⁴⁷*Ibid.*, p. 14.

⁴⁸*Ibid.*, pp. 17-30.

⁴⁹*Ibid.*, p. 19.

⁵⁰Prince Edward Island Housing Corporation, *Program Summaries* (Charlottetown: mimeographed, June 1975) p. 15.

⁵¹*Ibid.*, p. 5. The word "poor" does not appear in such program titles in any other province.

⁵²Prince Edward Island Housing Authority, *Annual Report* (for the fiscal year ending March 31, 1975) p. 9.

⁵³Newfoundland and Labrador Housing Corporation, *Statement of Programs* (mimeographed, not dated) not paged.

⁵⁴Government of Newfoundland, Statement by the Minister Responsible for Housing Policy in Newfoundland (mimeo., July 4, 1975).

⁵⁵Canada, Ministry of State for Urban Affairs, Statement by Barnett Danson to the House of Commons, November 3, 1975, pp. 1-2.

⁵⁶By the late 1970s, several thousand owners had given up their homes either by mailing in their keys to CMHC, or by filing a formal "quit claim"; apparently they moved to apartments at a lower shelter cost.

CHAPTER 6

Housing Policies in Ontario: A Case Study

In April 1964 the Government of Ontario passed "An Act to incorporate the Ontario Housing Corporation":[1] a short law (15 sections) covering in its first version not more than five mimeographed pages. This act did not effectively outline the nature of the new roles that a provincial housing corporation might play in the housing market and gave little hint of the furious activity in public housing that was to develop in Ontario within a space of three to four years.

Nevertheless, the Government of Ontario did in fact establish a corporation without share capital, under the name of the "Ontario Housing Corporation", to consist of not fewer than seven and not more than eleven members appointed by the Lieutenant Governor-in-Council. The most significant sections of the act were Sections 6-8 whereby the new corporation assumed, in the first instance, most of the responsibilities laid down for the Government of Ontario under the Housing Development Act of 1948[2] to make agreements with the Government of Canada under Sections 23 and 35 of the National Housing Act of 1954.

In Section 6 there was little mention of new activities in the field of housing, except in sub-section (4) which stated that "the corporation may acquire and hold real property and dispose of such property from time to time." In Section 7 the new corporation was deemed to be a management corporation under the terms of the Housing Development

Act. In Section 8 the Ontario Housing Corporation was given extensive power to raise its own funds by way of loans or the issue and sale of debentures, bills or notes, to be guaranteed by the Ontario government. Although these latter powers have yet to be exercised, they constitute what might have been considered an ace in the hole should the requirements within Ontario exceed the resources available from the federal corporation.[3]

With this very simple piece of legislation as background, the OHC began to communicate its intentions and its potential program throughout the more than 900 organized municipalities within the province late in 1964 and throughout the first half of 1965. It dissolved the Metropolitan Toronto Housing Authority towards the end of November 1964 and took over the administration of some 2,500 dwelling units within the metropolitan area. In fact, the new provincial corporation became a housing authority for the second largest municipality in Canada, while permitting the continuing existence of some 38 other federal-provincial housing authorities within the province. All federal-provincial public housing operations, however, were placed within the jurisdiction of the Ontario Housing Corporation, which permitted the remaining local authorities to administer and manage the existing accommodation. In municipalities where a housing authority had not previously existed the new corporation has, since 1965, assumed responsibility for the administration of newly constructed public housing and created regional offices throughout the province for this purpose.[4]

It was understood from the beginning that in an attempt to solve the critical needs of low or moderate income families for housing accommodation the OHC would have very broad powers. None of these powers were spelled out specifically in the legislation. The staff and board of directors of the OHC thus employed the most liberal interpretation of the 1964 amendments to the National Housing Act in an effort to create a much greater stock of public housing in Ontario than existed during the previous fifteen years.

During the years 1965-1968 the program of the OHC may be said to have passed through three distinct phases. In the first period, from the early months of 1965 and for about twelve to fifteen months thereafter, the corporation made every effort under Section 35D of the National Housing Act to acquire existing housing accommodation (in the form of row houses, maisonettes, garden-court apartments, and multiple dwellings, as well as a program to acquire some 200 or more individual houses scattered throughout the City of Toronto and the metropolitan area). The program of purchasing existing housing (whether partially or entirely vacant, or even fully occupied) soon built the stock in the metropolitan area to some 6,000 units. In large measure this new and radical attack upon the housing problem was made necessary by a formal request in the spring of 1965 to the OHC, from the Municipality of Metropolitan Toronto, for 4,500 additional public housing units to be provided within a year or two. There is little question that Metropolitan Toronto officials were dubious about the ability of the new corporation to fulfil such a large quota, and it is obvious that they had not envisaged the possibility that the response of the corporation would be to purchase existing housing.

There is much to be recommended in the purchase of existing housing during the early or formative stage of any new provincial housing corporation. This statement is based, of course, upon the assumption that there is a quantity of existing housing to be purchased and that the prices of such accommodation conform to federal and provincial regulations. In the spring of 1965 and for some months thereafter, all these conditions were met and the apparent success of the corporation was a major factor in influencing the passage of new housing legislation in several other Canadian provinces.

It soon became clear to the officials of the OHC that a full program could not depend for very long upon the purchase of existing housing which is relatively easy and quick to accomplish, provided the financial resources are available. These purchases simply transfer housing accommodation as quickly as possible from one sector of the population (say the lower middle-income group) to families in the lowest third of the income distribution. It does not add sorely needed housing to the total stock. The fact that such purchased housing could not easily be replaced and was not likely to be replaced by developers was not foreseen in the first instance. Moreover, the three largest municipalities within Metropolitan Toronto soon instigated a new form of resistance to the location of public housing within their boundaries, either by outright refusal to approve subdivision plans incorporating housing accommodation which might be suitable for purchase by the OHC, or by slowing down the process whereby approval would be granted.

A second phase of the operations of the OHC can be distinguished commencing about the autumn of 1965 and continuing throughout the ensuing two-and-a-half years; it may be described as "the encouragement of new construction through builders' proposals." This was not a new device prompted by the attrition of the purchase of existing housing, but had always been foreseen from the initiation of the corporation. By the beginning of 1966 it was apparent that entirely new construction was the only way in which public housing could be provided in most of the small and medium-sized municipalities within the province. Furthermore, the hope of greatly expanding the public housing stock over the ensuing five to ten years, particularly in the five largest urban centres (Windsor, London, Hamilton, Toronto and Ottawa), clearly lay in the development of large plans encompassing hundreds if not thousands of dwelling units. The corporation soon began to advertise for builders' proposals for specific amounts of housing for senior citizens and large families, and for traditional mixtures of bedroom counts within multiple dwellings, to be built usually on land owned or optioned by the developers themselves. Sometimes the site of the land was specifically mentioned, since the municipality was ready to sell such land to the corporation and sometimes the developers were asked to suggest appropriate locations.

These new techniques proved to be quantitatively as successful as the purchase of existing housing but of much more permanent value. Rarely did the corporation receive just one or two proposals in response to its proposal calls; customarily it received from six to fifteen and sometimes more – even in cases where the number of dwellings to be constructed in municipalities with populations of 10,000 to 25,000 was no more than twenty or twenty-five units. There clearly developed a substantial housing industry in Ontario which depended to a great extent upon the activities of the OHC and which was prepared to offer well located, sound and adequate housing at prices that appeared to be reasonable in the light of the rapid inflation which beset almost every phase of our economic activity since 1966.

It must be emphasized that the OHC acted only at the request of a local or municipal government within the province. At the time of its creation in 1964, some elected local officials were fearful that the new corporation would enter the field of housing within municipalities which had not previously shown any interest or initiative in this field and, perhaps, had shown outright prejudice against the location of public housing in their midst. If such were the fears of local governments, they had since evaporated. The minister and the chairman of the Ontario Housing Corporation made it clear in a series of symposia held in late 1964 and early 1965 that the corporation would take action only after the passage of a specific resolution by a municipal council asking the OHC to take action. This action usually consisted, in the first instance, of a brief survey to make some judgment of the need and demand for public housing in a given locality. A report was presented to the local council, which was required to request the OHC to construct a specified number of dwellings for families and/or senior citizens, often specifying the size of the accommodation and sometimes the location desired.[5]

A good deal of negotiation on the part of the officials of the municipality and the officials of the corporation then ensued; a proposal call would be issued and widely advertised; proposals would be received and examined; a specific recommendation would be made to the board of directors of the OHC; and then, and only then, would a contract be awarded to the successful proponent. Even at that stage the recommendation of the staff and board of directors was cleared with the mayor and local council so that the charge could not be made that public housing had been shoved down the throats of any municipality against its will.

A third phase in the operations of the OHC commenced towards the end of 1966 with the creation of a subsidiary corporation known as the Ontario Student Housing Corporation. In December 1966 the Lieutenant Governor-in-Council appointed this corporation, which included all of the members of the Ontario Housing Corporation together with the following members from appropriate departments of the Ontario government: the Deputy Minister of University Affairs, the Deputy Minister of Education, and the Deputy Managing Director (Development) of the OHC.

This new group began in 1967 to develop and construct residential accommodation for students at any university within Ontario which requested the services of the new corporation. In fact, the staff of the two corporations were one and the same, although some members were hired with particular responsibilities in the field of student housing. The important thing to observe is that the universities within Ontario were treated by the Ontario Student Housing Corporation in exactly the same manner as local governments were treated by the OHC. The universities were required to request the services of the OSHC, and this corporation acted only in response to a clear and definite request for its services by a fully recognized university or other institution of higher learning within the province.[6]

At the end of 1971 the Ontario Housing Corporation was responsible for the administration and social management of 42,630 dwelling units: 33,977 for families and 8,653 for senior citizens. The distribution of public housing between Metro Toronto and the balance of Ontario was almost exactly in the ratio of 45:55. An additional 7,339 housing units were constructed or acquired in 1972, bringing the provincial total to just under 50,000 and dropping the Metro proportion to 43.4 per cent.

Despite these evident physical and arithmetic achievements there was growing criticism of the OHC, the housing program, and the government. The housebuilding industry displayed increasing alarm at the significance of public housing in the province and the rising proportions of annual completions which were in the public sector. The municipalities were more critical than in the past of the growing public housing presence in their midst. Moreover, local governments were receiving demands from tenant groups for increases in local services: recreation, public health, day care and other social services. Elected and appointed officials tended to blame the activity in public housing for concentrating the needy and the demanding in large projects and for encouraging citizen involvement in public affairs. For their part, however, tenant and citizen groups under the guidance of the recently created Federation of Ontario Tenant Associations (FOTA) were critical of the social management in public housing programs, critical of admission procedures, critical of the rent scales and all manner of rules and regulations governing social behaviour. In addition, FOTA blamed the OHC for specific gaps in local, social, health and recreational services which were well beyond the corporation's mandate.

In response to these and various other criticisms of Ontario Housing Corporation and his government, Premier William Davis appointed, in November 1972, an Advisory Task Force on Housing Policy. He named Professor Eli Comay of York University, former Commissioner of Planning for Metropolitan Toronto, as chairman of the inquiry.

THE ONTARIO ADVISORY TASK FORCE ON HOUSING POLICY

The report of the task force describes its review as "the first major public examination of Ontario's housing". Its terms of reference were the following.

1. Examine the current housing situation in Ontario.
2. Make recommendations on "the appropriate role of the Ontario government in helping to meet the housing needs of the residents of Ontario."[7]
3. Make recommendations on the organizational requirements for developing and implementing suitable housing policies.[8]

The significance of this report for all provincial governments may first be exemplified in its statement of housing objectives. For the government to pursue its housing responsibilities properly, provincial housing activities should relate to the following housing objectives:

(a) to ensure the provision of housing for all households in adequate numbers, and at suitable locations to support community development in accordance with local and provincial development policies;

(b) to demonstrate government priority for housing by instituting suitable administrative procedures and providing required financial assistance;

(c) to assist in the provision of buildable urban land to implement development policies and to achieve stable land prices;

(d) to maximize the impact of available housing funds on housing production;

(e) to establish adequate programs and suitable administrative machinery at the provincial and municipal levels which clearly relate housing to social and welfare objectives;

(f) to maintain the quality of the existing housing stock;

(g) to provide equal and adequate help for persons with equal needs;

(h) to enable low- and moderate-income families and persons, and groups with special needs such as the elderly, native people, handicapped persons, students, and single persons to live in adequate housing conditions, at a price they can afford;

(i) to provide adequate choice in housing type and location and between owning and renting homes;

(j) to achieve the dispersion and integration of low- and moderate-income housing throughout communities generally;

(k) to secure the protection of the rights of home purchasers and tenants; and,

(l) to encourage improvement and innovation in housing construction, design and marketing, and land planning.[9]

The report of the task force indicated that a critical situation existed in the early 1970s. The following will illustrate the reasoning upon which the recommendations were based.

Several constraining circumstances have distorted the supply of housing and affected its cost. Among these are the continually rising standards which have led to production geared primarily to middle- and upper-income occupancy. Older houses are no longer available for the poor. With the shortage and rising cost of new housing, the price of old housing has risen sharply as well. The supply of serviced buildable land has not kept up with the urban growth in many areas. Environmental concerns, leading to stricter controls, have limited the supply of housing land. Planning procedures and regulations have seriously slowed down the development of housing land. Greater community participation has frequently slowed down or stopped housing production. The shortage of housing land and of housing had led to an accelerating price spiral, exacerbated by speculation and by panic buying in many areas. These circumstances prevail in varying degrees in most parts of the province, and apply to rental as well as ownership housing. As well, in the rural and northern communities, there are additional problems. peculiar to them.

These are not the only factors affecting the current housing situation. Certainly the rise in the cost of labour and materials, and the cost of financing, have played a very important role. These are outside the scope of the task force's review, but must command serious attention from the provincial and federal governments.

The constraints on production and the rising expectations of housing consumers have led to a widening gap between the kind and cost of housing which is provided and people's ability and willingness to pay for such housing. If the constraints are not overcome, housing Ontario's citizens will be increasingly difficult and will become increasingly a matter of subsidization.[10]

The major recommendations were an attempt to relieve these difficult situations, and they ranged from the basic question of governmental organization to protection for home owners and tenants within the law. Every facet of the problem within these two limits was covered in one way or another, however adequate or inadequate the recommendation and without regard to the position of the Ontario government on certain issues raised in this Report. The five major recommendations were as follows.

(1) *A Ministry of Housing, Planning and Local Government should be established within the governmental system in the province of Ontario.*

The task force saw the creation of a new ministry as a first step in the development of a new policy field towards governmental intervention to combine all the physical aspects of urban and regional development within which housing policy and housing programs would fit.[11] In the view of the task force the fields of housing and urban development must necessarily be combined. To effect this kind of governmental organization meant in 1973-74 the transfer of the physical aspects of urban and regional development from the existing Ministry of Treasury, Economics and Intergovernmental Affairs (TEIGA). This was a very significant and challenging recommendation and in substantial measure was soon implemented by Premier William Davis who announced, soon after receipt of the report, that a Ministry of Housing would be created within the province.[12]

(2) *Within the new ministry two Crown corporations should exist to deal with the problems of housing and community development in the province: These corporations would be:*

   (a) *The Ontario Housing Corporation (in existence since September 1964 and to be continued); and,*

   (b) *The Ontario Housing Finance Corporation*

The latter, which was a new organizational recommendation, would be responsible for all the financial aspects of housing assistance and residential land acquisition. Within a year following the tabling of the report in late summer of 1973 these recommendations were fully accepted. The OHC was continued and is described in its own publications as "an agency of the Ministry of Housing." In late August 1974, the Ontario Mortgage Corporation (the government's choice of title) was created and its membership announced by the Premier. It is interesting to note that the Chairman of OMC is W. H. Hignett who had completed his term of office and retired from the position of president of the Central Mortgage and Housing Corporation.

The task force saw the core function of the new ministry as establishing policy and planning and carrying out the province's housing development program. Three additional broad types of functions were visualized: development of assisted housing, land acquisition and new community development; urban and regional planning and local governmental services; and, the management of assisted housing.[13] The only major functional responsibility that was not fully assigned to the Ministry of Housing was urban and regional planning and local government services. Some important functions in the field of physical planning were transferred from TEIGA to the new ministry but the overall responsibility for urban and regional planning and local governmental services remained with TEIGA (in recent years TEIGA has absorbed two former ministries: the Ministry of Municipal Affairs and the Ministry of Economics and Development).

(3) *Municipalities in Ontario should have their responsibilities in the field of housing expanded.* (This is closely related to a further recommendation for the establishment of a Provincial Housing Development Program, within which the role of the municipalities would be defined.)

This recommendation constituted a significant reversal of governmental organization for the implementation of housing policies in Ontario. The establishment of the Ontario Housing Corporation, with its headquarters in Toronto, meant a significant centralization of responsibilities. The previous understanding that local governments and local housing authorities would have substantial responsibilities in the fields of initiation and management was changed dramatically. The Metropolitan Toronto Housing Authority was incorporated within the OHC. Moreover, local housing authorities continued with managerial roles but with firmer specifications and stronger controls from the corporation's head office.

As the program began to spread out into municipalities without any previous component of publicly-provided housing, a form of direct management was instituted from Toronto instead of establishing local housing authorities. It was not until 1973 that the OHC began to establish branch offices in Ottawa, London, Sudbury, and Thunder Bay. This development was the first indication that some decentralization was essential. Those employed in direct management could not be in constant touch with headquarters while commuting from Toronto to carry out their day-to-day managerial duties.

The most significant aspect of the task force's recommendation concerning delegated responsibility was the strong intimation contained in the final sentence of its discussion of this subject:

> . . . in the case of housing, municipal commitments and housing plans designed to achieve provincial as well as local housing objectives should lead to the delegation of responsibilities to the regional and local municipalities.[14]

This recommendation has since been implemented by virtue of the
Ministry of Housing's clear understanding that the application of its
programs within local or regional governmental areas would depend
on the formulation of a housing policy and a statement of plans and
programs by the local government concerned.[15]

(4) *The housing responsibilities of the Government of Ontario should
be met by a variety of actions, "all of which should be organized
and administered under a Provincial housing development program."*

Provincial involvement in housing should be directed to:

(a) restoring the effectiveness of the private market to the extent
most practical in the provision of housing;

(b) supplementing the private sector at those levels where it cannot
provide an adequate supply of housing;

(c) providing assistance to persons whose incomes are inadequate
to obtain suitable housing;

(d) taking primary responsibility for initiating a broad-based housing
program in all urban areas of Ontario. (This implies, where
necessary, assumption of total financial responsibility by the
senior governments);

(e) providing both short-term and long-term programs for assisted
housing at different levels (subsidized for low-income and
unsubsidized for moderate- and middle-income) so as to pre-
vent a serious imbalance at various levels of housing need.[16]

The report continued with a series of guidelines governing the
selection of different housing actions.

(a) Land supply should be given major emphasis, in both of its
public elements – land servicing and public land acquisition.

(b) The programs should lead to a housing supply which, in general,
more closely matches the distribution of incomes, thus reducing
the need for subsidized assisted housing. This implies a dual
approach to the future housing supply – to reduce housing
costs, and to adjust housing standards.

(c) Land servicing should receive primary emphasis in the joint
program of land servicing and land acquisition provided that
owners of developable land will meet an agreed commitment
to bring such lands into housing production at reasonable
prices which restore stability to the land market.

(d) Public land acquisition for strategic intervention in the market
should be subsidiary and should be used when the private
market is unable or fails to meet established provincial housing
goals.[17]

The most significant guidelines were those which placed emphasis on
increasing the supply of serviced land and the acquisition of land by

the public authority, in this case primarily the provincial government through the two proposed Crown corporations proposed; but this did not exclude municipal land banking.

It is noteworthy that on the day on which the task force report was published (September 13, 1979) Premier Davis announced that the chairman of the task force, Eli Comay, would be engaged at once to implement a "Housing Action Program" which conceived the development of 100,000 serviced building lots within a period of several months.[18] It is now well understood that the OHC embarked on a substantial program of public land acquisition in areas recommended by Comay, and that certain municipalities such as the City of Toronto also received funds for such purposes.

The overall recommendation – the establishment of a provincial housing development program – encompassed a series of important secondary recommendations which constitute the essence of the program. The report not only laid down directions and guidelines but a series of "main program elements", which included the following: land supply;[19] land servicing;[20] land acquisition;[21] assisted housing;[22] a short-term program designed to speed up the supply of single-family and multiple housing in the major urban areas of Metropolitan Toronto, Hamilton, and Ottawa, with some attention "possibly in some northern communities;"[23] and, other assistance to municipalities in the form of school building programs and other community services.[24]

The land acquisition program was specifically designated for the following purposes, presumably in order of priority:
- land for public housing;
- land for non-profit and co-operative developers;
- land for leased lots;
- land for new community development, and to implement regional planning policies;
- land for strategic intervention in the land market; and,
- land for municipal land banking.[25]

(5) *A comprehensive program of "housing assistance" whereby different sections of the community would get various kinds of assistance, both subsidized and unsubsidized, with particular reference to their requirements.*

"Housing assistance" is covered in depth in the report.[26] The recommendation begins with the specifics of "residential mortgage assistance" and delineates a provincial role in this field through the proposed Ontario Housing Finance Corporation. A strong provincial role in this area was not entirely an innovation, since the OHC was already involved in a series of programs in which mortgage assistance was available to builders: first, in terms of the provisions of the *Condominium Act 1968* (guaranteed provincial second mortgages); and second, when private developers were willing to make 25 per cent of their dwelling units available to low-income families under the provisions of the Integrated Community Housing Program (first mortgage assistance).

The major recommendation, however, was directed more towards grants and interest subsidies for low-income families, second mortgages for moderate-income families, and assistance to enable purchasers of older homes to undertake needed renovations. The recommendation included direct lending to individuals who were not served by the private market and subsidized interest rates to non-profit organizations and co-operatives for the construction and rehabilitation of housing for low-income families.[27]

The detail within the overall sphere of housing assistance is extraordinary. The recommendation included home-ownership assistance, assisted housing for low-income families and the elderly, public housing, community and social facilities, direct public housing for the elderly, and housing for other groups with special needs – native people, handicapped persons, the mentally retarded, roomers, students.

It is obvious that the task force attempted to cover every conceivable aspect of governmental intervention in the form of assistance, whether through adjustments in the mortgage field and in rentals; special provisions for groups disadvantaged by age, ethnic, physical or emotional disabilities; and students temporarily with little or no income.

A MINISTRY OF HOUSING WITHIN THE GOVERNMENT OF ONTARIO

In mid-1973 the task force's report emphasized that Ontario's current housing situation was substantially derived from two great strategic weaknesses:

1. "the absence of any guiding housing principles" at both the provincial and municipal levels of government; and,
2. the "protective and negative" character of the regulations and procedures which influence housing production where a "positive and productive" approach is required.[28]

The task force had been appointed on October 6, 1972. One year later (October 2, 1973) Premier Davis presented a statement "On Housing" in the legislature, in which he initiated a Ministry of Housing and tabled the *Ministry of Housing Act 1973*. The premier placed particular emphasis on programs that had already been initiated since the formal publication of the task force report three weeks earlier (September 13).

Mr. Davis announced that a new cabinet committee, under the chairmanship of the Treasurer and Minister of Intergovernmental

Affairs, would be set up; this committee would include the new Minister of Housing, the Ministers of Revenue and Government Services, and the chairman of the Management Board (formerly the Treasury Board). A further recommendation of the task force was also accepted, in principle, in the premier's statement that certain functions then in TEIGA[29] would be brought within the purview of the new Ministry of Housing. Moreover, more authority would be delegated to regional governments and certain municipalities. The premier reiterated that the government supported in principle the guidelines "set out by the Comay Task Force for the future development of the government role in the provision of housing for the people of Ontario."[30]

The *Ministry of Housing Act 1973* is a typical piece of Ontario Government legislation in the sense that it is relatively short, simple and direct, without in any way indicating the particular programs which might be created or the terms under which such programs would be offered within the province and within the realm of intergovernmental relations. In total, the act consisted of twelve sections and not more than 100 lines of text. The most important part of the legislation is Section 7, "Objectives of Minister", which reads as follows:

> The minister or the deputy minister, subject to the direction and control of the minister, shall,
> (a) make appropriate recommendations to the Government of Ontario on policies and objectives on housing and related matters with regard to the short-term and long-term housing needs of the people of Ontario;
> (b) make recommendations for the effective co-ordination of all housing and related matters within the Government of Ontario, with a view to ensuring the consistent application of policy;
> (c) advise and otherwise assist the Government of Ontario in its dealings with other governments regarding housing and related matters; and
> (d) advise and otherwise assist local authorities and other persons involved in local planning and development of housing with regard to realizing the objectives of the Government of Ontario for housing and related matters.[31]

The organization of the new ministry was quite rapid. The first minister was Robert Welch, formerly the Policy Minister for Social Development. By January 1st, 1974, the minister had appointed a deputy minister and had issued a brochure indicating in general terms the challenge which the ministry faced. Approximately 40 per cent of the total text was devoted to the "housing action program" which followed immediately upon the tabling of the Ontario Advisory Task Force Report. There was also a general description of the program of the OHC.

The brochure included a directory of services, which was an impressive roster of potential responsibilities and functions that had formerly been under the direction of TEIGA (such as committees of adjustment, the Niagara Escarpment Planning Regulations, the North Pickering Development Team, and sub-division approvals). The list of services also dealt with grants, subsidies, loans, urban renewal, and the Neighbourhood Improvement Program, introduced by the federal minister during the previous year.

AN INITIAL POLICY STATEMENT

In May 1974 the ministry issued its "Initial Statement of Policies, Programs and Partnerships", entitled *Housing Ontario '74.*[32] This first major policy statement was ushered in with considerable fanfare, including a press seminar to which the minister, the deputy minister, and both assistant deputy ministers spoke on May 28, some seven months following the formation of the ministry. This document and attendant remarks are worth examining in some detail to indicate the way in which a major province (which includes about 40 per cent of the Canadian population) regards its responsibilities in the fields of housing and urban development.

The statement begins with a ringing declaration that "adequate housing at affordable prices is a basic right of all residents in Ontario."[33] This is significant among the overall objectives, clearly committing the Government of Ontario to a series of housing policies and programs which it could no longer neglect or avoid. Nevertheless, it enunciates that "the people of Ontario, are by almost any standard of measurement, among the best-housed people in the world",[34] and the statistics supporting this statement are impressive.

In 1972 the 7.8 million resident of Ontario had available 2.3 million dwellings – an average of 3.4 persons per dwelling. Ontario was still substantially a province of homeowners with 65 per cent of the total available dwellings owner-occupied; 88 per cent of these were in the form of single-family detached houses. In the years that have elapsed since these figures were made available the ratio of people to dwellings has declined further, since the amount of new housing available continued to grow at a faster rate than household formations. In fact, throughout the 1960s the statistics for new persons per new dwelling averaged 2.5 and in the first three years of the 1970s this figure dropped to an average of 1.3.[35]

These statistical data should not necessarily be considered cause for rejoicing. The situation may very well have been brought about by the production of vast numbers of small dwelling units in high-rise multiple buildings; in 1973 a little more than one-fifth of all dwellings in Ontario had, on the average, fewer than one person per bedroom.[36] It would appear from these broad statistics that Ontario's housing accommodation is in reality under-utilized. On the other hand, a further decline in the ratio of new persons per new dwelling could be an additional factor in accentuating the very real housing crisis which exists, despite the apparently favourable statistical indicators.

The Ministry of Housing emphasized that the essence of the serious difficulties facing Ontario's housing market rests in the cost of housing. The cost of land and of building has risen so rapidly that many thousands of prospective homeowners and tenants can no longer afford home-ownership, at least for the time being. As tenants they continue to pay 25 to 50 per cent of their income for shelter which has the two-fold effect of restricting the breadth of an adequate standard of living and making it impossible for many families to save sufficient money to meet the downpayment requirements of home-ownership. The Ministry emphasized that

> it is not a simple matter of too little supply and too much demand. The home-building industries are producing, in total terms, more than enough new dwelling units to keep pace with growth in population and household formations.[37]

Nevertheless, the essential features of Ontario's housing policies must be focused upon supply and demand: on the one hand, ensuring the supply of adequate housing at reasonable cost; and on the other hand, introducing programs whereby demand can be supported to enable families, couples, and individuals to enter the housing market. On this basis the ministry stated a long series of commitments covering the entire gamut of housing production and distribution – from encouraging the rehabilitation of existing housing stock, through intervention in land and money markets, to the stimulation of new designs and building techniques to increase the supply of housing at relatively stable cost. The basic policy statement went on to indicate that translation of these commitments into action would necessitate that the ministry move simultaneously on five major fronts.

1. To increase the supply of new housing by bringing quickly into production serviced land that might otherwise be left undeveloped for two or three more years.
2. To improve existing housing stock by directly encouraging the rehabilitation of older housing and deteriorating neighbourhoods.
3. To discourage unproductive, pure speculation in land and in housing by engaging directly in extensive public land assembly and by empowering regional and municipal governments to do

the same, and through the application of the provincial government's new land speculation tax.

4. To broaden the mix of new housing by encouraging developers, and municipal or community non-profit housing groups, to provide more well-designed, lower-cost accommodation.

5. To reduce financial and regulatory obstacles to housing by providing substantial sums of money – through grants, loans, and mortgages – and by simplifying and streamlining government regulations and procedures at all levels that bear directly or indirectly on the cost of housing.[38]

The major programs introduced in *Housing Ontario '74* were for the most part familiar by virtue of both the Report of the Advisory Task Force on Housing Policy and the *Amendments to the National Housing Act* put forward by the federal Minister of State for Urban Affairs in mid-1973. The Ontario Ministry of Housing designated four main programs as follows:

(a) Ontario Housing Action Program (OHAP)
(b) Ontario Mortgage Corporation
(c) Assisted Rental Housing for Families and Senior Citizens
(d) Community-Sponsored Housing

The Ontario Housing Action Program was allocated $20 million for the fiscal year 1974-75 to achieve three main objectives:

1. to bring into housing production as quickly as possible significant amounts of serviced land that would not normally be developed until the late 1970s;

2. to increase rapidly, as a result of (1), the total supply of new housing;

3. to increase significantly the production of new housing available to families of low and moderate income.[39]

The efforts of the ministry would be devoted initially to Housing Action Areas located in major urban centres where cost and supply pressures were considered to be greatest. The ministry estimated that this program would directly influence the production in 1974 of 12,000 dwelling units which might otherwise have been built a year or two later, and as many as 28,000 such units in 1975.

OHAP was originally scheduled to end March 31, 1976 but the program was modified and extended to March 31, 1977.[40] In the first fiscal year of the ministry, ending March 31, 1975, the target of 12,000 units was exceeded, including "finally approved lots and blocks". Total production was reported as 12,877 units.[41]

In addition, two forms of mortgage assistance were made available through the Ontario Mortgage Corporation. Under the Direct Lending Program, OMC provided mortgage financing for home purchasers (with incomes up to $20,000) on the basis of OHAP agreements with developers. In fiscal 1974 seventeen developers and builders were assisted for twenty-one separate housing projects covering 3,999 housing units;[42] in fiscal 1975, 4,387 dwellings were started.[43]

In the following year mortgage financing under the Direct Lending Program reached $42.6 million and a second program, the Interest-Subsidy Program, announced July 7, 1975, made $26 million available for mortgage interest subsidies on homes started by March 31, 1976 for moderate-income purchasers.

Municipalities were assisted in a number of ways through grants under OHAP. The first annual report of the ministry listed development processing studies (nine grants to seven municipalities) and policy determination studies (eleven grants to ten municipalities).[44] A year later the annual report listed Capital Housing Incentive Grants to encourage municipalities to speed up final subdivision approvals and to offset the possible increase in municipal taxes (an implementation of a recommendation of the Housing Advisory Task Force). In fiscal 1975 nearly $6 million was granted to seven regional governments and three additional municipalities; and an additional $3.5 million was paid for fiscal 1974 starts.

Finally, there are the municipal housing study grants. Both regional and area municipalities are eligible for grants toward the cost of studies designed to facilitate residential development. Studies have included servicing requirements, and feasibility and planning studies. At the end of fiscal 1974, twenty-three applications had been received but only two had been approved by March 31, 1975. In fiscal 1975, however, forty-seven study grants were approved through OHAP to six regional municipalities and twenty-four area municipalities for 'a total of $1.7 million.[45]

The Housing Action Program was in fact a three-way partnership of the provincial government, local governments, and private industry. *Housing Ontario '74* indicated the roles of the respective partners as clearly as they could be stated in May 1974. The role of the Ministry of Housing was to:

(a) assist local governments to identify those specific areas of serviced or partially serviced land that can be brought quickly into housing production, and to help develop policies and production targets that are consistent with the province's overall housing policies;

(b) remove obstacles to housing development in those areas through such actions as accelerating review and approval of subdivision plans, and modifying where necessary – in co-operation with other provincial and municipal agencies – environmental or planning regulations which may unnecessarily delay development and add to its cost, but which, even with modification, still maintain sound environmental and planning principles;

(c) provide direct financing to municipalities where necessary to ensure that local levels of government do not incur unwarranted new costs as a result of accelerated housing development; and,

(d) work with the private development industry in meeting provincial and local government policies and production targets.

The role of local government was to:

1. give priority to identifying Housing Action Areas and to ensure that policies are implemented and production targets met with identified time periods; and,

2. accept and discharge, in a manner consistent with the objective of speeding housing development, those planning and development powers being delegated by the provincial government on a phased basis to regional governments.[46]

The role of private industry, which was required to enter into binding agreements with the appropriate levels of government, was intended to guarantee:

1. production of the numbers and price range of dwellings specified in the provincial, regional and municipal production targets;

2. stabilized lot prices; and,

3. specified amounts of land for the HOME Program.[47]

The Ontario Mortgage Corporation (established in August 1974) had the responsibility of consolidating and expanding substantially a direct interest in mortgage financing to assist in the production of new housing at prices more in line with the capacity of purchasers. The corporation supplied mortgages at below market interest rates to finance both lot-leased dwellings and condominiums under the Home Ownership Made Easy (HOME) plan. This activity was entitled the "Preferred Lending Program" and has been underway in Ontario since 1976.[48] In addition, OMC would finance the Community Integrated Housing Program (CIHP) whereby, as a quid pro quo, OHC would receive 25 per cent of the dwelling units created under the program to provide accommodation to low-income individuals and families.[49] In all, the ministry anticipated that the new mortgage corporation would assist in the production of up to 6,000 dwelling units in 1974.

ASSISTED RENTAL HOUSING

Assisted rental housing, in reality a new term for the more familiar designation "public housing", is accommodation for the elderly and for families on the basis of rents-geared-to-income. For the fiscal year

1974-75 the ministry expected to provide some 10,000 dwelling units along with the rent supplement program which would provide accommodation at reduced subsidized rental payments for another 1,500 dwelling units.

In that year the total budget for public housing accommodation for senior citizens and families was approximately $84 million. It was anticipated that 6,000 new units would be started for the elderly and 2,000 for family housing projects. No explanation was given for why these figures did not coincide with the ministry's statement that its budget would provide about 10,000 new public housing units.[50]

The new ministry offered to broaden the federal program of assistance to non-profit and co-operative housing groups under its Community-Sponsored Housing Program. Such groups might be sponsored by local governments, labour unions, welfare agencies, churches, educational or charitable institutions, and service clubs. The province's contribution was designed to reduce rent for lower-income groups through a grant of up to 10 per cent of the value of the housing project. Moreover, it would be possible to lease land from the province's land bank to such groups if a suitable site were available. The ministry also offered to provide technical assistance for the development and management of the project.

The totality of federal and provincial assistance might very well mean a 110 per cent mortgage, or a 90 per cent mortgage and 20 additional percentage points of outright grants contributed equally by the two levels of government. In return, the Ontario ministry expected such groups to make available up to 25 per cent of their dwellings for rental to families requiring rents-geared-to-income, that is those eligible to be placed on the public housing waiting lists. On its part, the ministry created a special branch for community-sponsored housing with an allocation of $4 million for the first fiscal year. Since the federal government had already allocated $75 million, this meant that over $79 million would be available to assist in the development of some 2,000 housing units in 1974 with additional starts expected in 1975. For the most part community-sponsored housing would serve the moderate-income rather than the lowest-income groups. A total of 23 applications were received between September 1974 and March 31, 1975, representing 2,528 dwelling units. At the end of fiscal 1974, 2,383 units had been approved among which 1,258 were recommended for inclusion in the rent supplement program.[51]

In the 1975/76 fiscal year 35 projects, representing a total of 2,274 units, were approved for provincial funding – 909 were included in the rent supplement program. For the first time a breakdown of "client groups" was provided as follows: neighbourhood groups and co-operatives, 14 projects for 573 units; charitable groups, 9 projects for 1,070 units; and, the City of Toronto Non-Profit Housing Corporation, 12 projects for 631 units. Of the 2,274 dwellings, 928 were for families, 1,160 were for senior citizens, and 189 were hostel units.[52]

OTHER NEW INNOVATIVE PROGRAMS IN ONTARIO

More than two years prior to the initiation of the Ministry of Housing the OHC had introduced a Rent Supplement Program whereby would-be tenants for public housing could be placed in privately-owned accommodation by agreement with the landlord.[53] If an agreement on a total rental acceptable to the corporation could be reached, selected tenants would pay the normal rent calculated on the appropriate scale for their income, and the difference between the landlord's market expectation and the rental capacity of the tenant would be made up by public funds on the following basis: 50 per cent federal, 42.5 per cent provincial, and 7.5 per cent municipal. (This was the basis for all subsidized public housing accommodation.) By mid-1974 the OHC had reached agreements throughout the province covering more than 2,600 dwelling units.[54]

The great advantage of this program is that low-income families are interspersed in the community with other families, often in single detached or semi-detached houses; and, to a significant degree in Metropolitan Toronto, in multiple dwellings. The obvious disadvantage of a rent-supplement program is that it does not add to the total housing stock but allocates a portion of existing housing to lower-income groups. At a time of inordinate tightness in the housing market, when vacancies in multiple dwellings are as low as one per cent (as was the case in Metro Toronto in the fall of 1974, again in 1976 and throughout 1979), there is little or no incentive for landlords to enter into such agreements. Nevertheless, many property management organizations, which are allied with large development firms, do co-operate with the OHC in this program; presumably they have so many varied relationships within the several housing programs in the province that such co-operation assists in the continuance of favourable relationships, including mortgage financing.

The new ministry declared in mid-1974 that it recognized the significance of conserving and improving the existing housing stock. *Housing Ontario '74* stated that the province's housing stock was relatively new, with more than 60 per cent of owner-occupied dwellings having been built since 1940. Most of the older dwellings are concentrated in the heart of the larger urban centres, as well as in a number of smaller cities and towns; moreover, they are for the most part occupied by lower-income groups. The Ontario Home Renewal Program (OHRP) which was announced by the ministry to begin in September 1974 would take advantage of the federally-sponsored Neighbourhood Improvement Program (NIP) to which the province contributed 25 per cent, and the related federal program known as Residential Rehabilitation Assistance Program (RRAP). Ontario, however, decided to extend its own financial aid to areas not covered by NIP and RRAP.

OHRP could be used in three different types of home-renewal activity. It would be possible to provide financial supplements for homeowners participating in the federal rehabilitation program. In the second place, the provincial funds would finance programs emphasizing structural repairs and sanitary improvements in geographical areas not covered by federal programs. Finally, Ontario hoped to finance programs of exterior improvement in predominantly low and moderate income neighbourhoods. It was estimated that about 3,750 dwellings might benefit from the federal-provincial home rehabilitation program during 1974.

In fiscal 1974, thirty-five Ontario Municipalities were allotted a total of $17 million by the federal government in its Neighbourhood Improvement Program.[55] A year later thirty-three municipalities were allocated a total of $15 million in federal funds. All of the municipalities referred to were selected by the Community Renewal Branch of the Ministry of Housing in consultation with the Provincial/Municipal Liaison Committee and CMHC.[56]

In the first annual report of the ministry the reference to the Federal Residential Rehabilitation Assistance Program (RRAP) and the provincial Ontario Home Renewal Program (OHRP) was largely explanatory. In fact, under OHRP 133 municipalities received $10.1 million to administer directly as loans to owner-occupants whose "adjusted annual family income" did not exceed $12,500. Applicants could borrow up to $7,500 from a participating municipality primarily for the repair of faulty structural and sanitary conditions, and the upgrading of plumbing, heating and electrical systems.[57] In 1975/76 the total amount awarded to 362 participating municipalities exceeded $15.2 million. Two regional governments, twenty-nine cities, eighty-four towns and thirty-eight villages participated in OHRP along with 177 townships and districts. By the end of the fiscal year 1977/78, 558 municipalities had entered the program.[58]

The third significant innovation (expatiated for the first time in *Housing Ontario '74*) took the form of a new thrust in the field of land assembly. The Government of Ontario expected to bring forward, late in 1974, legislation to establish an Ontario Land Corporation, which would assume financing and other responsibilities in connection with the land holdings of the province.[59] The ministry was determined to strengthen the role of local governments in many of these fields, and in the case of land acquisition it was committed to empower local governments to engage directly in the activity. In the first instance such powers were delegated through regional governments and thus to local governments within the eleven regional municipalities established in Ontario in recent years. Again, the province insisted that it must be assured that the local municipality would have available a prepared housing policy statement and that its land assembly proposals would be compatible with the overall housing policies and production goals of the province.

Nevertheless, regional governments are not in existence over much of the province (although they cover a large proportion of its total population) and those existing may in fact not wish to assume some or all of these responsibilities. In such cases the ministry would bear the direct responsibility or enter into agreements with local municipalities within or outside regions to enable them to carry out the program. However, an amendment to the *Housing Development Act 1948*, was put forward late in 1974 to enable a municipal council to acquire and hold land within the municipality for a housing project, including the preparation or disposal of the land for housing purposes. To make this possible the municipality must have an official plan in which a housing provision is encompassed or must have a statement of housing policy. In either case approval by the Ministry of Housing would be required regardless of the source of funds for land purchase.[60]

DECENTRALIZATION OF RESPONSIBILITY FOR HOUSING POLICY AND IMPLEMENTATION

The Advisory Task Force on Housing Policy was clearly concerned with the role of the municipalities and their attitudes as they affected the implementation of housing policies during recent years. Their report stated:

> Crucial to the implementation and success of the program would be the actual production performance at the local level. This is not only of significance to the housing development program but also to the provincial regional development program. Policy which is made at the provincial level can be frustrated at the local level, and the reverse also takes place. The task force is convinced that some method which has a chance of guaranteeing local as well as provincial performance should be instituted. The recommended approach is for a system of comprehensive long-term provincial-regional-local agreements on jointly developed programs, supported by financial incentives and financial sanctions . . . The municipalities in the province are generally concerned about their housing situation, are unable to cope with its

problems, recognize that it is the province's responsibility to deal with housing, and are by and large willing to co-operate to find a way of solving their housing problems.

Ready reception will be given by municipalities to financial assistance for services and community facilities; equally acceptable will be assisted housing programs for moderate-income families, such as the leased-lot program; senior citizen housing is also well received by municipalities. Subsidized family housing is less acceptable under present conditions. To the extent that this results from anticipated financial difficulties, this situation will have to be changed for many municipalities to begin to accept their share of responsibility. In addition to financial incentives, the municipalities and their residents should be called upon to take the initiative in dealing with their subsidized housing needs in the way that suits them best, rather than resist provincial efforts to provide housing for people in their community.[61]

The recommendations for the "delegation of housing responsibilities to Metropolitan Toronto and other municipalities" stated clearly,

Where municipalities are willing and able to undertake the responsibility for planning, developing and managing assisted-housing programs, this responsibility should be delegated to them. This should be based on the adoption of a joint plan for assisted housing which sets out the provincial and municipal housing objectives and how they are to be implemented, and the financial arrangements and sanctions to be used to secure municipal performance of the agreed targets. Relegation of responsibility for assisted-housing programs should allow for local circumstances and for suitable transition agreements. In many areas of Ontario, particularly in communities with little assisted-housing activity, the responsibility will remain with the province. OHC's duties should expand in those areas.

This responsibility should be delegated in the first instance to Metropolitan Toronto, which has nearly half the provincial stock of assisted housing, is willing to assume this responsibility, and has extensive experience and resources for planning, developing and managing housing.[62]

A decade after the formation of the OHC the question of local responsibility had in substantial measure completed a full circle. The Ontario Advisory Task Force Report became the basis of the statements in *Housing Ontario '74*. This initial statement of policies and programs of the new Ministry of Housing contained several significant references to local responsibilities which, taken together, make the clear point that the government of Ontario was firmly committed to increasing decentralization, at least in terms of the implementation of housing policies. The ministry was committed to

delegating to regional and municipal governments those powers and responsibilities which can be more efficiently discharged at the local level . . . encouraging the direct participation of community groups and municipalities in the production and management of low-cost housing.[63]

To ensure this, *Housing Ontario '74* indicated clearly that municipalities would be required to submit to the ministry statements of housing policy that would include production targets and levels of funding. In addition, the ministry would provide financial assistance to municipalities in preparing these policy statements.[64] Thus, housing policy, as far as the new ministry was concerned, involved some release of the firm grip which the OHC had developed in the previous decade, in favour of a renewed assumption of responsibility by those governments allegedly closest to the people in their communities and presumably more aware of individual and family needs and local requirements.

As far as the production of assisted rental housing for low-income families and senior citizens is concerned, the ministry proceeded rapidly with its avowed program of decentralization. Throughout 1975 and 1976 a number of changes were made in administrative practices to enable existing and newly created local housing authorities to carry out responsibilities previously carried at the head office in Toronto. At the same time a special committee on public housing management was engaged in discussions with regional governments and "municipalities at all levels in conjunction with the program to reorganize the systems of local housing authorities."[65] After two years or more of detailed discussions, many new LHAs were created where none existed previously, others were created for the first time within the scope of regional governments, and still others involved widening the geographical area of responsibility together with the elimination of small existing authorities.[66]

Early in 1977 the ministry announced, as a part of its longer-term plan for housing operations in Ontario, that it would offer municipalities two avenues of approach in the future. From 1964, for more than a dozen years, municipalities passed a resolution of council requesting a need-and-demand study for housing; and, the OHC (and later the ministry) implemented the requested survey. A recommendation would then be made to the local council for a certain number of family or senior citizen dwelling units and council would accept or reject the recommendation. When such recommendations were accepted, the OHC and the ministry carried out all the responsibilities of design, tendering, award of contracts, inspection of construction, and ultimately, takeover of the completed structure(s). At that point the operation and management of the building became the responsibility of either a local housing authority or the direct management branch of the OHC. In its 1977 announcement the ministry agreed to permit this sequence to continue, if the municipalities so wished, with the caveat that the ministry expected local housing authorities to cover all areas of the province before the end of the decade; thus direct management by OHC would cease.

The ministry, at the same time, provided local governments with an opportunity to assume much greater responsibility for the housing program within its jurisdiction. If the municipality decided not to follow the traditional route, it could notify the ministry that it chose, within its housing policy statement and/or approved official plan, to proceed more or less on its own. In this case, it was required to purchase the requisite land (within price guidelines set by the two senior levels of government), hire an architect or equivalent professional to create a design, call for tenders, and award contracts under its own supervision. Once again, however, the local government must abide by certain senior governmental price guidelines for housing construction within the federal-provincial-municipal subsidy system. Thus, the municipality would borrow 90 per cent from CMHC and provide the additional 10 per cent of capital, rather than the province; the subsidy system would remain as before – federal 50 per cent, provincial 42½ per cent, and municipal 7½ per cent, unless the price guidelines were exceeded.

By late 1974 there were already two significant policy statements published and available for study. The first required formulation of housing policy was issued by the City of Toronto in December 1973.[67] It is clear from the analysis presented that this document was not prepared in response to the initiatives of the Premier of Ontario in creating the Advisory Task Force on Housing Policy. It is also clear, by virtue of its timing, that it antedated the initial policy statement of the new Ministry of Housing. The fact is that within the "reform council" elected in the City of Toronto in December 1972, there were a number of interested and well-informed new councillors who were encouraged by the mayor to study the entire question of the role of the city in the housing field. The opening page of the city's document stating: "It's time for Toronto to get back into the housing business", was extracted from the inaugural address of the mayor to city council at the beginning of its two-year term on January 3, 1973. Thus, although the report is dated December, it fortuitously became the policy document which, the Ministry of Housing insisted some months later, must be prepared if a local government is to receive the delegated authority and financial assistance available from the province.

The City of Toronto's policy statement, described in the letter of transmission as "a proposed interim housing strategy", was prepared by a housing work group composed of members of city council and senior officials of several city departments. It is extremely interesting from a policy point of view because it not only encompassed almost every phase of a housing program, but, moreover, made it very clear that the City of Toronto was a governmental entity capable of implementing such a program.

It is not germane to this discussion to emphasize all the specifics of this policy statement but a number of interesting departures from past policies and programs throughout Canada, or at least new emphases within existing programs, are worthy of note. In the first statement of "goals", for example, the report included the following.

> The development of the capability of community-based non-profit corporations as producers of housing, to allow greater community involvement in the planning and operation of housing projects and thereby avoid confrontation and rejection of high density assisted housing imposed from above. . . .[68]

This was, indeed, a completely unsupported statement, since there was at the time little evidence of the capacity of non-profit corporations to produce substantial numbers of dwelling units. It does imply that the city would continue to obstruct the efforts of the OHC to produce large numbers of dwelling units for low-income families, the greatest number of whom actually reside in the city within Metropolitan Toronto. It is understandable, therefore, that the public and the media became incensed over the fact that in the first nine months of 1974 few more than sixty dwelling units of public housing were started in Metro Toronto in comparison with thousands, two or three years previously.

The document includes numerical targets and a clear enunciation of the work group's concept of the "city's role in housing":

> That the city explicitly adopt the role of co-ordinator of all housing programs implemented in the city and that the federal, provincial and metropolitan government be asked to concur in the housing program set out in . . . this report.[69]

This may very well be the strongest exposition of local government intent put forward in Canada during the past quarter-century. It calls for a reversal of past housing policies in which the federal-provincial partnership and its successors (after 1964) would no longer have the right to put forward programs to be implemented, following an examination by the planning board and approval by city council, without further reference (except in the case of technical matters) to the city and its staff.

In brief, the City of Toronto was asking:
- for legislation and financial assistance to produce 4,000 new dwelling units per annum during 1974 and 1975;

- that the city be permitted to enter the field of land banking with a proposed expenditure of $10 million during the first year, 90 per cent of which would be provided under Section 42 of the NHA;
- that the city would embark upon a public non-profit housing program with legislative authority to be derived from the province to enable it to establish "a city-owned, non-profit corporation", and with the further request that the province pass legislation enabling the city or its non-profit corporation to build housing without seeking *individual* project approval;
- that the city would commit $250,000 in 1974 and in 1975 for rehabilitation grants and loans to pay the material costs of the house repair groups if funding of labour costs were available under the Local Initiatives Program;* and,
- that the city council would urge the metropolitan corporation to assume full responsibility for the production and operation of the traditional public housing program.[70]

As 1974 drew to a close, the city had realized a number of its specific objectives. A new Department of Housing had been created within the civic administration and the first Commissioner of Housing had been named.[71] The city had also created its own non-profit housing corporation and was actively seeking suitable homes for acquisition and rehabilitation in a number of downtown neighbourhoods. The land banking program was approved by CMHC and funds were available to enable the new Department of Housing to undertake appropriate purchases.

However, during the first year of the new housing program no public housing was initiated let alone produced by the Department of Housing; moreover, there was no indication that any Toronto family was accommodated in housing, new or old, acquired, produced or rehabilitated under the new program. In short, the first year of the two-year program passed without any numerical increase to the public housing stock. In defence, however, the tooling-up process, required in 1974, did mean substantial progress in 1975 and 1976. It is often the case that the writers of a policy document underestimate the time involved in developing essential arrangements.

The Housing Department issued a progress report early in 1975.[72] The commissioner reported in detail the substantial planning which was required in 1974 to translate the projected targets of *Living Room* into reality within the housing market. A great deal was accomplished

---

*Local Initiatives was a federally funded program to stimulate employment via municipal projects.

in that first year, not merely in organizing the department but in detailed studies of projected programs of land banking, non-profit housing (both new construction and acquisition and renovation of older housing), and in developing relationships with authorities responsible for senior citizens housing and private housing production.

The first year was a year of study, of projection and initiation. In the City Land Banking Program, for example, four sites were identified amounting to more than 330,000 sq. ft. at a probable total price of nearly $2.9 million. On this land, the department projected 409 family dwelling units, and 246 non-family units. It expected that these projects would all be underway in 1975 or 1976 and would be completed for the most part in 1977-78. In two of the four cases zoning changes were required.[73] Similarly, programs were projected for the City Non-Profit New Housing Program, 1975. Fifteen sites, 271 family units and 687 non-family units were proposed with a total land and construction cost of nearly $24.3 million. In addition, the department identified, in co-operation with the Metro Parking Authority, six parking lot sites upon which an additional 131 family and 589 non-family units could be developed. Some of these latter proposals were under construction by mid-1977.[74]

The return of the City of Toronto to a direct active role in the housing field in 1974 was not achieved without serious administrative, organizational, and financial difficulties. A consulting firm examined the organizational needs of the Housing Department and submitted its final report to the mayor at the end of April 1975.[75] The consultants emphasized the special difficulties of developing a housing department in a large Canadian urban centre within the complexities of inter-governmental legislation and a public-private housing market. The report argued that the task of continuing to develop the city's non-profit housing at the current rate would be difficult. The report alleged that the department, by and large, had neglected the non-profit private sector organizations which had built 724 dwelling units in 1974 and were expected to create at least 700 per annum. "Although the department intended to work closely with the group, and designated (staff) positions for the purpose, it has devoted little effort to assisting this sector."[76]

The problem of devising satisfactory property management operations was emphasized in the report of the consultants. They alleged that there had been a failure to market the city's housing and that project managers and maintenance services were overloaded. While the city's programs provided mixed housing at both market and below-market levels, many low-income families found the city's market rents too high. At the time of the study 900 families were on the waiting list and the majority required below-market rentals. Although the city owned a mere 700 units at the time of the submission, city project managers were said to be over loaded with routine tasks and yet an additional 600-800 dwellings would be added before the end of the year.[77]

There can be little doubt that Toronto's housing department has been substantially strengthened since the spring of 1975 and that the operations of the department are considered a "model" of what can be done by a large urban community within the framework of federal-provincial legislation, programs and financial resources. The City of Toronto was one of the first municipalities in Canada to establish a non-profit housing corporation to take advantage of the new programs and has provided 1,800 units of accommodation since 1973.[78]

METROPOLITAN TORONTO'S INTERIM HOUSING POLICY

The recommendation (in *Living Room*) that the public housing program in Metro Toronto should be the "full responsibility" of the metropolitan corporation appeared during 1974 to be a major contradiction, in consideration of the other features of the proposed City of Toronto program. Furthermore, a serious conflict emerged when the Municipality of Metropolitan Toronto issued its own Interim Metro Housing Policy in May 1974.[79] Not only was this report a strong challenge to the proposed policy initiatives of the city, but the amendments passed by the provincial legislature in the early summer made it very clear that Metro would have the full responsibility for public housing. It is normally routine for a series of minor amendments to be made by the legislature each year to both the *Municipality of Metropolitan Toronto Act* and the *City of Toronto Act*. In 1974, however, many of the proposals were extremely important and contentious.

As far as housing policy was concerned, both the elected and appointed senior officials of the city and five boroughs within Metro alleged that Paul Godfrey, chairman of the Metropolitan Council, had negotiated secretly with cabinet ministers and senior officials to effect amendments which were not known in advance to the complainants. They argued that the matter of responsibility for housing policy was one of these secret arrangements. Although the Metro chairman denied this, the fact is that the *Municipality of Metropolitan Toronto Act* was amended as follows.

> 198a. – (1) The Metropolitan Council and the council of any area municipality may, by by-law by the Minister of Housing, adopt a policy statement related to housing, containing specific objectives, production targets and financial arrangements.

(2) Where a policy statement referred to in subsection (1) has been adopted by the Metropolitan Council and approved by the Minister of Housing, every housing policy statement that has been adopted by the council of an area municipality shall be amended forthwith to conform therewith and no housing policy statement of an area municipality shall thereafter be approved that does not conform with the housing policy statement of the Metropolitan Council and no by-law shall be passed by the Metropolitan Council or by the council of an area municipality that does not conform with the housing policy statement of the Metropolitan Council.[80]

Metro's own policy statement is labelled as a "draft" as well as an "interim document", and the issuing authority for the full report is listed as the "Office of the Metropolitan Chairman". The work of the document (issued some five months after the policy statement by the City of Toronto) is attributed to a "staff committee" which is reported to have spent a considerable amount of time on the question of appropriate production targets for Metro and the area municipalities. The "staff committee" turned out to be a group of officials representing the CMHC, the Ministry of Housing of Ontario, the departmental staff of the Municipality of Metropolitan Toronto with an additional consultant,[81] and certain other staff members representing each of the area municipalities.

The Ministry of Housing had stated that it would devolve responsibility for implementation of housing policy to local governments within recently constituted regional governments by the process of turning over responsibility in the first instance to the regional government or upper level in each case. Metropolitan Toronto is conceived as a regional government for these purposes, and antedates any other regional government in the province by at least fifteen years. The Municipality of Metropolitan Toronto began its policy statement by assuming that authority would be decentralized through the Metropolitan Council to the area municipalities: the five boroughs and the City of Toronto. It emphasized what it called "the concept of a shared responsibility for housing", and outlined a proposed system of consultation on all aspects of planning, land acquisition, construction and management of assisted housing in the metropolitan area.

It is not surprising, given the composition of the committee, that the interim policy statement of Metro Toronto bears a strong resemblance to that of the City of Toronto. The major exception was that all the responsibilities to be assumed by the city as outlined in its own policy document were now to be assumed by the Metropolitan corporation. In turn, such responsibilities would be assigned to the city or other area municipality within Metro after consultation and agreement that the local municipality (within the second tier of local government in Metro) had the necessary capability of assuming such responsibilities.

The report proposed a target of 20,000 new housing starts annually in the form of 14,000 apartment and 6,000 non-apartment dwellings. In addition, 8,000 low- and moderate-income units would be produced annually but it is not clear whether this figure was part of the afore-mentioned 20,000 new housing starts or over and above that total. Moreover, an objective of 1,000 rehabilitated dwelling units on an annual basis was affirmed.

The Metro report dealt with the familiar subjects that are part and parcel of the total housing problem and the overall housing program in Canada. The major policy initiatives put forward were two-fold. In the first place, Metro stated that it was ready to assume the management of OHC dwelling units and that such responsibility would be delegated later to area municipalities, as requested.[82] Secondly, the Metropolitan corporation was ready to assume administrative control and the placement of all tenants in rent-geared-to-income housing through a tenant placement bureau located in the Metropolitan Toronto Department of Social Services.

In order to accomplish these goals and specific targets the report estimated the yearly land banking requirements to be $25 to $35 million. In addition, the yearly program assistance from the two senior levels of government was estimated to be between $200 and $250 million – a possible grand total of nearly $300 million "to be invested . . . to help relieve . . . housing problems chiefly in the area of social housing."[83]

It is not difficult to "poke holes" in the Metro document and to indicate its inconsistencies. The annual program of the OHC had never exceeded $150 million. It is hardly likely, in view of the determination of the CMHC to assist all provinces in line with their respective capa-bilities, that the two senior levels would allocate approximately $250 million annually solely for Metropolitan Toronto. The curious indica-tion that Metro would take over responsibility for tenant placement by locating a tenant placement bureau within the Department of Social Services is surely an affirmation that all applicants for public housing were desperately poor; thus, they would best be treated by social service workers whose main preoccupations were the determination of eligibility for financial assistance and assistance with problems of social functioning.

The Metro policy statement included, as did that of the city, an indication that there should be a Department of Housing within the municipality, to be headed by a senior official. Metro also wished to form a non-profit housing company, although it had, for about fifteen years, maintained the Metro Toronto Housing Company Limited – a limited dividend housing company created under the original Section 16 of the NHA 1954 – for the purpose of constructing and managing housing for senior citizens. At the close of 1974, however, a Metro housing department had not been created and no senior official had been appointed. Neither had a Metro non-profit housing company been created under the terms of the *Housing Development Act of Ontario*, nor did it appear that there was any strong demand for the implementation of these recommendations.[84]

The explanation for the relatively rapid progress in implementing the City of Toronto's policy statement and the lack of progress on the part of the Municipality of Metropolitan Toronto may lie in the previously mentioned conflict concerning amendments to the *Municipality of Metropolitan Toronto Act*. The amendments of late June 1974, clearly made it necessary for any area municipality, including the City of Toronto, to develop a housing policy in conformity with that of Metropolitan council. On the day the amendments to the act were proclaimed by the Ontario government Karl Jaffary, of the executive committee of the City of Toronto, moved before the Metropolitan executive committee that legislation be sought to amend the *Municipality of Metropolitan Toronto Act*

> . . . so as to provide that no housing policy adopted by the Metropolitan council shall affect the official plan provisions of any area municipality or the responsibility of the area municipality for land use planning and the passage of zoning by-laws.[85]

In addition, the chairman of the City of Toronto's Housing Work Group, a local councillor, submitted a statement to the executive committee to the city in mid-June, in which he stated,

> It appears to be obvious that the Metro chairman's co-operative approach is preferable to the element of compulsion contained in the bill. If there is to be a Metropolitan housing policy, it should be the product of co-operation and consultation. If it is to be a tool to coerce area municipalities to take specific actions, then the representatives of all the area municipalities who sit on Metro Council may find that it is not in their interest to have Metro adopt any housing policy.[86]

The ultimate result of these submissions and contentions was a recommendation by the Metropolitan Executive Committee that its solicitor be authorized and directed to make application to the Province of Ontario for amending legislation to repeal subsection 2 of Section 198(a), a section that had just been enacted within the *Municipality of*

Metropolitan Toronto Act. The executive committee further recommended that the province adopt a policy of submitting proposed amendments to the governing legislation to the Metropolitan council for consideration prior to submission to the legislature. In short, the executive committee was convinced that Chairman Paul Godfrey had worked to amend the basic legislation without reference to Metropolitan Council.[87]

This detailed exposition of the development of housing policies within Metropolitan Toronto indicates the conflicts in the struggle for power over the implementation of housing policies and programs as the federal and provincial governments attempted to decentralize within this field. It was not that the OHC had determined to stop its program or to cease production while decentralization was effected; but, in the view of local politicians, there appeared to be a power vacuum into which both the area municipalities within a region or a metropolitan government, and the upper tier of regional government wished to move simultaneously. There are important lessons here for all major metropolitan areas in Canada, particularly Vancouver, Winnipeg, and Montreal which have developed further in the field of metropolitan government than any municipality other than Toronto.

Nevertheless, after careful study of the allocations and responsibilities for housing policy within Metropolitan Toronto, John P. Robarts made several major recommendations in his mid-1977 report to the Government of Ontario, all of which were designed to strengthen the resolve of Metro to accept responsibilities which the province was clearly willing to allocate to major regional governments, after appropriate negotiation. These recommendations were:

Recommendation 12.2   The Metropolitan council, in consultation with the area municipalities, be responsible for establishing housing targets as part of a comprehensive Metropolitan housing policy, and for the allocation of these targets among the area municipalities.

Recommendation 12.3   Metropolitan housing objectives be implemented through the planning powers of the Metropolitan council.

Recommendation 12.4   The Metropolitan council gradually assume responsibility for the existing housing stock of the Ontario Housing Corporation in Metropolitan Toronto.

Recommendation 12.5   The Metropolitan council be responsible for the direct provision of all low-income family and senior citizen housing in Metropolitan Toronto, and delegate this responsibility to any area municipality willing and able to undertake it.[88]

If these recommendations were acceptable to the Government of Ontario and assumed by Metropolitan council in due course, it seems clear that Metro Toronto would be functioning like a provincial housing corporation responsible for a population of nearly 3 million persons.

ANALYTICAL SUMMARY

A great deal of space has been devoted in this analysis to the experience within Ontario, the evolution of its legislative and managerial structures, and the political problems and inter-governmental in-fighting that has characterized the situation during the past several years. The reasons for this attention are simply that Ontario has accounted since 1964 for 70 per cent of all new public housing dwelling units financed through Section 43 of the NHA. The OHC initiated more new programs in the overall housing field than any other provincial corporation, and the province encountered problems and difficulties which should provide important lessons for other provinces. Whatever the experience in Ontario, the other provinces have not kept pace; for instance, from 1964-73 Quebec accounted for a mere 15.5 per cent of all new public housing dwellings financed under Section 43.

The argument is not intended to deny regional differences, regional preferences, and deliberate and clearly defined policies and programs within other provinces. It is difficult, however, to ignore the fact that almost twice as much housing activity, proportionate to population, has occurred on behalf of low-income groups in Ontario than in other provinces. When all programs are taken into consideration about 80 per cent of all governmental housing activity had been mounted during the years since 1964 in Ontario, which has about 40 per cent of Canada's population.

The other provinces, which argued before the federal Task Force on Housing and Urban Development in 1968-69 that the only way they could proceed to meet the needs of their residents would be through a diversion of federal funds from Ontario to the rest of the country, have proved conclusively that their arguments were false. The resources have been made available and the major applicants have not been those provinces which claimed that they were somewhat disadvantaged by virtue of the headstart and headlong activity of the OHC in its first five or six years. On the basis of statistical evidence, the will to develop major and innovative housing programs on behalf of low-income groups in some provinces appears to be weak or lacking.

Nevertheless, the record in Ontario is by no means entirely without flaw. Any analysis must begin with the totality of dwelling starts and completions (whether under private or public auspices) over a period of years. Dwelling starts in Ontario rose steadily from 1970 through 1973 reaching more than 110,000 in the latter year. Over the next three years the drop was equally dramatic, amounting to more than 20 per cent from 1973 through 1974; the recovery in Canada in 1975 and 1976 was not matched in either absolute or relative terms within the province of Ontario.[89]

It has been contended in the Ontario legislature that the annual percentage increase in housing starts in Ontario has lagged behind the national average since 1970 and the gap is widening. In 1975 Ontario experienced a decrease of 5.7 per cent in urban housing starts over 1974 while nationally, excluding Ontario, there was an increase of 16.6 per cent. While Ontario had an increase of 5.4 per cent in 1976, the national increase was 15.3 per cent.[90]

The Minister of Housing, in 1977, predicted a further drop of about 4,700 housing starts to a total of 80,000 – approximately 28 per cent below the 1973 figure. On the other hand, the Conference Board of Canada forecast 72,800 starts for Ontario in 1977.[91] In terms of the total housing effort, therefore, it it contended that Ontario has fallen behind and that the Ministry of Housing failed to take advantage of all financial funding available from the federal government through CMHC.

Ontario has, without question, implemented the most important recommendations put forward by the Advisory Task Force of 1973 and has implemented most of the proposals of its policy statement, *Housing Ontario '74.* There can be little question that the provincial government has taken seriously its responsibilities in housing. In a huge province with a growing population it may well be facing an impossible task. The downturn in economic activity which commenced in late 1975 affected entrepreneurial investment in all phases of construction in Ontario. The downward spiral of lessening investment, lessening employment and lessening demand for new housing for purchase resulted in a substantial number of completed housing units not being sold in 1977-79 – this sequence alone may account in large measure for the continued decline in housing starts.

Ontario is also the preferred location of about half of all newcomers to Canada. Many immigrants maintain the ownership of property and particularly the ownership of their own homes as a fundamental aspiration. The great majority of newcomers are neither particularly interested in assisted rental housing under private or public auspices. They have tended to strengthen the shift in public housing within Metropolitan Toronto and throughout the province, from the construction of rental housing for low-income families to the provision of housing for senior citizens. This latter trend is fully documented in a later chapter.[92]

Despite the allegation that Ontario has not made full use of available federal resources, the fact is that financial considerations are an increasingly important constraint in the development of housing for low-income individuals and families in the province. If traditional housing for families and senior citizens only is examined, there were nearly 85,000 dwelling units in 310 municipalities under management late in 1979.[93] If units acquired under agreements within the Rent Supplement Program (44 municipalities), Community Integrated Housing Program

(9 municipalities), Limited-Dividend Program (18 municipalities), the Accelerated Rental Housing Program, (27 municipalities) and the Assisted Rental Housing Program (30 municipalities), are counted, an additional 8,977 dwellings were occupied in November 1979.[94] Under modest assumptions of increasing numbers of dwelling units in all of these programs, it can be estimated that Ontario will have between 110,000 and 125,000 units under administration in 1985. The total number of people housed in such accommodation would be in the vicinity of 350,000 – 375,000.

This creditable performance is not without financial considerations which are worrisome to some members in all parties in the provincial legislature. Rising costs of construction together with stable incomes among applicants for socially-assisted housing have meant enormous per unit, per month subsidies in comparison with the past. In 1970 the total subsidy paid within Ontario was $26.8 million, of which the provincial share was $10.9 million. By 1975 the total subsidy had increased to $122.6 million, with the provincial share amounting to $50.6 million. The estimated number of dwelling units under administration in 1985 of 110,000 or more could mean a total subsidy in the neighbourhood of $325 – $335 million, of which the provincial share would be about $145 million. Such figures would mean that the subsidies alone would have risen between 1975 and 1985 from less than a fifth of the budget of the Ministry of Housing to more than 40 per cent.

In a huge province with high gross family incomes and an impressive gross provincial product, an annual housing subsidy approaching $150 million does not appear to be burdensome. But the fact is that some legislators and many people who have struggled on their own to acquire housing accommodation feel that this subsidy level is becoming burdensome. Moreover, it is emphasized that such subsidies continue during the entire period of debt repayment, usually fifty years, and that the total can only increase substantially during the balance of the century in response to inflation, unemployment, and the perpetuation of poverty in an affluent society.

It would appear, therefore, that Ontario's vast housing program will be under severe financial and philosophical examination in successive fiscal years. In the early 1980s the budget of the Ministry of Housing had not kept pace with increases in either the provincial budget as a whole, or the general price level. The government in power clearly wishes to restrain all public spending; there will be no exception for the field of housing. Moreover, there is considerable evidence that the general public believes that government has gone about as far as it should in its intervention in the housing market in Ontario. This is one meaning inherent in the process of decentralization of responsibility to local areas beginning in the late 1970s.

NOTES

[1]*The Ontario Housing Corporation Act*, R.S.O., 1970, c. 317.

[2]R.S.O., 1970, c. 213, as amended by 1972, c. 129 and 1974, c. 31.

[3]In the mid-1970s Ontario devised new housing programs which required the allocation of provincial funds without federal participation. These funds were made available without recourse to the borrowing powers of the Ontario Housing Corporation.

[4]By 1976 the Government of Ontario was committed to the development of local or regional housing authorities throughout the province; thus the "direct management" function was reduced substantially (within three years), except in Metro Toronto.

[5]In February 1977 the Ministry of Housing changed these administrative arrangements by giving municipalities a further option: constructing the housing itself (with OHC technical guidance, if required) with a federal loan of 90 per cent and local capital participation of 10 per cent. In any event, localities were, in the future, to acquire and zone land, whatever the development route to be followed.

[6]The Ontario Student Housing Corporation was formally dissolved in June 1978.

[7]Ontario Advisory Task Force on Housing Policy, *Report* (Toronto: Queen's Printer, August 1973) p. 1.

[8]*Ibid.*, p. 1.

[9]*Ibid.*, p. 7.

[10]*Ibid.*, pp. 2-3.

[11]*Ibid.*, p. 106.

[12]It is difficult to be certain because the provinces are slow in issuing annual reports of their housing activities, but it appeared in 1977 that the Ministry of Housing in Ontario was the only one with that exclusive responsibility. In both British Columbia and Newfoundland the ministry is entitled, Municipal Affairs and Housing. In other provinces responsibility for housing is assigned to the Ministry of Municipal Affairs (Alberta), the Ministry of Urban Affairs (Manitoba), and the Ministry of Labour (New Brunswick), among others.

[13]*Report, op. cit.*, pp. 107-108.

[14]*Ibid.*, p. 109.

[15]In mid-1977 there were 49 housing authorities. A number of new authorities had been created in 1975-76 on a county, regional or sub-

regional basis. In this process several small existing authorities were absorbed.

[16]*Report, op. cit.*, p. 11.

[17]*Idem.*

[18]*Infra.*, pp. 173-178.

[19]*Ibid.*, pp. 46-51.

[20]*Ibid.*, pp. 95-96.

[21]*Ibid.*, pp. 97-99.

[22]*Ibid.*, pp. 99-100.

[23]*Ibid.*, pp. 103-104.

[24]*Ibid.*, pp. 96-97.

[25]*Ibid.*, pp. 13-14.

[26]*Ibid.*, pp. 69-90.

[27]*Ibid.*, p. 70.

[28]Metropolitan Toronto Planning Board, "Report of the Ontario Advisory Task Force on Housing Policy, August 1973" (Toronto: mimeographed, January 9th, 1974) pp. 1-2.

[29]Ministry of Treasury, Economics, and Intergovernmental Affairs.

[30]Ontario, Statement by the Honourable William G. Davis, Premier of Ontario, to the Legislature, *On Housing* (Toronto: October 2, 1973) p. 6.

[31]Ontario, "Explanatory Notes", *The Ministry of Housing Act, 1973*, p. 2.

[32]Ontario, Ministry of Housing, *Housing Ontario '74* (Toronto: May 1974).

[33]*Ibid.*, p. 2.

[34]*Ibid.*, p. 2.

[35]*Ibid.*, Table 1. See "Appendix Tables".

[36]In 1977 many large homes and certain older apartment buildings in older districts in the City of Toronto were broken up into "bachelorettes" of about 350-400 square feet.

[37]*Housing Ontario '74*, p. 3.

[38]*Ibid.*, pp. 13-14.

[39]*Ibid.*, p. 15.

[40]Ontario, Ministry of Housing, *Annual Report 1975/76* (Toronto: Queen's Printer 1976) p. 8.

[41]Ontario, Ministry of Housing, *Annual Report 1974/75*, p. 13.

[42]Ontario, Ministry of Housing, *Annual Report 1974/75*, p. 11.

[43]Ontario, Ministry of Housing, *Annual Report 1975/76*, p. 8.

[44]Ontario, Ministry of Housing, *Annual Report 1974/75*, p. 15.

[45]Ontario, Ministry of Housing, *Annual Report 1975/76*, p. 9.

[46]*Ibid.*, pp. 16-17.

[47]*Ibid.*, pp. 17-18. The HOME (Home Ownership Made Easy) Program was an on-going activity of the OHC whereby serviced lots were made available to builders who were required to offer completed structures at agreed upon prices to the home buyer. In turn, the land could be purchased outright from the OHC at book value, or leased by the purchaser at a monthly rental for a period of five years or more. At the end of five years the purchaser could offer to purchase the land, which would then be available at its market value. *vid. Housing Ontario January/February 1976*, Vol. 20, No. 1, p. 10. 20,276 units were transferred to house buyers plus an additional 15,008 condominium units. *vid.* Ministry of Housing, *Annual Report 1975/76* (Toronto: Queen's Printer 1976) p. 25.

[48]*Housing Ontario, op. cit.*, p. 13.

[49]*Ibid.*, p. 14.

[50]In fact, *completions* of public housing dwellings for families and senior citizens in Ontario were 6,429 in 1974, 7,060 in 1975 and 4,183 in 1976. Cf. *infra.* chapter VIII.

[51]Ontario, Ministry of Housing, *Annual Report 1974/75*, p. 16.

[52]Ontario, Ministry of Housing, *Annual Report 1975/76*, p. 22.

[53]Under the authority of the National Housing Act, S. 44, 1973-74; *vid Ontario Housing, op. cit.*, p. 9.

[54]This figure was 8,977 units late in 1979. Ontario Housing Corporation, *Fact Sheet* (as at November 30, 1979) (Toronto: OHC, mimeo., December 1979) p. 2.

[55]Ontario, Ministry of Housing, *Annual Report 1974/75*, p. 7.

[56]Ontario, Ministry of Housing, *Annual Report 1975/76*, p. 17.

[57]*Ontario, Ministry of Housing, Annual Report 1974/75*, pp. 7-8.

[58]Ontario, Ministry of Housing, *Annual Report 1975/76*, p. 17; *Annual Report 1977/78*, p. 14. OHRP grants reached $23 million in fiscal 1978.

[59]Ontario Land Corporation was not in fact established within the Ministry of Housing but within TEIGA via *The Ontario Land Corporation Act*, assented to on February 14, 1975; the corporation was transferred to the Ministry of Housing on August 31, 1978.

[60]*Housing Ontario, op. cit.*, p. 12. In 1975 the federal allocation, under Sections 40 and 42 of the NHA was $35 million to the province. The Municipal Land Development Program received slightly more than $9 million which was made available to 13 municipalities. In February 1976 the minister announced the allocation of a further $18.3 million to 11 municipalities. See Ministry of Housing, *Annual Report 1975/76*, p. 21.

[61]Ontario Advisory Task Force on Housing Policy, *Report* (Toronto: Queen's Printer, 1973) p. 100.

[62]*Ibid.*, p. 109.

[63]*Housing Ontario '74*, pp. 11-12.

[64]In September 1974 the CMHC announced the first grant (the sum of $15,000 to the Borough of Scarborough within Metro Toronto to prepare its housing policy). A month later the Ontario Ministry of Housing announced its first two grants to Ottawa and Peterborough.

[65]Ontario, Ministry of Housing, *Annual Report 1975/76*, p. 27.

[66]The number of Local Housing Authorities was 58 at December 31, 1979; a 59th authority was formed in January 1980.

[67]*Living Room: The City of Toronto's Housing Policy*. An Approach to Home Banking and Land Banking for the City of Toronto (prepared by the Housing Work Group, December 1973).

[68]*Ibid.*, p. ii.

[69]*Ibid.*, p. iv.

[70]*Ibid.*, pp. ii-x.

[71]The first commissioner was Michael Dennis, co-author of *Programmes in Search of a Policy*. He was the former consultant on housing on the mayor's staff.

[72]City of Toronto, Housing Department, *Progress Report 1974* (Toronto: February 1975) p. 169.

[73]City of Toronto, Housing Department, *op. cit.*, p. 42.

[74]*Ibid.*, pp. 59-60.

[75]The Canada Consulting Group, *Continuing the Job of Building Toronto's Housing Department*. A Report to the City of Toronto, Executive Committee (Toronto: April 28, 1975) pp. 27, exhibits 1-34.

[76]*Ibid.*, p. 1-2 and exhibit 12.

[77]*Ibid.*, pp. 1-10.

[78]Ontario, *Report of the Royal Commission on Metropolitan Toronto* (June 1977 – issued July 4, 1977) Vol. 2, p. 229.

[79]Office of the Metropolitan Toronto Chairman, *Draft Interim Metro Housing Policy, Part I, Part II* (Toronto: May 1974). The confusion around "Part I, Part II" is soon dissipated when it is discovered that Part I simply contains the recommendations which "should be given immediate attention by the Metropolitan Council." The second part provides the background argument and data upon which the recommendations are based.

[80]Executive Committee of the Metropolitan Council of Metropolitan Toronto, "Proposed Amendment to the Municipality of Metropolitan Toronto Act", *Report No. 42*, Appendix A, p. 2158.

[81]Michael Dennis, not yet Commissioner of Housing for the City of Toronto.

[82]A special committee of staff members of the Ontario Housing Corporation and Metropolitan Toronto Council was created in mid-1976 to consider the principles involved in Metro's assumption of responsibility, and the administrative and financial arrangements which would be required to implement a new housing authority. Late in 1977 the committee had not yet reported but the question of delegating responsibility at a later time to the boroughs appeared to be moribund.

[83]Office of the Metropolitan Toronto Chairman, *op. cit.*, p. 10.

[84]The Metropolitan Toronto Non-Profit Housing Company was established in 1975.

[85]Metropolitan Toronto, *Report No. 42*, p. 2157.

[86]Statement by Michael Goldrick submitted to the City of Toronto Executive Committee on June 17, 1974, in *Report No. 42* of the Metropolitan Executive Committee, Appendix A, p. 2163.

[87]The Interim Housing Policy for Metro was adopted by council on November 5, 1974. The Office of the Chairman was requested to prepare a second draft Metropolitan Interim Housing Policy. This was submitted to the Social Services and Housing Committee and described as follows:

> This is an Interim Housing Policy. When an official plan is adopted for Metropolitan Toronto, that plan will contain a specific housing policy as part of the official plan.

See memorandum from J. P. Kruger, executive director, Office of the Metropolitan Chairman, to members of the Social Services and Housing Committee, January 23, 1975, p. 3.

[88]Ontario, *Report of the Royal Commission on Metropolitan Toronto* (Toronto: June 1977) pp. 235-238.

[89]CMHC, *Canadian Housing Statistics* (Ottawa: 1977) Table 4, p. 4.

[90]Legislature of Ontario, *Debates*, (Official Report No. 22, April 26, 1977) pp. 908-909, 927-928.

[91]*Idem.*

[92]cf. *infra.*, Chapter VIII, Table V.

[93]Ontario, *Fact Sheet* (Ministry of Housing, mimeo., as at November 30, 1979) p. 1. Metro Toronto is counted as one municipality in these data.

[94]*Ibid.*, p. 2.

CHAPTER 7

Constraints Upon Policies and Programs

Many Canadians, members of a group which appears to grow larger with the passing years, have no doubt that there is a simple solution to the "housing problem". The answer is clear, "Build more housing!" This declamatory proposition must be implemented by government, preferably by all three or four levels of government existing in Canada, through a procedure of mustering the resources of the nation in the interest of meeting a significant social and economic problem.

It should be obvious to all but the least thoughtful among us, that the simple solution to the question of providing adequate and affordable housing accommodation to all individuals and families is no solution at all. The major problems of Western urbanized and industrialized societies in the last quarter of the 20th century such as housing, unemployment, inflation, the roles of young people, women and the elderly, whether within or outside the labour force, are so complex that the ready dictum, "Let government handle it!" is an irresponsible denial of individual and social responsibility.

In the field of housing the situation is even more complicated than in certain other fields, such as the provision of health and social services, because absolutely contrary arguments are put forward with equal vigor by self-interested groups. The previously stated argument that governments can and will solve the problem of supplying housing for all if it were made a priority for public policy, is matched by the equally simplistic view that government is the major cause of the problem and should get out of the field entirely leaving the matter to private enterprise for solution.

The fact is there are several major constraints (and a host of minor ones) to the implementation of housing policies stated either by public or private entrepreneurs; and these forces apply almost equally to the projected efforts of both public and private intervention in the housing market. In the first instance, there are the traditional factors of production – land, labour, materials and money – which significantly constrain the supply side of the housing equation, with lesser and sometimes contrary influence on the demand side.[1]

Secondly, there is the whole question of public attitudes toward both housing policies and the programs which are developed to attain policy objectives. Twenty years ago it would have been substantially correct to argue that the members of the general public – whether individually reached or influenced by the media – were primarily concerned with the whole question of *public* intervention, including legislation, policy formulation and program development. This is no longer the case; rather, the pressures of individuals and small groups in both neighbourhoods and larger areas have been directed increasingly during the past decade toward the modification or outright rejection of housing policies, programs and developments initiated by *private* entrepreneurs.

Similarly, it would have been reasonable to argue two decades ago that elected and appointed officials at the municipal and provincial levels of government were almost unanimously dedicated to urban growth undertaken through the private market, with adherence to nominal planning controls such as subdivision approval and zoning, consistent with the approved "financial plan" and/or "official plan" of the municipality. This is no longer the position; rather, a proportion of elected and appointed officials in all levels of government are dedicated to a philosophy of "no-growth" or what is sometimes called "a conservor society". This group of persons has been far more influential than its numbers would suggest, by virtue of the qualities of literacy, devotion to principle and hard work evident in their efforts to ensure the maintenance of "a steady state" in urban development. The control of entrepreneurial activity by the enactment of new legislation, by the strengthening of existing legislation, and by administrative decisions based upon strict interpretation of the regulations, have proved to be powerful constraints in the 1970s.

Each of these important factors at work in our society, whether implicit within the factors of production or within the emotional and behavioural components of people's reactions to both policies and programs deserve full treatment in a descriptive analysis of housing policies. In the case of certain aspects, such as land, full-scale books have recently been published. There are, however, constraints upon an author with wider objectives than the intensity of specialized analysis. These subjects will, therefore, receive attention in the full recognition that far more might be said and indeed could be stated.

LAND AND HOUSING POLICIES

The subject of land, its availability, price, and servicing for urban development, has been under examination for at least two centuries. Adam Smith wrote,

> As soon as the land of any country has all become private property, the landlords, like all other men, love to reap where they never sowed, and demand a rent even for its produce.[2]

Perhaps the explanation lies in the fact, apparently obvious but recently restated by Blumenfeld, that "raw" land is not "produced", but a "free gift of nature".[3]

The availability and price of land for housing has occupied the attention of politicians, policy analysts, urban planners, individual and corporate building entrepreneurs, land speculators and almost everyone who aspires to acquire affordable housing in a nation which will have an estimated population of 30,655,500 in the year 2001, some 80 per cent of whom will reside in twelve metropolitan areas.[4] The clear implication is that the supply of land suitable for urban development is severely limited. For many observers, this fact is sufficient to explain the entire phenomenon of rapidly increasing lot prices in Canada's Census Metropolitan Areas. As stated before, the simple answer is insufficient; nor is it acceptable to point to pressures of housing demand upon the relatively fixed supply of land.

CMHC has maintained statistical data concerning the components of housing costs since 1961 for NHA bungalows.[5] There was little change to 1970 in Halifax, Montreal, Winnipeg and Edmonton but in Toronto the proportion of land cost to total cost rose from 29 to 35 per cent, and in Vancouver from 22 to 28 per cent.[6] The most recent data reveal that land costs for single-detached dwellings financed under the NHA doubled between 1971 and 1976 and increased a further 18.8 per cent through 1978.[7]

The rise in land prices, evident to every would-be home purchaser, became a major concern of Canadians in the 1970s, a focus for a good deal of technical research, and an inspiration for many innovative schemes launched through governmental legislation designed to stabilize at least, or reduce at best, the cost of land. Nevertheless, it became a well-advertised fact by the late 1970s that in the metropolitan area of Toronto, as well as in other growth areas such as Vancouver, Edmonton and Calgary, the cost of the lot in the price of new homes was equal to or greater than the cost of the house itself.

Land is in some ways an esoteric subject for consideration in a study of housing policies. This is not only because of different approaches taken by academic economists on the one hand[8] and private developers on the other, but because of the great confusion surrounding the concept of public land banking. The controversies about the nature and importance of land as a component in housing costs have ensured that none of the major literary contributions to Canadian housing and urban affairs in recent years have neglected the subject, at least in some of its ramifications. In his major report on urban Canada, Harvey Lithwick reviewed what he called "urban policy" in seven selected Canadian cities. His major interest was the projection of future urban growth and development and the policies which should be adopted to attain these goals.[9] Inevitably, his report directed attention to the impact of population projections upon housing demand and thus upon the supply of land for housing and other urban purposes.

As far as Metropolitan Toronto is concerned, Lithwick noted that available raw land within the political boundaries of Metro was not sufficient to provide new private family housing much beyond 1975 – in any event "there is none available within the reach of four-fifths of the population."[10] To quote a report of the Metropolitan Toronto Planning Board dated September 17, 1969:

> Proper sites for public family housing in Metropolitan Toronto are already nearly exhausted, while the demand continues to increase. To satisfy Metropolitan Toronto's request for 35,000 new units between 1971-1981, the Ontario Housing Corporation which has already agreed to the request will undoubtedly be forced to seek sites in the community outside Metropolitan Toronto. Metropolitan Toronto, in fact, depends on the urban land resources of the entire Toronto community to meet its public housing needs.[11]

In a research monograph in the *Urban Canada* series published a year later, I. Lithwick and his colleagues devoted attention to the spatial implications of Canada's urban future. Their statistical estimate for the three largest metropolitan areas – Montreal, Toronto and Vancouver – suggested a housing "demand"[12] between 1971 and 2001 of more than two and one-half million dwelling units. In terms of land this means

> a crude minimum estimate based on past high densities of 6,000 persons per square mile suggests an additional 400 square miles and a maximum of 650 square miles added to Toronto's land area alone. Similar amounts withheld for Montreal, and Vancouver would require between 125 and 250 square miles. It is impossible to estimate directly

the impact of these space requirements on land prices, although they will make our past trends seem flat by comparison. The secondary effects will be even more significant, since the competing demands for urban space lie at the heart of the full range of urban problems.[13]

The complexities of the politics, economics and administration of land have rarely been analysed more intensively than in two Canadian studies published in recent years. The Advisory Task Force on Housing Policy, appointed by the Government of Ontario in November 1972, commissioned a series of relevant investigations and published a working paper on land which has had a significant impact on provincial policies in the broad fields of housing and urban development.[14]

A second study, prepared by Peter Spurr for Central Mortgage and Housing Corporation, remains the most detailed available statistical analysis of "land and urban development" on a national scale.[15] This study had a very different impact than the Report of the Ontario Advisory Task Force because it was based upon a philosophy clearly explicated by the author[16] and because it was not published by CMHC. The publisher has argued that "months of public pressure" and a personal intervention by the Minister of State for Urban Affairs led to its release for private publication.[17] Moreover, the Spurr Report, as it came to be known, led many reviewers, analysts, and politicians to espouse an argument concerning "the land problem" which took the form of a theory of conspiracy.

In Ontario where the cost of building lots has escalated significantly since 1961, the task force posed the issue in a form which can be clearly understood.

> Without land, there can be no housing. New housing, housing re-development, community and commercial facilities supporting housing development all use land. Most of the housing development and redevelopment occur now in urban areas, so that the main issue concerns urban or urbanizing land. Equally, however, the satisfactory provision of land for urban purposes implies the suitable conservation of land for non-urban purposes.[18]

The research undertaken for this study showed that land costs had consistently increased at a higher rate since 1961 in all major urban areas of the province. In twelve cities which accounted for over 60 per cent of the population of Ontario, increases in land costs for houses ranged from 61 to 341 per cent during the decade ending 1971, while the cost of labour doubled and the prices of materials in housing construction rose just 45 per cent.[19] This discussion illustrates one of the analytical approaches which, in its various dimensions, cause confusion in the public mind. I refer to the several ways in which increased land prices may be viewed.

There are at least three sets of data which may be examined. First of all, there is the price of a serviced building lot in dollar terms.[20] Figures published by the task force as well as by Spurr clearly show a doubling or even tripling of the dollar price of a house lot in many Canadian cities from 1965 through 1973,[21] on top of a steady but much slower increase in such prices during the early 1960s. As far as the home buyer is concerned, it is the total price of the house including the lot which concerns him. It became widely understood that, cæteris paribus, an adequate house could be constructed in the mid-1970s for a reasonable price in most metropolitan areas, but the total purchase price was greatly influenced by the incredible rise in the price of the land.[22]

The second approach to the impact of land cost is derived by calculating the percentage of the total cost of a new house accounted for by land cost. As late as 1971 the latter represented between 20 to 40 per cent of the cost of a new house, but by 1973, in the metropolitan area of Toronto it accounted for over 50 per cent of the cost.[23] The socio-economic significance of this trend was expressed forcefully in the working paper.

> If for social reasons government action is required to deal with the effects of high land costs, then it is held that subsidies are in order for those who need them. As long as land costs constituted a lesser proportion of land development costs, this matter was not a public issue. When half the cost of a new house goes for the land, it becomes a matter of public debate.[24]

Spurr confirmed in his analysis the fact that there was substantial stability in the proportion of land costs to total housing cost throughout Canada during the years 1965-69. In the early 1970s, and particularly after 1973, there was a marked increase in this percentage. He emphasized that ". . . it is apparent that lot prices have escalated more rapidly than have house or total housing prices."[25]

The third method of examining the impact of land price involves a breakdown of the components of monthly ownership costs. At any point in time it is possible to describe the so-called typical new house in a particular Canadian metropolitan area and to analyse the proportion of monthly occupancy costs attributable to land, mortgage money, labour, materials, and other costs such as property taxes, fuel prices, and insurance rates. For the Ontario Advisory Task Force, Barnard Associates analysed the change in these components due to cost increases for the period 1967 – 1971, in twelve major Ontario cities.

In seven of these cities the percentage change due to rising land costs was the most important factor in the analysis. For example, in Toronto 41 per cent of the increase in monthly ownership costs was attributable to rising land prices; for Hamilton the figure was 37 per cent, and for Kitchener, it was 31 per cent. In Ottawa, London, Thunder Bay and Sault Ste. Marie the cost of mortgage money due to rising interest rates was the most significant component over the decade. In none of the twelve cities was the cost of materials most important, but in the case of Ottawa the "other" category, literally a combination of many sub-factors, was as important as the cost of mortgage money.[26]

Any member of the general public can be forgiven if these varied analyses tend to cause confusion. All that we know is that the prices of new or old houses in most urban areas have reached levels which seem astronomical in comparison with the past, even after allowing for increases in the general level of prices and wage rates. Nevertheless, we seek to understand the cause of these phenomena and to discover, if we can, the sequential nature of the economic and social events. Spurr points out that these empirical analyses raise a central question in land policy, that is, "What causes what, land price or house price?"

> Most people wrongly consider that lot prices are independent of house prices and thus high land prices are determinants of high house prices. Certainly, the cost of land and other production costs constitute the minimum price a builder would charge for a house. Moreover, as both house and lot prices are increasing quickly and the proportion of total housing price which pays for the lot is also climbing, people often conclude that the lot prices are pushing up the price of housing. Once this conceptual separation of the two prices are made, it becomes logical to conclude that lot producers (land developers) and the lot production process (involving producers and many government bodies) can control lot prices by direct manipulation and supply manipulation, respectively. Thus this conceptual distinction is at the heart of notions that lot prices can be controlled or lowered by interventions in the production process."[27]

Clearly, it is government which most people call upon to intervene. The Ontario Advisory Task Force made a detailed analysis of the provincial role in land supply and pointed out that the province of Ontario (and, by implication, all Canadian provinces) has a number of highly significant responsibilities bearing on the use of the land. These responsibilities range all the way from policies relating to environmental considerations and the power to expropriate land for public purposes, to provincial control over municipal borrowing, financial assistance for educational and community services and ultimate local government functions.[28]

The analysis concluded that provincial governments have the authority and sufficient powers to shape and time land development, but as far as Ontario is concerned, the provincial role in land supply had been ambivalent as the province had played only a minimal role in supply but a strong role in land use (which inevitably affects land supply). The provincial government was identified as an unwitting abettor of a land crisis by permitting land supply to be determined by two land demand forces – public land use considerations and a private land development market – without any conscious policy concerning land supply as such.[29]

The major impact of the task force in this area of concern was the initiation of an Ontario Housing Action Program by the new Ministry of Housing within the very month of its formation, October 1973. Professor Eli Comay, who chaired the inquiry, was appointed to stimulate housing production in ten high-growth areas in Ontario. Private developers and builders would receive mortgages for up to 95 per cent of the house price at a below-market rate of interest provided that the houses were priced for families of moderate and low income.[30]

The province agreed to provide interest-free loans to regional municipalities for major services for land development and to local municipalities for storm sewerage. Furthermore, the ministry would provide a direct unconditional grant to the local municipality (to offset possible increased municipal taxes) for every building created under the federal-provincial OHAP agreement. Local councils were further encouraged to determine the potential for new house-building through policy studies which would be financed with grants up to $100,000. Municipal councils were encouraged to process development proposals quickly and to determine local conditions of approval. These councils were to sign agreements with the ministry to ensure that services and facilities for the OHAP housing would be provided. For their part, building developers were required to provide 10 per cent of their units within the HOME income range and at least an additional 30 per cent for families with incomes up to $20,000.[31]

LAND BANKING

The Ontario Advisory Task Force defined land banking as ". . . the public assembly of large and small parcels of land, over short- or long-term use, for residential or other development purposes."[32] The major contribution of the Spurr Report, defined by the author himself as "the primary subject matter of the entire report", is a detailed examination of public land assembly programs, their goals, activities, and the many issues which surround them.[33] Nevertheless, this report attracted most public attention for its statistical revelations of private developers' land holdings within major metropolitan regions throughout Canada. From the private organization's point of view, land banking cannot simply be considered as "public assembly" because, surely, the private entrepreneur must plan ahead through forward purchase of the basic commodity upon which both his product and his ultimate profit rest.

Spurr's analysis of private land holdings encompassed six regional studies (Ottawa-Hull, Toronto, Kitchener-Waterloo, Winnipeg, Edmonton and Vancouver).[34] This research revealed that thousands of acres were located in corporate land holdings with substantial concentrations in the hands of a few development organizations in most regions. In the Toronto region, for example, a little less than 82 per cent of the total acreage was held by seven organizations; within this total four firms held 58.65 per cent of the total acreage.[35] Information of this sort, together with analyses of land development within the private sector, led a number of journalists to enunciate "a conspiracy theory", as suggested earlier in this chapter.

The argument ran as follows: the concentration of land holdings by a relatively few large development organizations in Canadian metropolitan areas was primarily in restraint of trade and the strengthening of oligopolistic firms in the housing market. Such vast land holdings would be released in small increments designed to maintain shortness of supply and thus to stabilize or increase high land lot prices. Needless to suggest, this was by no means the view of the development organizations who argued that they were doing no more than planning ahead one or two decades, that in any event much of their land would not be serviced for years to come, and that in fact they were ensuring a gradual rather than a catastrophic increase in the ultimate price of urban housing in the 1980s and 1990s.

The report on land and urban development did argue that developer land banks were increasing in size, value and importance. Moreover, there was no question that as the land moved "on stream" land sales yielded very high profits and provided a substantial proportion of the total revenue of most firms. A selected analysis of nine development organizations, with headquarters in seven large urban centres, revealed holdings of more than 33,000 acres, costing over $200 million but having a market value of at least two to three times its cost.[36]

Public land assembly is not inconsistent in purpose with private land banks. In both cases land is acquired in advance of its intended development, ". . . either in the sense that it is held for years before development begins, or because development follows acquisition immediately but the project is sufficiently large that it takes many years of regular construction to deplete (*sic*) the project."[37] Peter Spurr identified four distinct objectives a government body might pursue by undertaking a land assembly project and then analysed each of these objectives.[38]

(1) To reduce land costs for the ultimate consumer (i.e.: house prices).

This goal can be achieved when government buys suitable residential land, holds it until its cost is significantly lower than current prices, and then develops the site and sells it or leases it at below market prices. A case in point is the huge Malvern development in north-east Metro Toronto where 1,700 acres of raw land were acquired in the early 1950s at an average price of $900 per acre. Municipal services did not reach the Malvern area (approximately ten miles north of Lake Ontario in Scarborough) until the early 1970s. By this time, the Ontario HOME Program was in effect and building lots were leased to home buyers for five years at the "book value" then pertaining. This amount – as Malvern came into being – was at least 50 per cent below the current market value of comparable lots elsewhere in Metro Toronto.

As Spurr points out, buyers obtain one of two alternative kinds of benefits. Either they can obtain housing they could not otherwise afford *or* they can capitalize the amount of the price reduction by reselling the lot at market prices directly or by using the realized saving for other consumption. Since the federal-provincial partnership had banked the land in the first instance, no public official was ready to countenance attainment of the second kind of benefit. Thus, maximum prices were placed upon the homes to be constructed on the building lots subdivided in Malvern.[39] The land was leased for five years during which time the house could not be sold and consideration was given to the question of control over resales.[40]

In Spurr's view, the first kind of benefit is seen as a proper subsidy which goes only to families who could not buy a home without it. In practice, however, the technique raises difficult social questions. There are many families who can barely afford home ownership even with the subsidy, and may find it very difficult to maintain payments for increased taxes, rising costs of energy, and the cost of normal maintenance. These and other purchasers were likely to be in the front rank of sellers as soon as the five-year leasing period was completed. Since the Ministry of Housing had not evolved a method of controlling resales this was the experience in Malvern when many houses came on the market in late 1975 and early 1976 as the first leasing period expired.[41] Sellers made very substantial tax-free capital gains, surely a subversion of the original socio-economic purpose. The fact that these gains have been produced by public action is not lost on the general public.

(2) To control urban spatial expansion in support of planning goals, by leading or blocking the shape of a city's growth with the public land.

Some urban planners and elected representatives have viewed public land banking as a method of controlling the expansion of a city. It is reasoned that ownership of strategic acreage would impede spatial expansion in an unplanned direction or form and in particular, would block premature subdivision of raw land. Spurr considers that this form of public ownership of large acreages may be less effective and is certaintly more expensive than alternative techniques such as zoning. The exception to this conclusion would be the case where public land assembly is designed to create large greenbelts or regional parks intended to separate urban centres from rural land or recreational areas.

(3) To provide land for various social needs not met by private enterprise. One such need is low-cost land for subsidized housing projects for the elderly, public housing, and assisted ownership programs.

Governmental assembly of land for future development as public housing has been undertaken since the beginning of the 1950s by the federal government in co-operation with several provinces, and more recently by a number of provinces acting to implement their own housing policies, although supported with federal loans.[42] There are both short- and long-term instances of public activity in this regard. In many cases in Ontario, for example, municipalities have made land, which they own, available to the Ontario Housing Corporation to assist in the near-term development of social housing for senior citizens or families. In 1973, the corporation, on behalf of the government of Ontario, held almost 9,000 acres[43] and was in the process of additional acquisition, including the development of an entirely new satellite community known as North Pickering (25,000 acres).

The purchase of land well in advance of development can reduce substantially the total cost of a public housing project and thus should reduce the operational subsidies required for the half-century following occupation of the housing units. These comments apply to the case of rental housing but in situations like a vast development such as Malvern, and other large land holdings which are not yet under development, public land banking has raised difficult questions of public policy.

Whether or not government engages in land assembly, it can anticipate very strong criticisms. Those groups in the voluntary and public sectors dedicated to increase housing believe that government must plan ahead, must obtain substantial land banks, and must make this land available at or near cost in the development of socially-assisted housing both for rent and for sale. On the other hand, representative groups within the house-building industry believe that the vast public expenditures required in land assembly would be much better devoted to the servicing of land so that larger numbers of serviced lots would be available for building. In fact, at least in Ontario, the provincial government has undertaken both approaches without seriously affecting the cost of land in the form of lot prices. Both Spurr and the Ontario

Advisory Task Force agree that governmental activity has been insufficient to affect the market although it is suggested that "properly planned public land acquisition can have some effect in certain circumstances in moderating pressures on land and house prices."[44]

In 1976, as the housing market revealed substantial numbers of unsold houses in Ontario, the ministry determined to reverse the efforts of the previous quarter-century by announcing a new policy with respect to land which effectively ended some programs and presumably constrained certain social objectives – HOME was ended. Moreover, the ministry announced that it would gradually dispose of the major governmental land assemblies over a period of years. Building lots would be sold "at the lower end of the market range" in the particular communities in which such lots were located. These decisions might appear to be an acceptance of developers' viewpoints; they were not.[45] It seems apparent that the provincial government decided that its activities in land banking were, on balance, insufficiently productive. The inability to control windfall profits in the first assembly process and the inability to control resales of HOME and other development programs were important considerations in these decisions.

(4) To generate net revenue (profit) for governments.

The fourth objective identified by Peter Spurr was described as "the generation of revenue" through public land assembly projects. In reference to the banking and development of residential land, he wrote,

> As much as this is a profitable activity in the private sector, it is more profitable in the public sector as governments can achieve lower fiscal costs than their private counterparts.[46]

The decisions taken in Ontario in the late 1970s are a case in point. It is estimated that the provincial government will realize profits of $3 to $5 million per annum. As pleasant as this prospect appears, public land assemblies often involved expropriation, and previous owners have been strongly critical of the long delays in development during which the process of inflation added substantially to the "on paper" profits of government or future developers. Accordingly, the Ontario Ministry of Housing stipulated that these profits would be devoted to other housing programs in Ontario. As Spurr pointed out, in theoretical terms "the gain could be used to make the land program self-sustaining and finance development of infrastructure and other services, thereby off-setting property taxes and local improvement charges."[47]

The optimism concerning public land banking so evident in the literature and in the public debate of the past quarter-century has moderated significantly. The federal government had reserved $500 million for the five years following amendments to the NHA in 1973. Recent assessments, however, are generally pessimistic or negative.

> Despite a commitment by the federal government in 1973 to take action in the area of land, as well as similar commitments on the part of several provincial governments, the availability of lots or building sites from public land assemblies has not increased. In many market areas it has decreased. While the assembly, servicing and disposal or development of land for housing takes a long time, it is obvious that much more needs to be done through public land policies to influence or regulate the price of urban land as well as the form of urban land.[48]

No one can, of course, estimate accurately what would have happened to land prices in Canada in the absence of federal-provincial intervention in the 1960s and 1970s.

LABOUR, MATERIALS AND MONEY

In the 1950s the supply of construction labour was a cause for concern in some areas of Canada and a good deal of attention was devoted to restrictive practices of trade unions in controlling the number of apprentices in a variety of skilled building trades. This concern appeared to evaporate with the arrival in Canada of many thousands of newcomers, particularly from southern Europe, who were employed in construction labour.

By the mid-1960s attention had shifted from the supply of labour to union agreements, wage rates and the prices of certain building materials such as lumber, cement, and copper piping, which from time to time showed dramatic rises in unit prices. Once again there can be considerable confusion by virtue of the simultaneous examination of a variety of indexes, a variety of prices, a variety of wage rates for skilled tradesmen in several specialties, and a lack of knowledge concerning the proportion of increased house prices attributable to the cost of labour, materials and mortgage money.

The cost of residential construction during the years 1961-71 on a 1961 base showed increases of almost exactly 50 per cent.[49] When the base period was changed to 1971 the most recent indexes of construction costs revealed the following percentage increases by 1978 for Canada as a whole[50]:

prices of residential building materials	+ 84.0
wage rates of construction workers	+ 106.2
composite index of residential building materials and wage rates	+ 92.0
construction cost per square metre (NHA single-detached dwellings)	+ 98.9

Basic union wage rate indexes based on a 1971 index for selected trades revealed, by 1978, percentage increases of 116.7 for equipment operators, 117.8 for labourers, 104.4 for carpenters, 102.7 for cement finishers, 94.4 for bricklayers, 99.1 for plumbers, and 99.5 for electricians.[51]

Without the proportionate contribution to total price and/or cost increase through time from each of these components, it is difficult to judge the significance of labour costs as compared to the cost of materials or mortgage money as a constraint on the housing process. The figures do clearly illustrate, however, that the upward trend in all aspects of residential construction has accelerated in the 1970s.

The Barnard study for the Ontario Advisory Task Force did analyse all the reasons for change in monthly ownership costs for the years 1961-71.[52] For those years, changes in the cost of mortgage money ranged from 22 per cent of the increase in monthly occupancy cost in Windsor to as much as 29 per cent in Ottawa. The figure for Toronto was 25 per cent and the average for twelve large urban centres was 25.25 per cent.

The variation in changing costs of labour and materials was much greater. As far as labour cost was concerned, the change in monthly ownership cost due to rising wage rates was as little as 11 per cent in Ottawa and Hamilton and as high as 38 per cent in Windsor; the figure for Toronto was 15 per cent. Changes in the cost of building materials showed a wide variation ranging from 8 per cent in Ottawa, to 22 per cent in Thunder Bay and 25 per cent in Sault Ste. Marie. There does not appear to be cause for optimism that prices and wages will level off in the 1980s.

The cost of mortgage money, both in terms of the supply of available funds and the fluctuation in interest rates, has been the prime subject of several reports and numerous government studies.[53] There can be no question of the significance of the cost of home financing to the purchaser. In the 1960s interest rates rose from 7 to 10 per cent, "adding at least 20 per cent to monthly home ownership costs."[54]

In the first half of the 1970s first mortgage rates in Canada reached 12 per cent and effectively removed many moderate income families from the demand side of the housing market. In 1976-77 the Bank of Canada reduced its lending rate on several occasions so that by late 1977 first mortgages were commanding 10 per cent. By the spring of 1980 several increases resulted in rates in excess of 16 per cent. When all of the components of housing costs are taken into consideration the ultimate sale prices are far beyond the debt service capacity of perhaps two-thirds of Canadian heads of households. The familiar cry that Canadian governments must act to produce "affordable housing" was, therefore, particularly strident in the second half of the 1970s.

ADDITIONAL CONSTRAINTS

The number and variety of constraining factors in the housing market is almost infinite. Some of these aspects are within the control of government in the short run; others will involve longer term consideration and may not be resolved until the Canadian constitution is rewritten.

The controls exercised by provincial and local governments over the housing production process are a significant consideration. Provincial planning law has emerged during the past two decades as a specialized field within the discipline. Planning controls implicit within the development of "official plans", zoning, subdivision control, and, in particular, local by-laws governing the "maintenance and occupancy" of housing accommodation can be utilized either to stimulate both private and public activity in housing or, to effectively forestall such development. Building developers have complained incessantly since the initiation of the apartment boom in the early 1960s that governmental controls add years of time and thousands of dollars to the production of every dwelling unit.

The major response of municipal governments to these allegations is framed in terms of the financial disabilities of local government without home rule in a federal governmental system. Fundamentally, reliance by Canadian municipalities upon property tax is a significant consideration, they insist, in the process of housing production. The Minister of State for Urban Affairs pointed to the significance of the taxation dilemma facing local government in an important address in May 1977.

> I also think that the property tax can be a serious constraint on municipal governments . . . It is these variations in property tax burdens, caused by differences in the tax capacities of municipalities and in the ability of Canadians to pay property taxes . . . which I think serve(s) to reduce the ability of certain municipal governments to raise the revenues necessary to provide adequate levels of public services to their electorates.
>
> If a municipality levies a residential property tax at above average rates, the cost of shelter services will be higher in that community relative to the price in other communities. If a community levies a higher than average non-residential property tax, investments in factory buildings and other assets subjects to the property tax will be less profitable than elsewhere . . . What is of major concern to me is that Canadians living in communities with low taxable capacities find that their access to community facilities and the quality of their community and neighbourhood can only be met with tax burdens significantly greater than those faced by other Canadians.[55]

The fact is that the pressure on elected representatives is designed to stabilize such tax burdens rather than to increase them, with the clear result that many local areas have a much lower quality of community and neighbourhood than others.

The most subtle of all constraints on housing supply in Canada is difficult to pinpoint with accuracy. I refer to the whole question of attitudes on the part of Canadians toward the supply of housing in several respects. Attitudinal behaviour toward housing supply ranges all the way from resistance to "public housing", such as rental housing for low income families or housing for purchase by moderate income families, to private activity which appears to attract urban growth. These attitudinal sets which merit further explanation are the subject of the following chapter.

NOTES

[1]Shortages among the factors of production, such as mortgage funds, resulting in higher prices, have occasionally stimulated demand rather than depressed it. This has occurred because of the fear that house prices and rents will rise even more, a fear exploited openly by the real estate industry.

[2]Adam Smith, *The Wealth of Nations*, 1776, edited by Edwin Cannan, (New York: Random House, The Modern Library Edition, 1937) p. 49. In an edition in 1814, Buchanan agreed with Smith's observation but noted that "other men love also to reap where they never sowed, but the landlords alone, it would appear, succeed in so desirable an object." (Vol. 1, p. 80).

[3]Hans Blumenfeld, "Land Control and Land Prices", *Community Planning Review*, (Ottawa: Community Planning Association of Canada, February 1977) Vol. 27, No. 2, p. 1.

[4]Statistics Canada, *Population Projections for Canada and the Provinces, 1972-2001* (Ottawa: Information Canada, 1974) Table 6.2, Projection B (medium fertility), p. 61; and A. Goracz, I. Lithwick and L. O. Stone, *The Urban Future*, Research Monograph 5 (Ottawa: Central Mortgage and Housing Corporation, 1971) Table II, Method N4, p. 30. The latter projections of total population in CMA's include about half of the metropolitan areas recognized in the census.

[5]For Canada as a whole, bungalows accounted for 75 per cent of all NHA single-detached dwellings over the decade 1961-70. In Toronto, however, the proportion was about 35 per cent for the same period. Dennis and Fish, *op. cit.*, pp. 78-79. These data revealed that the ratio of land costs as a percentage of total costs for Canada as a whole, increased by only one percentage point (from 17 to 18 per cent) during the years 1961-70. Lithwick, however, lists the increase in land costs 1964-68 at 19.3 per cent. See N. H. Lithwick, *Urban Canada* (Ottawa: CMHC, December 1970) p. 21.

[6]Dennis and Fish, *ibid.*, p. 79.

[7]Central Mortgage and Housing Corporation, *Canadian Housing Statistics*, 1978, Table 112, p. 92. Using 1971 as a base equalling 100, the index for

1961 was just 56.7; for 1976 it had reached 201.0 and by 1978, 239.0. Similar data were not published for the metropolitan areas.

[8]L. B. Smith, "Housing in Canada," *Urban Canada,* Research Monograph 2 (Ottawa: Central Mortgage and Housing Corporation, January 1971) pp. 31-37.

[9]N. H. Lithwick, "Problems and Prospects," *Urban Canada* (Ottawa: Central Mortgage and Housing Corporation, December 1970) pp. 186-191.

[10]*Ibid.,* p. 187.

[11]Metropolitan Toronto Planning Board, September 17, 1969. At the time, Lithwick wrote, the OHC received an annual request from Metro's Social Services and Housing Committee for a specific number of public housing dwellings for families. Metro itself was responsible for public housing units for senior citizens. OHC responded to these annual requests, sometimes projected over a five- or ten-year period, through a variety of techniques which, by the mid-1970s resulted in a portfolio of more than 30,000 dwelling units under direct management.

[12]The authors did not mean "effective" demand but simply the requirements based upon statistical projections of increasing numbers of families and non-family households.

[13]A. Goracz, I. Lithwick, and L. O. Stone, *The Urban Future,* Research Monograph, No. 5 (Ottawa: Central Mortgage and Housing Corporation, January 1971) p. 118.

[14]Ontario Advisory Task Force on Housing Policy, *Land for Housing,* Working Paper C (Toronto: Queen's Printer, June 1973) pp. 67.

[15]Peter Spurr, *Land and Urban Development: A Preliminary Study* (Toronto: James Lorimer and Co., 1976) pp. 437.

[16]Spurr expressed his personal belief that the relationship between Canadians and urban land is essentially exploitative. Land is space, space has become "owned" and a method for obtaining significant financial gains. He considers urban development to resemble an "excessive machine", consuming enormous and increasing volumes of energy and other resources which he describes as a horrendous, deliberate, short-term exploitation of this planet. *op. cit.,* pp. 8-11.

[17]See back cover of 1976 paper edition.

[18]Ontario Advisory Task Force on Housing Policy, *Land for Housing,* p. 1.

[19]*Ibid.,* Appendix, Table 1, p. 62. These data were developed by Peter Barnard Associates in a commissioned report entitled, *Developments in the Cost, Supply and Need for Housing in Ontario,* April 1973.

[20]"Serviced" lot, as defined by the task force, is land with water supply, sewer lines leading to treatment plants, and roads suitable for cars, trucks and buses. In addition, urban land for housing must include school sites and other community facilities.

[21]Ontario Advisory Task Force on Housing Policy, *op. cit.,* p. 2, and Table 3, p. 64. See also Spurr, *op. cit.,* Table 2.0, p. 15.

[22]The task force reported that in the Metropolitan Toronto area the average price of a serviced lot in March 1973 at $22,000 represented an increase of about 100 per cent over the previous year. Within three years this price exceeded $30,000.

[23]Peter Barnard Associates, *op. cit.*, pp. 12-13.

[24]Ontario Advisory Task Force on Housing Policy, *op. cit.*, p. 31.

[25]Spurr, *op. cit.*, p. 21, and Table 2.2, p. 20.

[26]Ontario Advisory Task Force on Housing Policy, *op. cit.*, Table 2, p. 63.

[27]Spurr, *op. cit.*, p. 21-22.

[28]Ontario Advisory Task Force on Housing Policy, *op. cit.*, pp. 29-30.

[29]*Ibid.*, p. 30.

[30]The income ranges were those pertaining to the HOME Plan, with differential income limits for the various areas.

[31]Ontario Ministry of Housing, "Housing Programmes in Ontario", *Housing Ontario* Vol. 20, No. 1, (January – February 1976) p. 11.

[32]Ontario Advisory Task Force on Housing Policy, *Land for Housing*, p. 39.

[33]Spurr, *op. cit.*, p. xvi.

[34]Spurr, *op cit.*, pp. 81-182, *passim.*

[35]*Ibid.*, Table 3.5, p. 112.

[36]Spurr, *op. cit.*, pp. 239-241.

[37]Spurr, *op. cit.*, p. 246.

[38]*Ibid.*, pp. 246-257.

[39]This was true, of course, in all HOME Programs.

[40]In extenuating circumstances, such as the transfer of the householder to a new job in another community, the individual owner was required to appeal directly to the Board of Ontario Housing Corporation for permission to sell. There have been very few such appeals and some were denied because it appeared that the owner's objective was the realization of a capital gain. In the few cases where permission was granted, stringent financial controls were exercised; the land lease was transformed to the new owner at the original terms.

[41]Perhaps the only way to exercise such control would be a stipulation that houses must be resold to a government organization at a fair market value, excluding an increase in land cost.

[42]The most recent annual reports of several provincial housing corporations indicate substantial interest and activity in public land banking. The Manitoba Housing and Renewal Corporation, for example, had land banked 4,717 acres including 3,554 in the Winnipeg area by the end of 1975. Manitoba Housing and Renewal Corporation, *Annual Report*, 1974-75 (Winnipeg: Queen's Printer, February 1976) p. 6.

[43]Ontario Advisory Task Force on Housing Policy, *Report* (Toronto: Queen's Printer, August 1973) p. 39. In the spring of 1977 the amount of land controlled by the Ministry of Housing and the Ontario Housing Corporation was listed at 23,000 acres. (*Housing Ontario*, Vol. 21, No. 3, March/April 1977) p. 15.

[44]Ontario Advisory Task Force on Housing Policy, *Report* (Toronto: Queen's Printer, August 1973) p. 49.

[45]In a series of speeches in March 1977, the Minister of Housing, John Rhodes, stated that his ministry would sell land sufficient for 3,000 to 4,000 "land units" per year depending upon demand. Land units are defined as single lots, semi-detached lots, or blocks of land on which a specific number of residential units will be built. The minister emphasized that serviced land would be marketed to the building industry for the construction of no-frill, modest homes which must qualify under AHOP assistance. *Housing Ontario*, *op. cit.*, p. 16.

[46]Spurr, *op. cit.*, p. 253.

[47]Spurr, *op. cit.*, p. 255.

[48]Canadian Council on Social Development, *A Review of Canadian Social Housing Policy* (Ottawa: CCSD, January 1977) p. 163-164.

[49]Statistics Canada, *National Income and Expenditure Accounts* (Ottawa: Statistics Canada, Cat. 13-001, 1971).

[50]Central Mortgage and Housing Corporation, *Canadian Housing Statistics 1978*, Table 110, p. 91.

[51]*Ibid.*, Table III, p. 91.

[52]Peter Barnard Associates, *op. cit.*, *Land for Housing* (Ontario Advisory Task Force on Housing Policy, June 1973) Vol. 2, Table 2, p. 63. Their findings on land cost have previously been reported in this chapter.

[53]L. B. Smith, "The Canadian Housing and Mortgage Markets", *Bank of Canada Staff Research Studies*, 1970, pp. 110.

[54]Ontario Advisory Task Force on Housing Policy, *Report* (Toronto: Queen's Printer, August 1973) p. 35.

[55]Canada, Ministry of State for Urban Affairs, Remarks by the Honourable Andre Ouellet to the Annual Meeting, Canadian Federation of Municipalities (Toronto, May 18, 1977) pp. 5-6.

CHAPTER 8

Housing for Low-Income Families: The Importance of Attitudes

Public housing projects are seen as particularly burdensome since they generally require municipal cost-sharing and may, in addition, bring social and other problems into a community. New housing of all types generates short-term demands and long-term commitments for municipal expenditures on physical services, transportation facilities, schools, and the full range of human services. Although the federal and provincial levels of government sometimes subsidize the provision of these services, and developers in many instances provide physical services, it is easy to understand how municipalities may decide to discourage further residential growth in times of restraint. Such a policy may be adopted even though its social implications are recognized to be great.[1]

For more than a century, in Western industrial nations, there has been particular concern about the housing conditions of persons and families who were attracted to the new employment opportunities consequent upon the industrial revolution. In Great Britain and Western Europe the thrust toward improved housing conditions was led by public health doctors and other professionals in the health care field and by so-called social reformers and social workers. These pioneers in housing reform had one substantial argument no longer applicable in advanced western countries – the danger of widespread infectious disease. In Great Britain and Western Europe it was possible to point to past outbreaks of cholera, typhoid, smallpox and even the bubonic plague, and to emphasize that the entire community was potentially threatened by recurrent epidemics associated with inadequate housing conditions and inadequate sanitation within rapidly expanding urban areas.

Fear is a pre-eminent additional force and certainly not without powerful effect in influencing the passage of legislation intended to overcome the worst evils of "slum living". The statistical associations between poor health and poor housing, between the incidence of crime and poor housing, between mental illness and poor housing, between family breakdown and poor housing, were not difficult to demonstrate.[2] Nevertheless, progress in the enactment of laws restraining perpetuation of the most inadequate housing conditions could not be expected to overcome the basic problem, namely poverty.

In the decade following World War One, North America emerged as an "island of prosperity" in the midst of serious economic difficulties throughout Western Europe and the rest of the world. When the Depression struck the United States and Canada with full force in 1931, these nations were ill-equipped to deal not only with unemployment and consequent poverty, but with the enormous impact of these manifestations upon housing conditions. A good many families lost their homes when they could not meet the mortgage payments and/or local tax levies. A great many former homeowners thus became tenants and characteristically, tenants have very little choice in periods of either great depression or great prosperity.

In those years, however, the view emerged in Canada that unemployment was not the responsibility of the individual worker in a worldwide economic depression, and thus the miserable housing conditions of hundreds of thousands of households were a consequence of their lack of employment and income, and not due to their lack of thrift or good management. This acceptance of a more reasonable attitude toward poor people was by no means universal but it did penetrate the legislative chambers of the federal government and to some degree those of the provincial governments. Moreover, at the local level there were active reform movements with the objective of improving the housing conditions in such cities as Vancouver, Winnipeg, Toronto, Montreal and Halifax. Groups of concerned persons and associations made some headway during the 1930s but were forced to wait until the post-Second World War years to achieve objectives which were often enunciated in the 1920s and particularly in the early-1930s.

The years 1945-49 were critical in Canadian housing history. A movement had developed toward housing reform, a concept which encompassed physical and social planning, the improvement of transportation facilities and a variety of community improvements. Implicit within all these objectives was the clear drive toward slum clearance, visualized as a simple program whereby the worst housing would be eliminated and those who lived within it would be rehoused in physically and socially adequate housing accommodation. Those who strove for such accomplishments were unaware of the strong resistance they would encounter and the attitudes of a substantial proportion of the general public toward their activities. They were soon disabused of their innocence.

The early struggles towards urban redevelopment, particularly in Vancouver and Toronto, were strongly opposed by organizations of home builders, boards of trade, chambers of commerce, associations of ratepayers and/or home-owners, and a variety of groups which alleged that public intervention in these matters was a form of "communism" at worst, "creeping socialism" at best. Other opponents to public housing who were members of social, charitable and religious organizations viewed the provision of public housing as "immoral". In their view, there was something different about the provision of housing for persons from the provision of food, clothing and medical care for those who could not afford to meet their own needs.

More than forty years later these sets of attitudes have by no means disappeared. In the meantime, the society has become "affluent", in the sense that a far greater proportion of Canadians have substantially greater incomes and greater purchasing power than would have been conceived possible in 1945. Most Canadians, even those in poverty, abound with physical possessions – stoves, refrigerators, television sets, automobiles, electrical appliances of one sort or another – which were generally restricted before World War II to the few fortunate wealthy. The onset of affluence has not, however, made the lot of the poor more pleasant or more socially accepted. Rather, in a so-called affluent society, those individuals and families who are unable to provide adequate housing accommodation with their own resources are less accepted than in the years when the great majority of Canadians were not relatively well-off.

Programs of public intervention in housing just before and following World War Two rested upon the basic concept that it was desirable for the state to ensure adequate housing accommodation for certain individuals and families, not merely to protect the great majority of citizens from the threat of crime and disease but because the costs of slum dwelling had to be inevitably met by expenditures for social services, health services, correctional services, and the protection of persons and property. It seemed logical for government to create housing at rentals or prices which could be "afforded" by the poorest families, with the full knowledge that the difference between the costs of construction and the capacity to pay of those needing accommodation – the "subsidy" – would have to be met by the taxpayers of all levels of government. Those who required such subsidization were quickly seen by the general public as "those people" who required assistance by comparison with other people who managed with their own resources.

The stigma attributed to the residents of public housing was prevalent from the very beginning of efforts towards slum clearance in Canada and the United States. Those persons who had struggled to meet their own problems with their own resources resented those who required and received assistance. The latter group were generally perceived as poor, shiftless, and immoral. Attitudes towards those who require assistance have not changed much in more than four decades. Those families who are the prime applicants for socially-assisted housing accommodation are the focus of disrepute, resentment and a whole set of negative attitudes which set them apart from other Canadian families.

THE CHANGING POSITION OF THE FAMILY WITHIN HOUSING POLICY

During the years from the early 1930s through the late 1960s, the concept of the family appeared to assume a position of centrality within both public (governmental) and private (market) housing policies. The origin of this emphasis was both economic and social. In the depths of the Great Depression, in both the United States and Canada, unemployment among workers in the construction trades was extremely high as the decline in housing building from 1929 through 1933 was incredibly steep. In terms of the economy, stimulation of housing construction appeared to have substantial favourable consequences.

On the social side it had been apparent to many voluntary groups and governmental organizations that a substantial proportion of families in both urban and rural locations in North America were living in what could only be described as slums. Thus the early efforts in the United States to build housing through the Public Works Administration and to improve existing housing through the Works Progress Administration were to some degree the economic and social sides of the same housing coin.[3] Similar objectives were implicit in Canada's enactment of the Dominion Housing Act, 1935, and the National Housing Acts of 1938 and 1944.

In those years, there was little or no doubt that the beneficiary of housing policies and programs ought to be "the family", defined as two parents with one or more dependent children and perhaps one or more persons related by blood or marriage, living together in the same household. These arrangements were considered both the normal and desirable state of social development within the society. Since the proportion of persons over age 65 was less than 6 per cent, the housing requirements of the elderly were not considered to have the same priority. Similarly, since there was little or no sympathy for the unmarried mother who wished to retain her child or for the separated or divorced person with responsibility for dependent children, little or no thought was given to the housing requirements of these groups. Rather, the twin thrusts of economic benefit resulting from increased activity in housing construction and social benefit consequent upon the re-housing of disadvantaged families from the most inadequate housing, were considered the top, if not the only, policy priorities.

During the 1970s, these emphases were altered. The reasons for a shift away from the centrality of the family within housing policy toward other priorities are both economic and social in origin. Economic problems of the 1970s in North America – simultaneous unemployment and inflation – were very different from those of the pre-war period. Moreover, the social circumstances in which a great many family units or households now find themselves are quite different from those which were the norm in the pre-war period. Whatever the explanation, there can be little doubt that the family, and particularly the low-income family, has lost its position of highest priority within public and private housing policies.

A "family of low income" is defined in the National Housing Act[4] as a family that receives a total family income that, in the opinion of CMHC, is insufficient to permit it to rent housing accommodation adequate for its needs at current rentals in the area in which the family lives. In several of the major legislative acts passed by the governments of the provinces in recent years, this definition has been expanded to include the possibility of purchasing as well as renting housing. It is significant that the federal definition does not include this concept which seems to imply that families of low income are expected to be tenants rather than home owners. Paradoxically, a good many of the federal-provincial housing programs initiated in the 1970s were intended to enable families with quite modest incomes to assume the responsibilities of home ownership.

THE HOUSING CONDITIONS OF CANADIAN FAMILIES

In Canada's written presentation to Habitat (The United Nations Conference on Human Settlements) in June 1976, a considerable degree of justifiable satisfaction was expressed officially. The presentation on "Shelter" began:

By any standard, Canadians are among the best-housed people in the world. For example, in 1971, only 2.7 per cent of all Canadian dwellings lacked piped water and the average number of persons per room was perhaps the lowest in the world at just 0.7. Some 60 per cent of all dwellings were single-detached houses. A similar percentage were occupant-owned. The level of household amenities was remarkably high.[5]

Canada does have generally a high-quality stock. The average number of rooms per dwelling in 1971 was 5.4, a slight increase from 1961.[6] The proportion of crowded dwellings (defined as dwellings in which the number of persons exceeds the number of rooms) has dropped from 18.8 per cent in 1951 to 16.5 per cent in 1961 and 9.4 per cent in 1971.[7] This fortunate reduction in crowding is in part a reflection of an increase in the size of new houses but is due also to the decreasing size of the Canadian family.

An examination of all the traditional housing indicators conceals significant regional variations. For example, although less than 3 per cent of all Canadian dwellings lacked piped water, the figure in 1971 for the Prairie provinces was 8 per cent.[8] In the same year in the Atlantic provinces, 27 per cent of occupied dwellings lacked exclusive use of a bath or shower compared with only 3.6 per cent in the province of Ontario.[9] Approximately 500,000 dwelling units in Canada (about 8 per cent of the total stock) lacked basic facilities in 1971, that is, an indoor toilet, running water, a bath or shower.[10] Most of these dwellings are in rural areas or smaller urban centres. Very often the situation is due to a lack of municipal water and sewage systems outside the traditional built-up areas. The Canadian presentation to Habitat noted, however, that "the other major factor is poverty."

> In 1971, over 25 per cent of "low-income" families occupied dwellings without bath facilities. Poor people also tend to occupy old dwellings. Of households earning less than $4,000 in 1971, some 40 per cent owned houses built before 1940.[11]

"Low income", in this context, consisted of families with incomes below a threshold for each family size, implying that those urban families falling below these figures must spend at least 70 per cent of total income for food, shelter and clothing. This measure is acknowledged to be crude and somewhat arbitrary. In recent years, a family is considered to be "low income" when its income is somewhere between 50 and 56 per cent of the national average, with adjustments made for community size.[12]

The most recent major study of housing conditions in Canada was undertaken in 1974 by CMHC in conjunction with Statistics Canada.[13] This survey is described by the corporation as "the most detailed study of housing ever done in Canada." The overall impression conveyed by a brief summary of a 23-volume survey of housing units is captured in the following paragraph.

> The basic picture that emerges is that by almost any measure Canadians in the urban part of the country are well housed. The majority of the stock is less than 25 years old, is of good quality, has most of the facilities generally considered necessary, and provides a relatively high average amount of space per person. Some problems of distribution are apparent in specific cities, however, and gaining access to adequate housing apparently imposes a high financial burden on some special groups. In addition, although most Canadians are well housed, some are spending a large part of their income on shelter.[14]

This summary reinforces the view of most Canadians that, with the exception of a very tight market in such cities as Toronto, Ottawa and Vancouver, Canadians do not face a housing crisis. Moreover, the dividing line between the so-called "high financial burden" and an appropriate proportion of income to shelter cost is 25 per cent. Since a large proportion of Canadian home-owners and tenants who have acquired accommodation within their own resources have, at one time or another, and sometimes for long periods, devoted more than 25 per cent of their gross income to shelter cost, this argument will fail to change the attitudinal position of most who will read the results of the survey.

In terms of the adequacy of the Canadian housing stock the 1974 survey was designed to overcome enumerator bias by eliminating judgments of physical condition through the preparation and checking of a list of eleven undesirable characteristics. These were later combined into an overall measure of "good, fair, and poor" according to the nature of the fault.[15] Nearly 90 per cent of the 3.3 million housing units surveyed were judged to be in good external condition, only about 8 per cent were classed as poor, and less than 3 per cent as fair. In absolute terms this means that about 350,000 dwelling units only, were rated as poor or fair.

Although it is clear that serious problems continue, the general impression of the 1974 survey (in which all twenty-three census areas were included) is the most satisfactory picture of Canadian housing stock that has emerged throughout the forty years in which housing conditions were surveyed as a part of the decennial census. Renters were more than twice as likely as owners to be living in poor housing conditions – nearly 12 per cent of the rental stock was in poor external condition compared with less than 5 per cent of the home-ownership units. Sharing or lack of facilities are no longer significant problems in most of urban Canada – only 1.8 per cent of all units surveyed, or 59,000 dwellings, suffered from such inadequacies.

The whole question of the use of space as a measure of crowding was carefully studied. By the traditional definition – households with an average occupancy of less than one room per person – only 4.4 per cent of the units (148,000) were crowded in the 23 census metropolitan areas in 1974.[16]

The survey devoted much attention to house prices and rents, although it must be recognized that substantial increases have occurred since 1974. The significant measurement was that of "affordability", where the traditional definition of a payment of more than 25 per cent of household income on shelter was considered a form of deprivation. Around 600,000 or one-fifth of all metropolitan households paid more than 25 per cent of their income on shelter; more importantly, 180,000 of these households paid more than 40 per cent of their income to obtain and maintain their dwellings.[17] Tenants have greater problems in this context than owners, a situation which is apparently explained by the fact that the average income of renters is substantially lower than that of owners.

The most serious problems for Canadian society are implicit in the conclusion, which confirms many previous studies, concerning overall housing needs: lower income households are most likely to have problems of affordability. At the lower end of the income scale, many households spent more than 50 per cent of their income on shelter; by contrast, households at the higher income levels spend less than 10 per cent. The survey claimed a significant discovery was that large numbers of middle or upper-income groups have apparent problems of affordability.[18] The survey concluded that, overall, about 60 per cent of all households in urban Canada had none of the problems described as: dwelling-unit inadequacy, over-crowding or problems of affordability. About one-third of all households (1,025,000) had one problem only: 180,000 were living in inadequate dwellings, 298,000 were over-crowded and 547,000 were paying more than 25 per cent of total household income. "Affordability, therefore, emerges as the largest single housing problem."[19]

A significant proportion of so-called "low income" families are in receipt of social assistance payments made available through federal-provincial or provincial-municipal social welfare programs. In fact, for the poorest 20 per cent of families in 1971, about one-third of total income was earned as wages and salaries and almost half was received as payments by governments,[20] either through universal transfer programs such as family allowances and old age security allowances, or through direct social assistance payments. While it is true that an important proportion of such families in the lowest income levels do occupy satisfactory housing, particularly elderly persons and couples, the evidence in both urban and rural areas pointed conclusively to the fact that the condition of housing and income levels are directly related. The poorest housing in every community is occupied by the poorest families; since the poorest families often include larger numbers of children than the average, they tend to be crowded and their needs for the basic physical amenities are often unmet. It is these families for whom, in the years 1945-64, most attention was paid when the concepts of slum clearance, urban redevelopment and urban renewal were under consideration, both for purposes of program definition and for purposes of program implementation.

The housing conditions of Canada's native peoples are generally the most unsatisfactory and indeed deplorable. When substantial numbers of members of such groups migrate to urban centres, as in the case of Winnipeg, Regina and Toronto, they move almost immediately to the bottom of the socio-economic distribution, exist for the most part with income provided through public social welfare programs, and occupy some of the poorest housing in the nation. This is not as evident in Toronto where a group of native people have formed a non-profit housing company which, with federal and provincial funds, has purchased accommodation which its rents to families within its community[21] and has recently constructed an apartment building for elderly persons.

It can readily be understood, therefore, that Canadian families of lowest income, of largest size, or where one of the two parents is deceased or has left the family unit, constitute the majority of applicants for public housing accommodation. If, as seems desirable, the housing management organization created under federal-provincial-municipal or provincial auspices considers the need for housing as the prime determinant in selecting families for accommodation in relatively scarce public housing, the social situation in such housing projects becomes a deterrent to normal family life on the one hand and an obstacle to further public participation in housing programs on the other.

There are, depending upon the definition used, perhaps 150,000 publicly provided non-institutional dwelling units available for "low-income families" throughout this country. At the same time, there are approximately one-half million one-parent families,[22] most of whom have very low incomes and would score highly on any point-rating system designed to determine priority for public housing accommodation. It is thus entirely conceivable that every public housing dwelling unit in Canada could be occupied by a one-parent family, if need were the sole criterion.

Alternatively, the needs of the elderly in Canada for decent and adequate housing accommodation are substantial, when one considers that more than half of all Canadian individuals over the age of 65 receive a guaranteed income supplement, determined on a means test, in addition to the basic old age security allowance. Elderly couples and individuals might well occupy a great deal more of the available public housing accommodation if need were the only criterion. In both cases, however, need is not the only criterion because the desirability of social viability (community) within the housing project itself is central in the thinking of every intelligent public housing administrator and because the size of the available accommodation is a factor which must be taken into consideration.

More important perhaps than these observations, is the fact that the nature and distribution of poverty in Canada is such that antagonism has developed toward the nuclear family, particularly in its role as applicant for public housing. Many municipalities who must initiate the requests for intergovernmental housing activity throughout the country have not only been overly cautious, but often entirely discriminatory in their choice of housing programs so as to exclude poor families, regardless of whether they were headed by one or two parents. The reasons for such discrimination are entirely clear from a management standpoint, but from a policy point of view are entirely unacceptable.

HOUSING DEMAND: CHANGING SOCIAL PATTERNS

The facts of change within the Canadian family are now so well-known that they merit but brief reiteration in this discussion. Large families, so fashionable during the period of the baby boom from 1944-1959, have given way to the newly-fashionable small family with one or two children at most and sometimes none at all. Although the number of marriages has been maintained at a relatively high level in comparison with the pre-war period, it is known, even in the absence of accurate data, that in the 1970s a great many two-person families (households) were formed by unmarried couples.

In addition to these facts there are other personal social innovations which strongly affect the relationship between supply and demand in the housing market. There are a great many more non-family households than ever before and they are of unusual composition. In the 1950s a non-family household might consist of the following: two sisters, one sibling taking care of another sibling of the opposite sex in their old age, or a son or daughter living with an elderly parent and providing care and support. The household compositions now so prevalent were relatively unknown.

Today, a demand for housing may come forward from: households composed of two, three or four persons of the same sex who are unrelated; common-law partners without children; or, single persons who in the affluence of the 1960s or early 1970s were able to accumulate the capital required for a downpayment on a single detached or condominium home or, if not, certainly possess sufficient resources to rent a privately marketed apartment. Whatever the nature of the households which constitute the demand for housing units, the facts are that firstly, the nuclear family is no longer the pre-eminent source of demand for housing, for sale or for rent;[23] and secondly, the newly-constituted households of the 1970s demand a somewhat different type of housing accommodation. Their requirement is a set of spaces and facilities which would not usually meet the requirements of the traditional family of parents and children.

It cannot be argued, with the exception of the situation in certain housing markets at certain times within certain communities, that the housing demands of these new types of social arrangements have made it impossible for families to acquire housing accommodation. But it is certainly worth arguing that these new demands have induced investors in housing development to concentrate their energies in meeting the requirements of these new markets, rather than to continue building accommodation that might be more adequate for traditional family requirements. Moreover, it is possible that this shift, which became evident in the early 1960s, did reduce the push toward innovation in housing construction which might have reduced the cost of traditional family housing. These tentative arguments will never be settled because it is a fact that the entire Canadian housing demand-supply situation changed relatively suddenly and very strongly in the early 1960s in the direction of multiple housing, primarily for rental, rather than single-detached housing, primarily for sale.

It is important then, in this context, to separate out the private market from the public or assisted-housing sector. In the private market, the housing industry responded very quickly after 1960 to the changing demands of the newly-formed family or household types by shifting the kind of construction in which it was engaged. It would not have done this if it were not a fact that multiple housing in high-rise form in the large urban centre was far more profitable than the building of four or five single-family detached homes on an acre of ground in the typical suburban municipality. High-rise apartment buildings, which became particularly evident by the late 1960s throughout Canada's twenty-three census metropolitan areas, were both an economic and social response to changing family conditions. Although we know how many single-parent families exist at the time of the census and although we know how many dwelling units are occupied at any particular time of estimate, we do not know exactly how many dwelling units are occupied by each of the substantial variety of household relationships which have developed in recent years.

In the private market, however, the shift in response to social change was not only relatively quick and extremely profitable but painless, both for the developer and the host municipality which welcomed the in-migrants to the community because they brought needed manpower to the labour market and expenditures to the retail and wholesale enterprises of the community. Moreover, private market multiple housing in the 1960s was almost entirely designed for rental accommodation and tenants in the private sector were notoriously undemanding from the point of view of local politicians. It is only in recent years that the costs of these housing responses (in terms of the provision of municipal services) have been carefully considered and have been found in many cases to have exceeded the benefits of increased local tax revenues.

In the public sector, however, which combines a mixture of self-interest and charitable impulses on the part of local politicians, local community groups, and elected representatives in higher levels of governments, the changes in the family were not so welcome. Fewer and fewer intact families consisting of two parents and one or more dependent children presented themselves as candidates for public housing accommodation. By the mid-1970s, in Ontario at least, applications from one-parent families headed by a woman constituted from one-half to two-thirds of all applications received by public housing registries in the medium-sized and larger urban centres. In 1971, 80 per cent of all single-parent families were headed by a woman but, in the area of publicly-provided accommodation for low-income families, more than 95 per cent of applicants from one-parent families were headed by a woman. These facts, together with the point-rating systems which had been developed to evaluate the needs of applicants for housing accommodation, would have led directly to a form of social segregation which the community could not countenance, even if there were not strong tendencies towards discrimination at work.

There is now sufficient experience and knowledge of the situation over the past decades in Halifax, Montreal, Toronto, Winnipeg and Vancouver – to name some of the centres of greatest activity – that few elected and appointed officials in our towns and cities are unacquainted, at least by hearsay, with the problems of operation and management. To be blunt about it, they are both prejudiced and/or frightened of the problems which might arise if they were to initiate substantial construction of assisted rental housing for low-income families. Although they have been assured again and again that only a very small proportion of such families are troublesome (perhaps 2 to 3 per cent), they have toured housing projects in various provinces, particularly in Ontario, and they do not like what they see. What they like to see is well-maintained, well-trimmed, beautifully painted apartment buildings such as those inhabited by families in the upper 15 per

Table V

Public Housing Provided for Families and Senior Citizens (Ontario, 1951-1979)[1]

Completions and Acquisitions Under F/P and OHC Programs	1951-1971	1972	1973	1974	1975	1976	1977	1978	1979[4]
Metro Toronto									
Family	13,300	2,370	4,785[3]	1,994	776	57	—	—	—
Senior Citizens[2]	—	—	—	—	—	—	—	—	—
Balance Ontario									
Family	14,540	1,267	1,321	1,198	521	331	292	144	18
Senior Citizens	8,370	3,537	3,343	3,167	5,515	3,555	3,261	2,469	1,254
Acquired by Purchase or Take-Over									
Metro Toronto									
Family	5,885	141	—	28	24	132	11	—	19
Senior Citizens	—	—	—	—	—	—	—	—	—
Balance Ontario									
Family	252	24	48	42	224	108	65	73	8
Senior Citizens	283	—	—	—	—	—	—	—	—
Sub-Totals[5]	42,630	7,339	9,497	6,429	7,060	4,183	3,629	2,686	1,299

[1]Excludes dwelling units acquired through Rent Supplement and Accelerated Family Rental Housing Programs.
[2]Municipality of Metro Toronto is responsible for Senior Citizens in Metro Toronto. Housing stock approximates 11,000 units.
[3]Includes 333 hostel units.
[4]As at November 30, 1979.
[5]Total (1951-1979) equals 84,752.
Source: Ontario Housing Corporation

cent of the Canadian income distribution. What they do see are some of the evidences of poverty – the difficulties of maintaining property in its spanking new condition, the well-used outdoor spaces and facilities, the occasional evidence of vandalism, and the kinds of pressures on physical structures which come about as a result of densities per dwelling unit of five to six or more persons. Moreover, the decision-makers, primarily the elected and appointed officials of local government, have discovered a much safer group upon which to devote their energies and their charitable instincts: our increasingly large elderly population.

The evidence is now clearly at hand and some figures may be of some interest. Table V illustrates the declining proportion of family housing and the increasing share of senior citizens' accommodation within public housing programs initiated in Ontario, the province in which the greatest activity has occurred since 1951. It is clearly evident that the construction of new accommodation for families in Canada's most populous province has almost dried up. The situation may be more noticeable outside the municipality of Metropolitan Toronto in terms of numbers but within Metro itself, it is quite clear. Family accommodation within public housing is out of favour within local initiating bodies and little or no pressure is being exerted by provincial governments to reverse this trend.

On the other hand, almost everyone is pleased that elderly couples and single elderly individuals are attracting the bulk of attention and that most new housing accommodation is provided for them. Such persons are uniformly grateful, do not have children, cause very few problems of operation and management, pay their rent on time, and rarely engage in vandalism or other anathemas for public housing management.

HOUSING SUPPLY: CHANGING PHYSICAL PATTERNS

The response of the house building industry to changes in social patterns and the new modes of family life which induced new housing requirements is reflected in the statistics of housing completions by type of dwelling. From 1961 to 1971, single detached houses in Canada increased in number by just 20.6 per cent whereas apartments and flats increased 47.6 per cent.[24] As a proportion of total dwelling units completed in specific year, the changing figures were equally dramatic. In 1949, 13 per cent of all dwelling units completed were apartments and flats; in 1959, 25 per cent of the completions were in this form. As the apartment building boom progressed strongly, this proportion rose to 42.5 per cent in 1965 and 50.5 per cent in 1970.[25] In the late 1970s, however, as costs increased and as resistance to high-rise multiple dwellings in downtown urban centres increased significantly, the proportion dropped to the point where, in 1975, it was just 34.6 per cent.[26] It must be remembered that this proportion is still substantial as it is based upon a greater number of dwelling units completed than in the 1950s and early 1960s.

The simple facts of arithmetic do not provide information, however, concerning the size of accommodation. Almost by definition, the new apartments of the 1960s were not meant for nuclear families or even for the one-parent family with dependent children. There were very few accommodations constructed in Canada in the period 1959-75 which were apartments of three bedrooms or more. The greatest proportion were one-bedroom and bachelor accommodations with many variations on these themes, for example, junior one-bedrooms and the like. These accommodations appealed to the single, unmarried person maintaining his/her own household and to households consisting of two persons of the same or opposite sex who were a couple but not a married couple. Such construction, in response to the new life styles, was easily marketed.

The pressure on costs significantly increased the subsidies (the difference between the actual full recovery costs of accommodation provided for families and the rentals which would be collected on a rent-geared-to-income scale) required in public housing accommodation. These subsidies began to mount and passed the $100 per unit per month mark and by the time they passed the $200 per unit per month mark, there was a considerable negative impression upon the entire field of assisted rental housing. At the same time that costs increased faster than incomes, the sale price of houses for purchase exceeded the financial capacity of families who were considered to be in the lower half, or even in the lower two-thirds of the middle-income group. This situation, which was put very clearly in an annual report of the Nova Scotia Housing Commission under the heading "Low Rental Family Program", is the situation in which the Canadian housing industry found itself in the mid and late 1970s.

> Problems are being met in this program as a result of rapidly rising costs. The capital costs of the program and the returns from the rents bear little relationship to each other now and the amount of subsidy to be paid out over the fifty year mortgage term is significant. On the other hand, the demand for such housing continues to increase because private market rentals and purchase prices are rising at a correspondingly rapid rate, removing more and more families from the private market.[27]

INTERGOVERNMENTAL HOUSING POLICY
AND THE FAMILY

The response of both the Government of Canada and the governments of several provinces to this situation was not to create additional public rental housing for families but to develop new programs designed to encourage home purchase by families whose incomes were in the lower middle or upper segments of the lowest third of the income distribution. Such programs as the Assisted Home Ownership Program (AHOP), launched in 1973, and the provincial equivalents, were designed to push the capacity for home ownership down the income distribution to the lower portions of the middle income segment or even below.

It has already been indicated that the cooperative ventures of two or more levels of government to create assisted rental housing no longer seriously encompass the needs of Canadian families whose resources are insufficient to enable them to acquire adequate and affordable housing in the private market. The shift away from family accommodation has been demonstrated and the inevitability of increased activity on behalf of the elderly on the one hand and further encouragement to non-profit and cooperative housing corporations on the other, is likely to continue through the first half of the 1980s.[28] In consideration of this substantial reduction in the availability of housing for the lowest half of the income distribution, governments have substituted a variety of programs designed to encourage home ownership by Canadian families who would normally not have sufficient income to carry the monthly burdens of principal, interest, taxes and repairs.

The reasoning of the federal government was clearly stated in its written presentation to Habitat.

> Throughout most of the country, home ownership has been viewed as a social good, conferring stability on both communities and families. When, suddenly, it is no longer possible for many persons of average and even well-above average incomes to become home owners it is natural to conclude that something is seriously awry.[29]

It is very difficult to be optimistic about the future of such home ownership programs because they are based inevitably upon major assumptions that may prove to be weakly based. There is, first of all, the assumption in AHOP that five years hence the income of the family will have increased. Moreover, a sufficient increase is required to enable the family to meet the much higher scale of payments when the mortgage is rewritten at the effective rate of interest then pertaining.

If the prospects for economic growth and development and thus the prospects for expanded employment were encouraging, these assumptions might be reasonable. All the forecasts in the late 1970s, however, appeared to indicate that economic growth for the first half of the 1980s would be relatively modest and that unemployment would continue to be a serious problem for the Canadian economy. When one realizes that it would be considered a triumph for the federal and provincial governments, working together, to reduce the percentage of unemployment in the labour force to 6 per cent, it is sobering to reflect upon Beveridge's classic contention that full employment would suggest a tolerance of perhaps 2 per cent frictional unemployment at any one time. In Canada unemployment has successively increased from 4 to 6 per cent and now we appear destined to have an 8 per cent rate of unemployment accompanied by inflation. Under all these circumstances, family policy in Canada can scarcely count upon appropriate housing policies to meet the significant need of an additional 148,000 families and/or 215,000 households formed annually in the period 1976-1981.[30]

NOTES

[1]Ontario, *Report of the Royal Commission on Metropolitan Toronto* (Toronto: June 1977) p. 232.

[2]J. M. Mackintosh, *Housing and Family Life* (London: Cassell and Co. Ltd., 1952); Albert Rose, *Regent Park* (Toronto: University of Toronto Press, 1958); D. M. Wilner et al., *The Housing Environment and Family Life* (Baltimore: John Hopkins Press, 1962).

[3]Nathan Strauss, *The Seven Myths of Housing* (New York: Knopf, 1945) pp. 12-28, 127-143.

[4]Canada, *The National Housing Act*, Revised Statutes, c. N-10, as amended through 1978-79 (Ottawa: 1979) S. 2, Definitions.

[5]Canada, Ministry of State for Urban Affairs, *Human Settlement in Canada*, distributed at Habitat, June 1976, p. 15.

[6]*Ibid.*, Table 2.2, p. 17.

[7]*Idem.*

[8]*Human Settlement in Canada*, pp. 15-17.

[9]*Ibid.*, p. 17.

[10]*Idem.*

[11]*Human Settlement in Canada*, p. 17.

[12]*Ibid.*, p. 17, fn 1.

[13]CMHC, *Housing in Urban Canada: An Overview Based on the 1974 Survey of Housing Units* (Ottawa: 1977) p. 12, plus eight tables.

[14]*Ibid.*, p. 2.

[15]*Ibid.*, p. 5.

[16]*Ibid.*, p. 7.

[17]*Ibid.*, p. 10.

[18]*Idem.*

[19]*Ibid.*, p. 12.

[20]*Human Settlement in Canada*, op. cit., p. 5. See also, *Canada Year Book, 1975*, Table 6.4, p. 254. Nevertheless nearly 600,000 households of the one million considered to be below the poverty line in 1972 owned their own homes, and 85 per cent of these were free of mortgage debt. (*Human Settlement in Canada*, p. 21.)

[21]Wigwamen Incorporated, *Housing Programs in Ontario*, a special edition of *Housing Ontario*, Jan./Feb. 1976, Vol. 20, No. 1, p. 15.

[22]*Human Settlement in Canada*, p. 5.

[23]This is closely related to greatly increased costs of home purchase and rental housing. It has been estimated that only 30 per cent of Ontario families in 1974 could carry the costs of home purchase with less than 25 per cent of their gross family income. The comparable figure for 1967 was 70 per cent of families. *Ontario Economic Council, Issues and Alternatives 1976, Housing*, Table 4.

[24]*Human Settlement in Canada*, Table 2.2, p. 17.

[25]Canada, Central Mortgage and Housing Corporation, *Canadian Housing Statistics, 1975* (Ottawa: March 1976). Percentages calculated from Table 9, p. 9.

[26]*Ibid.*

[27]Province of Nova Scotia, Nova Scotia Housing Commission, *Annual Report* (for the fiscal year ending March 31, 1974) p. 9.

[28]Late in 1978 the Ministry of State for Urban Affairs announced that the traditional financial arrangements for public housing for families and senior citizens would cease on December 31, 1978. Henceforth, provinces, municipalities, and non-profit organizations were to seek mortgage financing in the private market in lieu of the 90 per cent federal (capital) loan.

[29]*Human Settlement in Canada*, p. 15.

[30]*Canadian Housing Statistics, 1978*, Table 115, p. 94.

CHAPTER 9

Canada's Housing Problem: Insoluble Crisis or Intractable Dilemma?

It is still apparent, as I wrote in 1968,[1] that Canada does not suffer from a lack of "housing policy", if housing policy is equated in any substantial measure with housing legislation. More legislation, in terms of both the quantity and quality of enactments, has been passed since 1964 than in the whole of the previous century. Legislation, however, is not tantamount to housing policy per se or to the implementation of a course of action intended by the government enacting such legislation. Nevertheless, within the past fifty years we have progressed from the first awakening of federal concern to a situation in which all levels of government – federal, provincial and municipal – are deeply involved with the housing of every individual and family in the nation.

Housing policy never built a housing unit. The mere enunciation of the objectives of a public or voluntary body, and the passage of legislation through which such objectives are intended to be attained, are not sufficient by themselves. All the protestations of elected and appointed officials, of house builders and land developers, and all the pleas and pressures of voluntary groups and citizens' organizations, will be of little avail unless the national economy can afford an allocation of resources commensurate with the measurement of human need for housing.

The limits of housing policy become clearer with each passing year.

The federal government can indeed supply funds for investment in residential building activity, but the major portion of such activity will, and must, continue to be financed through private financial institutions (unless we find ourselves, through revolution, war or anarchy, in an entirely different society than at present). Although it is desirable that investment in residential building for the public sector increase considerably, most Canadians still prefer to acquire accommodation within the normal or traditional housing markets; that is, they prefer to buy their own homes if they can manage to do so, or they prefer to rent apartments under private management.

If these assumptions are correct, federal housing policy is primarily an instrumentality to encourage the assumption by the provinces of their rightful constitutional responsibilities. In my view, the federal stance has been basically correct. Canada Mortgage and Housing Corporation[2] should stimulate, encourage and work in every way – short of encroaching on the constitutional prerogatives of the provinces – towards better housing and living conditions for all. It could accomplish this in part through education, research and active involvement in conferences and programs designed to improve public understanding of the whole situation and its constituent parts.

More important are the resources – the hundreds of millions of dollars per annum assigned by the federal government to CMHC for the implementation of programs permissible under the NHA. The corporation, as an agent of the Government of Canada, must act as the custodian of federal housing policy implied by the NHA or enunciated by the Government of Canada. Nevertheless, CMHC faces severely realistic limits which become the boundaries of national housing policy. For example, if all provincial housing corporations emulated, in full measure, the activity of the OHC in past years, there might not have been sufficient resources for allocation by the CMHC; and if all provinces had been equally active, the total public housing program would be in the neighbourhood of some 25,000 to 35,000 dwelling units per annum.

Allegations that there has never been a national housing policy have been made continuously since the 1930s. More important than criticism is an effort to understand and work for an elevation of the priority assigned to residential building within total capital investment. While this is a desirable objective it must be seen within the context of the total requirements of this nation. We require a vast investment in all forms of social capital – specialized educational facilities, roads and other forms of transportation, hospitals and other forms of medical institutions, and special institutions for the elderly, the mentally retarded, and the emotionally ill. At the same time, we require a vast investment in human resources – the training and retraining of hundreds of thousands of persons who are economically unfit to take their place in the society that is rapidly emerging in the last two decades of this century.

The list of requirements is almost endless. If it can be argued that there is no national housing policy, it can also be argued that there is no national transportation policy, no national policy in the utilization of natural resources, no national policy with respect to the utilization of human resources, no national social welfare policy, and so on. The heart of this argument is that housing must take its place within the context of all needs, demands, and pressures which our entire political and economic system faces today and will probably always face in varying degrees. This is not to suggest that housing must take a back seat and that the priority for housing expansion must always remain low; but it must be seen as one major requirement among many. If this could be clearly understood, the limits of housing policy may be more readily amenable to appropriate political and social action.

There is now emerging within the provinces a new spirit of recognition of the need for decent, safe and sanitary housing. It is important to ensure, through pressure upon elected and appointed officials in municipal and provincial governments, that the enunciation of fine phrases, excellent legislation and stated objectives will be translated into the reality of physical accommodation adequate to the needs of the various segments of our population.

There was consternation in some metropolitan areas, in the early 1970s, that the list of applications for public housing was growing each year or remained generally stable at a high level. In the field of housing, as in many other fields of human activity, it can be argued that "nothing succeeds like success." There were more applications for public housing than in the past because applicants came to believe that they had a chance to be accommodated, even though the time lapse from application to occupancy might be from six months to two years. Furthermore, an applicant always has the right to decline at the critical moment and to reaffirm his faith in his capacity to make his own way without the assistance of this new form of "social service".

Since 1976 the number of applications for both family and senior citizens' accommodation has been declining steadily throughout Ontario. The Metropolitan Toronto Housing Registary reported that total active applications at December 31, 1979 were less than 50 per cent those in June 1978. In the midst of unemployment and inflation the needy appeared to have given up the hope of obtaining assisted housing. For some bureaucrats, however, the figures demonstrated that the need had been met.

Provincial housing policy can be seen, therefore, to face limits as serious as those surrounding federal housing policy. The ritual of passing legislation required for any province to participate in the new array of programs available under the NHA has been observed. It is almost as if we were back in the days of the phrase, "there ought to be a law". Now there are many laws and relatively little affordable housing. The provincial governments must demonstrate within the next few years that they mean serious business in attempting to provide housing for those least able to meet these needs. Alternatively, they must give up their role in favour of the federal government or turn it over to local or regional governments which are allegedly closest to the people who really need the housing. This latter decision would have profound financial and tax implications.

Most provinces face serious financial strictures in their attempts to elevate the priority previously assigned to housing within their jurisdictions. Many of their constitutional responsibilities have become of the utmost importance in the lives of urban residents – education, health care, the social services, labour relations, the development of human resources and, of course, the provision of housing accommodation. Thus, it is not only at the federal level that housing must compete for an appropriate share within the totality of scarce resources. When one considers that the combined population of all four Atlantic provinces is less than that of Metropolitan Toronto and the total taxable capacity (as represented by income on the one hand and property assessments on the other) is far greater in Metro Toronto, one can appreciate the difficulties faced by certain provincial and municipal jurisdictions.

Within provincial legislatures there is also the traditional distrust of urban society and its members. It is well known that, despite increasing urbanization, most provincial legislatures continue to be dominated by members who represent rural areas. Redistribution of electoral constituencies has had some effect during the past thirty years but it is still true that the vote of a person who resides in an essentially rural constituency is worth three, four or five times the vote of a person who resides in a large urban centre. In Ontario some 30 per cent of the population resides within Metropolitan Toronto, yet only one-fifth of the seats in the legislature are derived from constituencies within that metropolis. In considering the views of legislators with respect to the social and economic problems of our cities, rural influence in the provincial governments is an important fact. It can scarcely be denied that in such provinces as British Columbia, Alberta, Manitoba, Quebec, and New Brunswick, domination of the legislature by non-urban-oriented members has played a substantial role in restricting provincial activity in the fields of housing and urban renewal.

The scope and limits of housing policy can be visualized more clearly than in any other political jurisdiction when one examines the record, the present situation, and future prospects within municipalities. It is here, at the heart of the urban society, that a great many poor people tend to live – alone or with families, young or old. (There are some exceptions – Canadian Indians living on reservations, Canadian Eskimos who are nomadic, and persons in various provinces who live in "unorganized territories".) Although there is a good deal of rural poverty and underdevelopment in Canada, the physical and social inadequacies of the housing conditions of the urban poor are a stark reality and in our cities the impact of inflation becomes most obvious.

It is within this climate of social and economic conditions that local governments are expected to fulfill all the roles expected of them. It has become patently obvious that they cannot fulfill all these functions, even with the best of good will and motivation; but one cannot take for granted that the motivation necessarily exists. Legislators in municipal government tend to be self-made men and women, small businessmen and a few members of the professions. They are generally quite conservative in their views towards the poor and those who require assistance or subsidization in any aspect of their living conditions such as the provision of housing accommodation.

In the largest urban centres the situation may gradually change, as the trend towards cosmopolitanism grows and as legislators who are more urban and sophisticated in their views attain office. I do not anticipate, however, that the extent of local governments' participation through initiatives in the fields of housing and urban renewal will increase radically during the balance of the century.

After careful examination of the "brave new words" of federal and provincial housing legislation of the past few years, it is precisely this point that is most disturbing. Because of the reliance upon local government initiatives in many provincial enactments, it will be unlikely that much will occur within the field of assisted housing unless the interpretation of the legislation includes many more incentives than are apparent in the enactments themselves. There is the possibility, of course, that the provincial housing corporations will become more aggressive in their operations and adopt a posture more like that of the early OHC. This is not apparent within the legislation, but aggressiveness is often the result of administrative decision and the attitudes of those appointed to the senior posts of such corporations. Perhaps it is too soon to insist that several of the newer housing corporations appear, on paper at least, much more passive than active. Nevertheless, it seems important to raise the question for consideration.

Many Canadians have written and spoken in the past twenty-five years of Canada's "permanent housing crisis". In part, this phraseology was used to counter the argument that the situation at any one time was particularly unusual, particularly threatening to more families and individuals than in past years and perhaps even more unusual than in the period of intense shortage following World War Two. For those Canadians who urgently required housing accommodation in the second half of the 1940s there were literally no houses to buy and none to rent, unless one was relatively well-off financially. Yet, in July 1946, C. D. Howe[3] enunciated a national housing program with a goal of 80,000 new dwelling units per annum. This seemed an incredible target for a nation which averaged some 43,000 new dwelling units per annum during the previous twenty years. Yet the target was reached by the early 1950s. However, there have been additional periods of critical shortage, particularly in the mid-1950s and again in the early 1960s after several years of severe economic recession.

As stated earlier, Canadians are among the best-housed people in the world. The fact must be accepted, however, that whatever the achievement of previous housing goals, attainment of such objectives has always been followed by increasing expectations, increasing demands, and a significant reduction in the utilization of our housing stock when measured by the number of persons per dwelling unit. Ontario, in particular, is very much aware of this phenomenon, which in a real sense means that all governmental action in stimulating continued activity in the private housing market and direct public housing production is a form of tail-chasing. Policies change in order to develop new programs to enable the supply to accommodate the demand only to produce a further set of demands which make production appear continuously inadequate.

In this sense Canada's housing problem is an insoluble crisis. The statistics for Canada, like those enunciated earlier for Ontario, reveal far higher achievements in the early 1970s than in the 1960s. Thus, there is no question that for a number of years housing production exceeded the number of new family formations. The product was not, however, disseminated throughout those households that constitute the essence of the urgent demand for housing. The result was not, in short, a simple process of meeting housing need and cutting into the backlog of unmet housing requirements, but a substantial reduction in the number of persons per dwelling unit. There are far more units now occupied by one- or two-person households than ever before and there are far more units occupied by two or more unrelated single persons.[4] This is in part a function of expanded income, but it is also a function of the distribution of both production and absorption of housing accommodation.

Despite an increase in the proportion of housing production designated for sale or for rent to low- and lower-middle groups, most of the produced housing is designed for those who can command the resources to meet their personal or family requirements without assistance. This takes two forms: single family dwellings of a very high standard for sale to persons in the upper-fifth or upper-quartile of income recipients; and, bachelor apartments, junior one-bedroom apartments, one-bedroom apartments and, perhaps, two-bedroom apartments which constitute a substantial amount of all rental accommodation built since the beginning of the apartment boom in 1959-60. The proportion of newly built private accommodation for rental consisting of more than two bedrooms has been a very small fraction of production during the past quarter-century.

The sub-group which has suffered most severely during the very substantial housing production of the 1960s and the 1970s is usually described as "the working poor". These individuals and families would, in several provinces, receive more income and additional benefits (depending upon the size of their families) if they were in receipt of welfare assistance. They remain employed at very low salaries and, unless they happened to have purchased a home at least ten or fifteen years ago at quite modest mortgage interest rates, they will be tenants. As such, they face not only the problem of rentals that are high in comparison with their income, but also the fact that very little rental accommodation is available for large families. It has been estimated that the "working poor" number as many as one-quarter of the entire Canadian population – some five to six million persons within perhaps one to one-and-a-half million households. Some are intact families, some are families where the mother is attempting to support dependent children without a male adult figure in the household, and some are persons over the age of 65 who continue in the labour force but whose income is relatively modest either because of lack of skill or because they work only part-time.

The group described as the "working poor" face not only a shortage of housing accommodation but an incapacity to survive in the housing market, even if they can enter it because of very low downpayments required, as is the case from time to time, or because of new innovations such as condominium ownership, assisted home ownership, co-operative housing, and so on. Their problem is essentially that of meeting the regular payments, whether they be in the form of repayments on a mortgage together with rapidly rising municipal taxes, whether they be payments to the co-operative organization which provided them with the accommodation at a very low downpayment, or whether they are in fact attempting to struggle in an increasingly tight rental market.

THE ASSUMPTIONS UNDERLYING PROPOSED SOLUTIONS TO AN INTRACTABLE DILEMMA

The most significant set of assumptions concerning solutions to Canada's housing problem relates to the degree of governmental intervention to be taken in the housing market. Politically, there are persons with a leftist approach (not confined to any one political party) who believe that massive intervention by one or more levels of government will solve the entire crisis. The fact is that, by contrast with the situation in the 1940s and 1950s there is a tremendous amount of intervention or activity by the Government of Canada, by provincial governments, by regional governments, and by municipal governments. One must maintain an attitude of constructive scepticism towards the view that government or intergovernmental activity will somehow provide the answers to these extremely difficult problems.

The essence of the dilemma with respect to the role of government rests in the nature of the housing industry. It remains true that all dwellings (with the exception of a small number built by individuals or small groups who form a true co-operative) are built by private enterprise. The house-building industry in Canada – large development institutions, small builders and some traditional craftsmen who build two or three houses a year – produce all the housing that is added to the total stock each year; about 85 per cent of this total production is on the builder's own account. The total capital investment in residential construction (public and private) is now of the order of $13 to $14 billion per annum.[5]

There is, in fact, no merit in the contention that further massive governmental intervention will solve the problem. This is not to deny that governments will develop new programs, and that governments will stimulate the house-building industry through financial programs, design competitions, and emphasis on innovations in construction – all intended to cut the costs to the ultimate purchasers, whether they be individuals, families, or public housing corporations. The allegation that house building should, however, be a government activity only, has no merit; there would be absolutely no advantage in such a take-over. This proposal, sometimes made by politicians and by some so-called liberal-progressive organizations in our society, would simply mean that civil service organizations would embrace huge staffs of construction workers. This would surely not cut down the complexities of housing production, would not simplify the process of housing production, or cut down production costs.

The dilemma consists in the nature and amount of governmental intervention that would be sufficient to achieve the social goals of housing policies. There is no easy answer but our experience during the past twenty-five years indicates that we have not yet reached the limit of government intervention in this area. Governmental activity is bound to increase, if only for the fact that house building, as an economic activity in Canada, may have a significant contra-cyclical impact on the period of little or no growth frequently predicted for the early 1980s by a wide variety of economists, public officials and politicians.

Governmental intervention is bound to increase and spread into new programs as certain activities either reach their peak or fail to meet their objectives because of tremendous price inflation. It is no longer sufficient to advocate (as I did some years ago) that a larger proportion of total housing production must be assigned to the lowest income groups; this has been done and the housing crisis has not dissipated.

The three main constituents of this phenomenon in Canadian urban life are as follows.

1. A substantial increase in immigration occurred in the first half of the 1970s; net immigration was nearly double that of the second half of the 1960s. Moreover, in-migration to the larger urban centres from smaller areas of population, villages and towns coincided with increased immigration to Canada.

2. The proportion of non-family households, as well as those without children or with only one child, increased significantly. The housing industry reacted to a large group of relatively affluent small households and created a substantial amount of housing accommodation to meet their specific requirements. The absence of children is a factor of considerable importance to the profitability of those firms which have concentrated upon the construction of multiple dwellings, most often in high-rise form.

3. Very substantial numbers of the most highly educated, relatively young families with few children have come to view the heart of our urban centres – the downtown core of such metropolitan areas as Montreal, Toronto, Winnipeg, and Vancouver – as prime residential areas and the most desirable living sites for the last quarter of the twentieth century.

It is probable that, among 23.5 million Canadians (the estimate for 1978),[6] more than 6 million are persons who arrived in Canada since January 1st, 1946 and children they have borne in this country. Immigrants have had a profound effect on the housing market in all aspects. A substantial number are individuals and families who place a great deal of emphasis on home ownership and they work hard in order to achieve home ownership. Moreover, many older areas in the central cities of our large metropolitan areas have been preferred by certain groups of newcomers who have devoted much effort and money to home improvement and, indeed, rehabilitation of entire neighbourhoods. To a substantial degree they have been responsible for reversing the downward slide of many older neighbourhoods which, before 1950, were identified as severely blighted or vulnerable to blight and slum conditions. If such conditions had continued to prevail throughout downtown Toronto and other cities, there might have been a great deal more slum clearance than has been evident to date.

The largest group of new young entrants in the housing market are Canadians born during a vast upsurge in the birthrate during the years 1944-61. For some years in the 1950s births approximated 500,000 – about twice the number for the second half of the 1930s. Even though there was a rapid decline in the 1960s and 1970s, new births are still at the rate of about 350,000 per annum. The generation born after 1944 continues to reach maturity and those entering the housing market in the early 1980s are most likely to have been born between 1950 and 1955. Similarly, the OHC has noted that among their applicants there is a comparable trend towards those under the age of 25 in contrast with the experience during the years 1965-71.

The trend towards a preference for housing accommodation in previously elegant downtown neighbourhoods (which had deteriorated somewhat over many years) has meant a revitalization for such neighbourhoods and has had significant consequences for older residents and their tenants.[7] It has recently been noted that one of the most important industries in Canadian urban centres is the renovation industry.[8] In the mid-1970s older homes commanded much higher prices than they did in the 1960s. This eliminated many long-term residents in older areas of the heart of metropolitan areas. The older middle or low-income homeowners did not fare badly as they probably received a much higher price than would be anticipated a decade before; it was the displaced tenants who were the victims because of their inability to find accommodation elsewhere.

In years past these now displaced tenant families and individuals were an additional source of income to the older resident owners. If public housing were available they may have been accommodated as a consequence of their displacement; but for that group known as "roomers" – single persons, particularly middle-aged and older – there is little likelihood of alternative accommodation, except in even more deteriorated neighbourhoods at probably higher rentals.

These interrelated trends in the core of central cities have raised the question: "If the city is to be denied as a site for housing accommodation for 'poor people' or low-income families, and if there is not sufficient accommodation in publicly-provided housing (particularly beyond the boundaries of the city), where are these individuals and families to live?" For the first time in Canadian history it appears that the lowest third, or even the lowest half of the income distribution have no alternative to the overly expensive and, for the most part, physically and socially inadequate accommodation they must seek in the most crowded and least desirable neighbourhoods in our communities.

PROSPECTIVE SOLUTIONS TO HOUSING DILEMMAS

The presumptive solution lies surely within the realm of resource allocation. Herein, however, rests a series of interconnected dilemmas and difficulties facing both public and private managers of our economic development. It is easy to grossly over simplify the situation and state that, were we to allocate a more substantial proportion of our annual product to residential housing, we would very soon solve the problem of insufficient housing accommodation for all Canadians.

The question remains: "From which sectors of the Canadian economy shall we divert resources to meet what was, in the mid-1970s, the most significant and burdensome housing crisis since the end of the Second World War?" Is it possible to argue that our gross national product is expanding rapidly and that further resources could be diverted to residential construction or housing improvement and modernization; and that, at the same time, we could take care financially of all the social requirements, as well as investment in non-residential construction (factories, plants and equipment), let alone such public expenditures as roads and transportation facilities, in a society approaching total urbanization?

It is difficult to escape a pessimistic conclusion. Although it could be suggested that additional resources should be diverted to residential construction (and this proposal will be made again and again), the fact is that there is a statistically sufficient amount of housing available for Canadian requirements. At the bottom of the income distribution the situation remains much the same as it has during the 1970s. In Ontario there has been a very substantial expansion in most forms of housing accommodation available through federal-provincial programs for low and moderate-income groups. Nevertheless, the need appears to remain at a high level. The problem is not supply, therefore, but effective demand; it is not simply a question of housing but a matter of income.[9]

Such reasoning has been influential in promoting one major federal-provincial housing initiative of the 1970s – the rent supplement program – and one significant proposition now under debate – the provision of housing or shelter allowances to the needy. A rent supplement program has both social and economic advantages. The dispersion of a proportion of families in need of housing assistance throughout the privately owned housing stock has clear potential for the integration of low-income households within neighbourhoods containing middle and upper-middle income families. In its original form, however, whereby the housing authority paid the landlord the difference between market rental and the tenant's rent paying capacity, the program diverted but did not add to the housing stock.

In recent years a variety of federal-provincial programs (described in Ontario as the Community Integrated Program, the Accelerated Rental Program, the Assisted Rental Program and the Community Sponsored Housing Program) encouraged new housing construction with a stipulation that up to 25 per cent of the dwellings could be rent supplement units, with tenants to come from low-income groups or selected from housing authority waiting lists. By the end of the 1970s there were nearly 12,500 such dwellings under management or agreement in Ontario.

Shelter or housing allowances are a late 1970s concept to strengthen or maintain demand and security of tenure among low-income households. In British Columbia the SAFER (Shelter Allowances for Elderly Residents) program was instituted by 1976-1977. Older persons paying more than 30 per cent of income for shelter (subject to certain income and rental limits) could receive a monetary allowance. A report evaluating the program was not available early in 1980 but it is known that the program has not increased the quality of accommodation.

From the governmental point of view rent supplement and shelter allowance programs have distinct economic advantages. They do not require major capital expenditures in expanding the opportunities of low-income households in the housing market. At the same time total subsidies may be very heavy in years of scarce rental accommodation and near-zero vacancy rates.

Some of the basic questions include such complete unknowns as the proportion of the housing stock that should desirably be under public ownership and management on behalf of low-income groups. In recent years there has been increasing resistance, in Ontario as well as elsewhere in Canada, to the provision of public housing on two bases. There is the well-known and traditional opposition to the location of such projects within many neighbourhoods, particularly in the communities of the 1950s and thereafter which constitute the suburban and dormitory areas within census metropolitan areas. There is the related resistance by many municipal authorities to the provision of public housing in any form except for the elderly. The traditional prejudices against failure in an affluent society on the part of a family head continue strong.

There is also a widely held attitude throughout the nation that "troubled" families – families of low income, families who are included within the definition of the "working poor", families with a male head who has little skill and little capacity within the labour market, families without a male head – are "troublesome" in terms of behaviour with neighbours and concerning relationships within the family unit. There is no doubt that some of these prejudices are founded on experience in that poverty, particularly within large groupings, breeds maladjustment between parents, between parents and children, and between families and their neighbours. There is not the slightest doubt that the system of determining priorities among public housing applicants does and must give weight to families with relatively little income, families that have many members and who may find it extremely difficult to cope with the problems of child development and socio-economic progression in a rapidly changing urban society.

A similar question may be raised with respect to the proportion of public housing accommodation that should be allocated to the elderly. In the mid-1970s estimates revealed that the great increase since the late 1960s in the number of public housing units for senior citizens, both individuals and couples, resulted in accommodation for about 5 per cent of those in Ontario who were 65 years of age or over. What should the proportion be? Since about one-half of all elderly persons in Ontario have little income other than the Old Age Security Allowance and must apply for part or all of the Guaranteed Income Supplement, it could be argued that as many as one-third to one-half of the elderly need to be accommodated in publicly-provided housing. Is this conceivable as a social objective and, more important, is it conceivable as a physical objective?

In the late-1970s the great majority of senior citizens resided in their own homes; many of these homes are their own by virtue of past purchase. Yet each large urban centre has its proportion of single elderly men and women who must rent rooms for a high proportion of their income, and such communities also have a group of elderly couples who are tenants. These persons certainly should be provided with public housing accommodation and it is conceivable that between 10 and 15 per cent of the elderly households should be accommodated under intergovernmental programs. Nevertheless, no Canadian should be permitted to forget that the older people are increasing rapidly in absolute terms; by 2001 this group may number nearly 11 per cent of the total population.[10] There will then have to be a continuous and substantial production of public housing for senior citizens to maintain even the current 5 per cent level in such provinces as Ontario; in other provinces the proportion has not yet approached 5 per cent.

The only way in which our determined and clear-cut statements of policy will be translated into reality will come as a result of federal-provincial planning, not from year to year, not for five years at a time, but for one or two decades ahead if not for the balance of the century.

Each year the federal government should be able to provide the provincial governments with a statement of the anticipated total housing programs within the entire nation, whether under private or public auspices. It should also be able to tell its provincial partners the financial resources apparently available, and the cost of proposed housing programs. The next step would be federal-provincial planning of the allocation of these resources towards the several segments of our national population requiring housing accommodation.

The private sector should know well in advance: the proportion of our resources that could be devoted to the well-to-do purchaser of housing accommodation; the proportion of our resources that could be made available on terms similar to those of the NHA, to another segment who may wish to become home-owners; and, the proportion that will be made available to provide housing, for sale or for rent, to the mass of our population who require a great deal of assistance.

The time has come for provincial governments to reconsider their permissive view of local governmental activities in housing and community planning. A reversal of the traditional approach would mean that our local governments would be required to plan future development within their jurisdiction and, in this course, create housing plans encompassing annual target objectives and perhaps goals for five or ten years ahead.

The local option to undertake such planning should be removed and each *urban* area (at least to begin with) should set a housing objective within which the public housing component would be very clearly identified. If the target objectives were not appropriate in the view of the responsible provincial ministry or agency, the local plan should be returned; probably just as many would be returned as the number of draft "Official Plans" now sent back in Ontario without the approval of the minister. The targets would include urban renewal, as well as firm additions to the housing stock to be allocated appropriately within the several housing markets in the community.

The search for solutions would be easier if the three or four levels of government (including regional governments) would only plan ahead. Since the end of the war planning has become commonplace; however most economic, social and physical planners would argue that our housing progress is distinguished by lack of planning. This may indeed be so, since the major decisions in terms of the number of dwellings constructed are made by private entrepreneurs whose overriding consideration is the profitability of their enterprises. These decision-makers are strongly affected by housing policies at every level of government, but they are not primarily concerned with the priorities of social needs. The main evidence available for these contentions rests on the fact that never have so many dwellings in Canada been built as those built since 1970.[11] We have a substantial surplus of family units for sale, yet an increasing shortage of rental units and dwellings for small households.

The crisis has worsened and the plight of low-income groups has become increasingly worse. The group unable to take care of its housing requirements within its own resources has widened substantially to include a significant proportion of all those families and individuals who fall within the lowest half of the Canadian income distribution.

THE PERSISTENT ISSUES AND THE ULTIMATE SOLUTION

In the early 1980s Canadians face serious economic and social problems, all of which pose dilemmas for the direction of future housing policy formulation. The nation is affluent beyond the wildest expectations of the decade following 1945; yet the proportion of persons in the labour force who are unable to find employment ranges from one in four to one in fifteen, depending upon the season and the region. The nation is affluent, yet one in every five has a standard of living below that desired for all our citizens. In addition to more than one million persons who are almost totally dependent upon public funds for basic support there are probably three times as many who work full-time (or who wish to work full-time but manage only part-time work by virtue of the scarcity of employment) and whose annual earnings bring them within the category of the working poor.

The mystery is that a nation which by every physical, social and statistical measure is among the best-housed in the world cannot maintain a sufficient supply of dwellings to meet the needs of approximately one in every ten of its population, and that another three in every ten experience increasing difficulty in meeting their needs within the housing market. How can this nation (with the third or fourth highest living standard in the world) convert or divert its resources, wealth and riches to the solution of a problem which rests within one of the three basic elements in living standards?

The argument has been waged for half-a-century as to whether the solution rests in an increase in overall supply or increasingly stringent governmental controls. In the late 1970s this argument again took the form of demands for controls on rentals and prices of homes rather than policies and programs designed to substantially increase the total supply.

It must be admitted that those who demand controls are correct in their assertion that to increase the supply of high-priced dwellings for sale or high-priced apartments for rental will be little improvement. Controls, on the other hand, will do nothing to increase the supply and, unless they are extended into the process of allocation of scarce housing accommodation to those who need it most, will do little to help the overall problem. Thus, to improve the supply is insufficient unless additional financial resources by both the federal and provincial governments, and even by our regional governments, are directed towards those groups most in need.

The trouble is that most Canadians have had so many tales of woe brought to their attention that they know not which policies to advocate. A great many families have found great difficulty in raising the resources to purchase their own homes. They occupy apartments at high rentals in relation to their income, find it increasingly difficult to save for the downpayment on a home purchase, and inevitably, as their families expand, are forced to borrow from lending institutions at record-high rates and from other members of the family, if this is possible, to meet their own family housing requirements.

We can, therefore, be forgiven if we seem at times to be overwhelmed by the load of social and economic responsibility thrust upon us. The issue becomes one of social versus individual responsibility. Since the 1940s Canada has not been backward in assuming such responsibility through its various levels of government, in enacting legislation, formulating policies, developing housing programs, and implementing such programs at enormous cost and dedication of public and private effort. Yet every improvement in the situation appears to mean increasing demands, higher expectations, and a circular process in which there is no beginning and no end.

Although we have assumed an increasingly aggressive role in the housing market, there is not the slightest question that governments will have to do more, will have to intervene more, and will have to demand more of independent private house-building organizations and taxpayers. The key lies in the command of governments over resources. The residential construction industry can only thrive if both private and public resources are made available, not only to enable them to build, but to provide those in need with the opportunity to acquire adequate housing.

As housing purchasers must inevitably rely upon the resources of non-governmental lending institutions, government could intervene more in the manner in which these financial resources are dispensed. Government could prescribe banks, trust companies, insurance companies, and other lending institutions to devote a greater proportion of their privately held resources to housing accommodation or could prescribe rates of mortgage interest by subsidizing either the lending institutions or the ultimate consumers.[12] Governments could prescribe the total framework within which residential construction would take place without stifling the house-building industry, without nationalizing the lending institutions or the house builders, or, for that matter, without turning the nation into a totalitarian state.

Nevertheless, in a democratic society, government cannot force the building industry to restrict its activity to any one province or even to Canada. In the mid-1970s several large development organizations turned their attention to more profitable markets in the United States and to the development of shopping centres rather than house building.

Government could prescribe that a proportion of residential house-building activity be devoted to those who are most disadvantaged in the housing market. We have certainly not yet reached the limit of providing for the lowest-income individuals and families by rent-geared-to-income housing, housing for sale at subsidized interest rates, and housing on leased government-owned lots, despite the fact that such programs are currently out of favour; nor have we reached the limit of the proportion of housebuilding activity directed to the lower half of the income distribution.

If this means that there will be fewer costly dwellings built in Canada over the next five, ten or twenty years, very few Canadians will suffer. It may be that the upper-third of our income receivers will have to devote resources to enlarging, remodelling or rehabilitating their existing dwellings to meet their higher aspirations. If we build more standardized and less customized housing, and more of medium density rather than in the style of the great apartment era of the 1960s, very few Canadians will suffer. There is nothing sacrosanct in the proposition that an acre of serviced land can only accommodate one to five dwellings. Neither is there anything sacrosanct in the doctrine that high density multiple apartment dwellings should be built wherever possible in urban areas; this is only likely to involve a greater return to the entrepreneur and less likelihood of accommodating family house-holds with children. Somewhere between these extremes, which constitute our experience over the past thirty years, is the middle position of medium density, intensive urban development, but controlled and planned urban growth.

One issue has certainly been settled during the past twenty-five years. Canadians are no longer afraid of government interference in the housing market, of vast governmental allocations of funds (particularly since they take the form of repayable loans), or of a public role in the development and allocation of housing accommodation. "Subsidy" is no longer a dreaded word to those who must be taxed to assist the "dependent" poor, the working poor and the working class. Nevertheless, the social attitudes of Canadians formed during the years 1919 and 1949 have by no means disappeared. Public housing still conveys the notions of charity, worthlessness among the poor, and troublesome people residing in neighbourhoods where public sanitation has replaced the disorder of the slum without removing entirely the social breakdown which characterized the slums of the first half of the twentieth century.[13]

The ultimate solution to Canada's housing dilemma lies in an aspiration. There must be a fundamental change in the attitude of Canadians towards housing in general. Housing must be provided for all members of society, not only for those who have adequate resources to meet their own needs. This proposition must take the form of a concept of housing as a public service.

In the language of social administration, housing must be regarded as a "social utility" – a requirement of all people which must be provided by the society for all its people. Housing accommodation must be viewed as we conceive the requirement that supplies of pure water be provided to all, that facilities be made available to dispose of waste products through sewage treatment, that roadways, sidewalks and street lighting be provided, and that educational facilities be available for children. The truth is that without decent and adequate food, without clothing appropriate for our climatic conditions and without housing accommodation adequate in both physical and social terms, all other public and social utilities are eminently wasted.

There is a solution to the long-term housing problem but a major change in the attitudes of Canadians towards the provision of housing as a *social* need is required and a great deal more planning than has been evident during the past thirty-five years is necessary. We can no longer aspire to be primarily a nation of home owners, because the very pace of our urban economic development makes it absurd to remain wedded to the assumptions of 1945 or 1955. The assumptions of the past with respect to those in need of assistance must be swept away. Furthermore, the term "public housing" should no longer be used to mean assistance only to the very poor. Social housing policy must mean the intervention of all levels of government to ensure that the distribution of housing shall be in the *national* interest. Moreover, the terms "assisted rental housing" and "assisted home ownership" are infinitely preferred to "public housing".

It is not easy to formulate a statement of solution, although the words come easy. The problem is one of maintaining a balance between optimism and dire pessimism. As a serious student of Canada's housing progress during the past forty years I find it very difficult to be optimistic but it would be fatalism to be otherwise.

NOTES

[1]Albert Rose, "Canadian Housing Policies", a background paper prepared for the Canadian Conference on Housing, October 20-23, 1968, sponsored by the Canadian Welfare Council.

[2]The name was changed from *Central* Mortgage and Housing Corporation as of January 1, 1979.

[3]A senior member of the cabinet during the years 1946-56, and at the time, the Minister of Reconstruction and Supply, responsible for housing policy. See H. S. M. Carver, *Houses for Canadians* (Toronto: University of Toronto Press 1948) p. 4.

[4]The number of family households in Canada increased from 3,024,285 in 1951 to 5,633,940 in 1976 – a rise of 86.3 per cent. During the same quarter-century non-family households rose from 385,010 to 1,532,150 – an increase of 398 per cent. CMHC, *Canadian Housing Statistics, 1978,* Table 119, p. 96.

[5]CMHC, *Canadian Housing Statistics, 1978* (Ottawa: 1979) Table 23 and Table 26, p. 21-22. See also Statistics Canada, *Canadian Statistical Review* (Ottawa: December, 1979) p. 18.

[6]*Canadian Housing Statistics, 1978*, Table 120, p. 97.

[7]The Canadian Council on Social Development, *Housing Rehabilitation* (Ottawa: 1974) pp. 159, *passim.*

[8]CMHC, Speaking Notes for Mr. R. V. Hession, president. An address to the Canadian Association of Housing and Renewal Officials (Fredericton, N.B., June 28, 1977) pp. 7-11.

[9]L. B. Smith, "Urban Canada: Problems and Prospects, *Housing in Canada,* Research Monograph 2 (Ottawa: 1971) pp. 31-37.

[10]Those over 65 will thus number 3 million persons or more. See Statistics Canada, *Population Projections for Canada and the Provinces, 1972-2001* (Ottawa: Information Canada) June 1974, pp. 74-76.

[11]CMHC, *Canadian Housing Statistics 1978* (Ottawa: 1979) Table 1, p. 1.

[12]This is precisely, of course, what was intended in the Assisted Home Ownership Program, now terminated. Most provinces supplemented the federal subsidies to home purchasers.

[13]Toronto Real Estate Board, *How to Build Canada Better,* A study of public and private housing (Toronto: July 1979) p. 44.

APPENDIX A

Provincial Legislation in Housing and Urban Renewal in the 1960s

---

BRITISH COLUMBIA

Title and Date of Legislation

The British Columbia Housing Act 1960. This legislation was formally cited as The Housing Act, R.S.B.C. 1960, C. 183.
The Provincial Home Acquisition Act, 1967.

General Objectives

The early legislation was designed to consolidate previous enactments, particularly sections of The Municipal Act, and to clarify the provincial role in participating with Central Mortgage and Housing Corporation within the National Housing Act, 1954. The Home Acquisition Act followed the Provincial Home Owner Grant Act of 1957, which was essentially a property tax rebate for home owners.

Major Provisions

Until 1967, when a housing management commission was created, the 1960 act basically enabled the province to operate within Section 35

201

(later Sections 40 and 43) of the National Housing Act. With the development of a housing management commission the two existing local housing authorities, Vancouver and Prince Rupert, were disbanded.

The Provincial Home Acquisition Act provided grants or second mortgages for first time purchasers of both new and existing housing. More favourable terms were available in the case of new housing, in line with the government's strong preference for home ownership.

Special Features

None in the 1960s; British Columbia already had one of the most active programs for elderly citizens housing through the Elderly Citizen's Housing Aid Act of 1955.

ALBERTA

Title and Date of Legislation

"The Alberta Housing Act". An Act to Co-operate with the Government of Canada and Other Public Authorities for the Provision of Housing and Urban Renewal, April 1965.

An Act to Amend the Alberta Housing Act, April 1967.

General Objectives

To enable and encourage provincial and municipal participation in public housing and urban renewal under the 1964 amendments to the National Housing Act.

Major Provisions

The Alberta Housing Act placed the onus of responsibility upon the municipalities to acquire, undertake, carry to completion, maintain and operate public housing projects or other housing accommodation within the municipality with the approval of the province.

Amendments of 1967 authorized the Government of Alberta to establish the Alberta Housing and Urban Renewal Corporation.

Special Features

The new corporation issued a brief mimeographed statement of the "Programmes under the Purview of the Alberta Housing and Urban Renewal Corporation". These included: urban renewal, public housing, co-operative housing, land assembly programmes, university student housing, provincial staff housing, housing for migratory workers, and elderly citizen housing.

SASKATCHEWAN

Title and Date of Legislation

"The Housing and Urban Renewal Act, 1966". An Act respecting Public Housing, received Royal assent March 30th, 1966.

General Objectives

To enunciate the powers of the province to enter into agreements with the various parties involved in federal-provincial housing projects and to delineate the powers of a municipality to enter into such agreements.

Major Provisions

The onus of responsibility was placed upon the municipalities which were given relatively broad powers under 5.6. These included most of the programmes specified in Section 35A to D of the National Housing Act.

Municipalities were encouraged to carry out urban renewal studies, aided by a 25 per cent provincial grant, and to prepare and implement urban renewal schemes. The act also gave municipalities the power to pass by-laws prescribing standards for the maintenance and occupancy of property in urban renewal areas, providing for appeal against enforcement of such by-laws.

Special Features

The Saskatchewan legislation did not include a provision for the creation of a provincial housing corporation.

MANITOBA

Title and Date of Legislation

"The Manitoba Housing and Renewal Corporation Act" received assent on May 4, 1967.

General Objectives

To create a Crown corporation with appropriate powers including the right to enter into agreements with all of the respective governmental bodies involved in programmes under the aegis of Section 35 of the National Housing Act.

Major Provisions

Part II of the Act entitled "Public Housing" stated the objectives of public housing, the circumstances under which it should be undertaken and permitted the broadest possible activity of a provincial government in this field. It specified further that the sites of proposed projects must be chosen within approved planning schemes of local governments or the Metropolitan Corporation of Greater Winnipeg.

The corporation was permitted to lend moneys to a municipality or a housing authority equal to the usual provincial capital contribution in the 90-10 arrangement propounded in the 1964 NHA amendments.

Part III of the Manitoba Act permitted the new provincial corporation to enter into agreements with respect to urban renewal schemes; the latter, again, must be defined within local or metropolitan planning proposals.

Special Features

The Manitoba legislation encompassed 49 sections within 5 major parts, running 26 pages in length. On prima facie evidence it appeared to be a full-blown development of provincial assumption of responsibility.

ONTARIO

Title and Date of Legislation

"An Act to incorporate the Ontario Housing Corporation" was passed in April 1964, the first of the major provincial initiatives following the 1964 amendments to the National Housing Act. The formal citation is *The Ontario Housing Corporation Act*, R.S.O., 1970, C. 317.

General Objectives

The legislation established a corporation without share capital, under the name of the "Ontario Housing Corporation", to serve as the agency of the Government of Ontario in its relationships with the Government of Canada.

Major Provisions

This was a short law (15 sections) which did not effectively outline the nature of the new roles that a provincial housing corporation might play in the housing market and gave little hint of the activity in public housing that was to develop within two to three years in Ontario.

The most significant sections of the act (Sections 6-8) empowered the new corporation to assume most of the responsibilities laid down under the *Housing Development Act*, originally passed in 1948. (R.S.O., 1970, C. 213). The new corporation could acquire, hold and dispose of real property from time-to-time and was deemed to be a management corporation under the terms of the previous legislation.

Special Features

The Ontario Housing Corporation was given extensive powers to raise its own funds by way of loans or the issue and sale of debentures, bills or notes, to be guaranteed by the Ontario government. Such guarantees appear in just one other provincial housing statute of the 1960s: that of Newfoundland.

QUEBEC

Title and Date of Legislation

The Quebec Housing Corporation Act received formal assent on June 29, 1967.

General Objectives

In the language of "notes" appended to the act,

> This bill proposes a general law whereby all municipalities will now be able to renew any part of their territory and equip low-rental lodgings for persons with small incomes, with the assistance of the Quebec Housing Corporation constituted by this act; the corporation will be able to grant subsidies and make loans for such purposes.

Major Provisions

The Quebec legislation was divided into seven "sections" (French) or "divisions" (English). Division II formulated the organization of the Societe d'habitation du Quebec (Quebec Housing Corporation) to be composed of five members. Two persons would be appointed for ten years, one of whom would be appointed president of the corporation; the other three members were to be appointed from public servants, one of whom would become vice-president.

Division III, entitled "Renewal of the Territory of a Municipality", contained four main sections: (i) renewal projects (urban renewal schemes); (ii) renewal programs; (iii) approval of renewal programs; and (iv) carrying out of renewal programs. Municipalities were required to submit proposals to the corporation for approval through the various stages of project definition, plan preparation and implementation of renewal programmes. Steps to rehouse persons displaced by renewal were to be specifically described, taking into account their income.

"Low-Rental Lodgings" was the title of Division IV which comprised five important parts. These encompassed municipal programs, municipal housing bureaus (non-profit housing corporations), financing of municipal low-rental housing activities, loans to non-profit organizations, and the establishment of grievance bureaus in each municipality.

The remainder of the act dealt with technical matters concerning by-laws, agreements, financial provisions and the like.

Special Features

The Quebec legislation was the most extensive passed by any of the provinces in the 1960s. It was further distinctive in that it contained a series of explanatory notes which were, to some degree, a statement of provincial policy in housing and urban renewal.

The success of the Quebec legislation appeared to depend in large measure upon local planning and local initiatives.

NEW BRUNSWICK

Title and Date of Legislation

The New Brunswick Housing Act, assented to May 19, 1967.

General Objectives

To empower the government of the province to enter into agreements with, and to borrow funds from, the federal government and its agency, to conduct special studies, to prepare and implement urban renewal schemes, and the like.

Major Provisions

The legislation initiated the New Brunswick Housing Corporation, consisting of a president (to serve as general manager and chief executive officer) and four other members. The objects and purposes of the corporation were stated in Section 9 and nine sub-sections of description were required.

The governing objective appeared to be "to obtain the participation of municipalities in housing projects" but additional objectives included: the study of new housing types and construction methods, and studying "the usefulness and application of co-operative, condominium and other forms of housing ownership and their application to housing needs in New Brunswick."

Special Features

The legislation was unique since it permitted the province to make agreements with respect to "training in the construction and designing of houses, in land planning or community planning or in the management or operation of housing projects." This provision presumably permitted subsidization of the educational programmes of students in urban and regional planning, or in housing administration.

New Brunswick was the only province to table a white paper on housing in the legislative assembly prior to royal assent. The *White Paper on Housing* was composed of two major parts: a brief history and exposition of Canadian housing development during the twentieth century with particular reference to the role of the provinces, and "A Housing Strategy for New Brunswick" outlining government policy and the specific roles contemplated for the new corporation in public housing, limited-dividend housing, rural housing and urban renewal fields.

NOVA SCOTIA

Title and Date of Legislation

The new legislation was cited as "The Housing Development Act, Bill No. 38 of 1966". (R.S.N.S., 1967, C. 129, amended by 1969, C. 52).

General Objectives

To establish a commission to be known as the "Nova Scotia Housing Commission" (to consist of not fewer than eight and not more than fifteen members) which would assume all the rights and privileges of the previous Nova Scotia Housing Commission which had existed for more than forty years.

Major Provisions

The duties of the housing commission were specified as follows: to study housing needs and conditions; to make recommendations for the improvement of housing conditions; to encourage and promote public and private initiative in housing and urban renewal matters; and to carry out and perform such other duties regarding housing and urban renewal as may be directed by the governor-in-council.

Part I of the legislation contained the usual clauses which permitted the government of the province to make agreements with all other levels of government through the housing commission. Other parts of the legislation encompassed public housing and co-operative housing.

Special Features

The unique part of the Nova Scotia legislation was Part III, entitled "Co-operative Housing". The housing commission was enabled to "encourage and promote the formation and organization of companies for the purpose of building and providing sufficient and suitable housing units in any part of the province and selling and leasing the housing units." Moreover, the commission could advance loans to such companies, was responsible for inspecting the plans and the construction, and would determine and fix the maximum rentals to be charged by co-operative housing companies.

PRINCE EDWARD ISLAND

Title and Date of Legislation

The Prince Edward Island Housing Authority Act was given royal assent on April 7, 1966.

General Objectives

An authority (corporation) of not less than seven members was established by the act "to provide family housing units for families of low income".

Major Provisions

The authority could undertake housing projects either alone or in conjunction with any municipality together with the Central Mortgage and Housing Corporation.

The legislation specifically empowered the new provincial organization to "purchase, lease, acquire, convert or construct, maintain and operate property, both real and personal, required or useful for the carrying out of the functions of the authority."

Special Features

The new authority was given the power to borrow money either under the provision of the National Housing Act or by temporary or other loans from any chartered bank.

NEWFOUNDLAND

Title and Date of Legislation

The Housing Act 1966, (S.N., C. 87) was followed by "An Act to Incorporate the Newfoundland and Labrador Housing Corporation" which received royal assent on April 25, 1967. This act required twenty-two printed pages encompassing forty-four sections.

General Objectives

The legislation created a corporation to act for the province in the broad fields of housing and urban renewal. The new organization was deemed to be a housing authority constituted under Section 15 of *The Housing Act 1966* to enable it to expropriate land and buildings within the purposes of *The Expropriation Act, 1964.*

Major Provisions

Exactly one-half of the act was concerned with the financing of the activities of the corporation. The corporation could borrow money for any of its purposes through the issue of bonds, debentures or other securities. The minister, acting for the province, could unconditionally guarantee any loans in Canadian or "United States of America currency" to be raised from time-to-time by the corporation.

Although the term "research" was not used, the corporation was empowered "to foster, through scientific investigation and technology, knowledge of housing and of the means of dealings with any conditions relating to the development, control and direction thereof."

Special Features

Newfoundland was the only province, other than Ontario, to specify guarantees of loans raised by the housing corporation, and the only province to refer to the possibility of borrowing in the United States.

The new legislation included in Section 25, a series of powers which gave the new corporation the complexion of an urban development organization rather than a housing organization. These features included:

1.   the power to service land through the creation of streets, bridges, sewers, pavements, and the like, "necessary to the development

of lands for urban or suburban uses and for housing and community development";

2. the power to develop open space and the landscaping thereof
   through the creation of parks, recreation grounds, swimming
   pools and similar places for recreation;

3. the power "to procure the installation of tramway lines, trolley
   bus lines . . . power and light distribution systems . . . gas
   distribution systems, telephone systems and the like".

Newfoundland was the only province to suggest that the new
corporation might enter the fields of public transportation and public
utilities.

Development of the National Housing Act

TITLES OF PARTS OF THE ACT

Part	1938	1944	1954
I	Dominion Housing Loans	Housing for Home Owners	Insured Mortgage Loans
II	Low-Rental Housing	Housing for Rental Purposes	Housing for Rental Purposes and Land assembly
III	Assistance to Municipalities in Respect of Low-Cost Housing	Rural Housing	Housing Redevelopment (1954) Urban Redevelopment (1956)
IV		Home Improvement and Home Extension Loans	Home Improvement Loans and Home Extension Loans
V		Housing Research and Community Planning	Housing Research and Community Planning
VI		General	Federal-Provincial Projects
VII			General

TITLES OF PARTS OF THE ACT

Part	1964	1973	1979
I	Insured Mortgage Loans	Insured Mortgage Loans	Insured Mortgage Loans
II	Housing for Rental Purposes and Land Assembly	Housing for Rental Purposes and Land Assembly	Housing for Rental Purposes and Land Assembly
II.1			Land Acquisition and Leasing
III	Urban Renewal	Urban Renewal	Urban Renewal
III.1		Neighbourhood Improvement Program	Neighbourhood Improvement Program
IV	Home Improvement Loans and Home Extension Loans	Home Improvement Loans and Home Extension Loans	Home Improvement Loans and Home Extension Loans
IV.1		Rehabilitation and Conversion of Existing Residential Buildings	Rehabilitation and Conversion of Existing Residential Buildings
IV.2		Loans to Facilitate Home Ownership	Loans to Facilitate Home Ownership
V	Housing Research and Community Planning	Housing Research and Community Planning	Housing Research and Community Planning
VI	Public Housing	Public Housing	Public Housing
VI.1		New Communities	New Communities
VII	General	Loans for Student Housing Projects	Loans for Student Housing Projects
VIII		Loans for Municipal Sewage Treatment Projects	Water and Sewerage Projects
VIII.1			Community Services
IX		General	General

Index

Andras, Robert K., 48-49, 50, 69, 70
Assisted Home Ownership Program,
    55f., 92, 97, 178

Barnard Study, 156
Basford, Ron, 54, 64
Blumenfeld, Hans, 145
British Columbia Housing
    Management Commission, 82

Central Mortgage and Housing
    Corporation, 11, 24, 29, 31,
    34, 49, 50, 58-59, 62, 63,
    78-79, 125, 168
City of Toronto Non-Profit Housing
    Corporation, 22
Comay, Eli, 75, 111, 150
Curtis Report, 28, 30
Community Integrated Housing
    Program (CIHP), 118
Co-operative Housing Assistance, 57,
    91

Davis, William, 75, 111
Danson, Barnett, 82
Dennis, Michael, 11, 52
Dennis and Fish Report, see
    *Programs in Search of a
    Policy*
Donnison, D. V., 3
Dominion Housing Act, 1935, 3, 166
Dunhill Development Corporation,
    82, 83

Eligibility, for public housing, 9

Federation of Ontario Tenant
    Associations, 106
Filtering down process, 2, 53
Fish, Susan, 11, 52f.

Galbraith, John K., 36
Godfrey, Paul, 129

Hellyer, Paul, 43, 48, 61, 69
Hignett, Herbert, 70

Home Ownership Made Easy
    (HOME), 118, 150
Housing,
    cost of construction, 5
    co-operative, 60
    crisis, 143, 191f.
    crowding, 168-170
    for Canada's native people, 62,
        171
    function of, 11
    public, see Public housing
    rental, 169
    type of, 5.10, 173, 176f.
Housing Ontario '74, 75, 114, 116,
    117, 120, 121, 123, 124, 135
Housing policies, 16, 145f., 181
    constraints upon, 18f., 144
    decentralization of, 21ff., 36, 122
    definitions of, 17
    economic context, 5f., 167
    families, 170, 178
    formulation of, 16, 74
    goals of, 20f., 35
    "housing by headline", 15
    municipalities, 185
    non-family households, 166, 172
    underlying philosophy, 18
Housing and Urban Development
    Association of Canada
    (HUDAC), 63

Income determination, 9
Intergovernmental relations, 29f.
Interim Metro Housing Policy, 76

Jaffary, Karl, 132

Land banking, 60, 91, 128, 150ff.
    definitions of, 150ff.
    in Ontario, 97
    objectives of, 60
Limited Dividend Housing
    Corporations, 38
Lithwick, Harvey, 11, 51, 53, 146

Lithwick Report, 51
Living Room, 75, 127
Local Housing authorities, 4, 37, 64

Marsh Report, 28, 30
Metropolitan Toronto Housing
    Authority, 25
Ministry of State for Urban Affairs,
    11, 48f., 50
Mortgage rates, 5, 156

National Housing Act,
    of 1938, 3, 166
    of 1944, 18, 19, 28, 160
    of 1949, 21
    of 1953, 18, 19
    of 1954, 19
    of 1964, 38ff.
    of 1973, 54ff., 58
Neighbourhood Improvement
    Program, 57f., 63, 64, 121
New Communities Program, 61
Nicholson, Lorne, 82

Ontario Advisory Task Force, 75,
    106f., 122, 123, 147, 156
Ontario Home Renewal Program,
    120, 121
Ontario Housing Action Program
    (OHAP), 116, 150
Ontario Housing Corporation, 63,
    69, 101ff., 124
Ontario Land Corporation, 121
Ontario Mortgage Corporation, 116

Poor law philosophy, 90
Programs in Search of a Policy, 5,
    52f.
Public housing,
    administrators of, 23
    applicants for, 174, 183
    assisted rental housing, 116, 118,
        177, 187
    attitudes towards, 3, 143f., 163ff.
    attitudes towards recipients, 166,
        184, 193
    decrease in amount constructed,
        76, 81
    determination of eligibility, 7f.,
        9, 168
    following World War Two, 23, 31,
        32
    for families, 85, 167, 177
    hostility towards, 30, 31

local housing authorities, 124
Non-Profit Housing Assistance, 57
    for one-parent families, 9, 171
    policy shift in, 96
    pressures for slum clearance, 31
    by provinces,
        Alberta, 84
        British Columbia, 81
        Manitoba, 86
        New Brunswick, 90
        Newfoundland, 94
        Nova Scotia, 91
        Prince Edward Island, 92
        Quebec, 87
        Saskatchewan, 85
    quantity constructed, 37
    reasons for, 163
    schools of thought, 24
    for senior citizens, 82, 84, 85, 86,
        91, 93, 171, 176, 193
    for students, 105
    types of dwellings, 9, 77
Purchaser protection, 62

Satellite communities, 61
Slum clearance, 63, 164, 165, 171
Spurr, Peter, 147ff.
Subsidies, 6

Randall, Stanley, 70
Regent Park, 31, 47
Rent control, 28
Rental scale, 9, 82
Residential Rehabilitation Assistance
    Program (RRAP), 59, 63,
    64, 121
Robarts, John P., 133
Rose, Albert, 33, 47

Task Force on Housing and Urban
    Development, 43-46, 50, 61,
    69
Toronto Housing Company, 2
Trudeau, Pierre E., 43, 48

Urban Canada, 146
Urban development, 30
Urban renewal, see Slum clearance

Veteran's Rental Housing, 30

Wartime Housing Limited, 28, 29
Welch, Robert, 113
Winters, Robert H., 21
Wolman, 7